Danielle –

It's a joy to know you.
Keep your light shining bright.
I hope these words will inspire
and bless you. Thanks!

Danny Stevens

Psalm 119:18

The Speaking God

Denny Stevens

WestBow
PRESS®
A DIVISION OF THOMAS NELSON
& ZONDERVAN

Scripture taken from Holy Bible, New International Version ®, NIV®
Copyright © 1973, 1978, 1984, 2011 by Biblica, Inc®
Used by permission. All rights reserved worldwide.

Scripture quotations [marked NIV] taken from the Holy Bible,
New International Version Anglicised
Copyright © 1979, 1984, 2011 Biblica, formerly International Bible Society
Used by permission of Hodder & Stoughton Publishers, an Hachette UK company
All rights reserved
'NIV' is a registered trademark of Biblica
UK trademark number 1448790

Scripture taken from the Holy Bible, New International Version®, NIV®
Copyright© 1973, 1978, 1984, 2011 by Biblica, Inc.™
Used by permission of Zondervan. All rights reserved worldwide. WWW.ZONDERVAN.COM
The "NIV" and "New International Version" are trademarks registered in
the United States Patent and Trademark Offices by Biblica, Inc.™

WestBow Press books may be ordered through booksellers or by contacting:

WestBow Press
A Division of Thomas Nelson & Zondervan
1663 Liberty Drive
Bloomington, IN 47403
www.westbowpress.com
1 (866) 928-1240

ISBN: 978-1-5127-1828-7 (sc)
ISBN: 978-1-5127-1829-4 (hc)
ISBN: 978-1-5127-1827-0 (e)

Library of Congress Control Number: 2015918148

Print information available on the last page.

WestBow Press rev. date: 11/20/2015

Dedicated to my wife and best friend, lovely Alaine, and our daughters—Kelly and Jana

I keep asking that the God of our Lord Jesus Christ, the glorious Father, may give you the spirit of wisdom and revelation, so that you may know Him better. I pray also that the eyes of your heart may be enlightened …
    —*Ephesians 1:17–18a*

This is the one I esteem: he who is humble and contrite in spirit, and trembles at my word.
    —*Isaiah 66:2*

God is a Speaking God

Every book has a pitch. Here is mine: I want you to know the joy of discovery when the Holy Spirit illuminates a truth to you, and the light goes on. It's the "Aha" moment! It's when the pages of Scripture come alive. Now, they are more than words … they are life.

My whole motivation for writing this devotional book is to share just a little bit of the daily joy I find in reading God's Word. I want to share with you the quiet thrill of discovery and revelation. When I set out to seek the Lord and explore what God would say, the Spirit of God unveils truth in a way that I am able to apprehend. My soul is truly satisfied when I get a glimpse of what is on His heart. There is delight in my spirit and it triggers a thirst for more. That's what happens when you come honestly and earnestly before the Lord. God will pour out His Spirit upon you that will take you by surprise. You will be blessed beyond measure!

The format of a one year Bible has always worked well for me. I don't preach from it, but it is my most-read, everyday Bible. For me, I have to have a plan that actually works. Since I was a bi-vocational senior pastor for thirteen years, I know all about the pressures of life that squeeze out personal time with the Lord. I understand that this is more common than we care to admit. *Who has the time to read the Bible?* Yet for anyone who knows His voice understands that one word from God is worth it all. It's His Word to **me** that gives me confidence to walk out my faith boldly.

Fifteen minutes is all it takes. This is workable in any schedule. The commitment of purposeful intention is rewarded in your desire to fellowship with God. There will always be an endless reservoir to draw from. In this format is an amount that you can eat and enjoy, and yet will keep you coming back for more. Sure, you can read on and go deeper. That is the nature of eating. You taste and see that the Lord is good, and you create an appetite and longing for more. The purpose of a regular diet, as this, is to get the routine established. Get the flow of faithfulness going. There is a stability and health developed when I commit to an everyday diet. Also, a systematic approach to reading the Bible gets you into topics that you might not choose otherwise. There is balance and wisdom in that.

I also understand that for me to become a *disciple*, I need *discipline*. I mean that I must embrace those things that are going to have long-term implications for health. I cultivate prayer. I create an environment for worship. I put the Word of God in front of me. I schedule it. I trip over it— because I need it more than I know. My schedule for fellowship with God has to become non-negotiable. There will always be distractions to draw me away. There will always be fires to put out. But I dig my heels in. I resolve to be steady.

For me, I have always enjoyed a good devotional alongside my Bible. Nothing replaces the Word, but God has raised up godly men and women that speak our language pretty well too. It has always been a pleasant addition to give me another perspective. I have been impacted by devotionals from Oswald Chambers, Mike Bickle, Neil Anderson, Les & Leslie Parrott, to acknowledge a few. I hope that your time in *these* pages will give you another perspective, as well. They come from a pastor's heart.

So the idea behind this devotional is simple. Read it alongside the Bible readings for each day listed at the top of each devotional. The topic of the day will be found in the passages you just read. Stay with it and you will have read the Bible through this year and you will have picked up a newfound appreciation for the voice of the Lord in your own life. A heart-felt prayer completes the reading that makes a personal application.

Growing in the knowledge of the Lord is always the goal when we open the pages of His Book— *"to know Him better" (Ephesians 1:17)*. The revelation I receive is priceless. Sometimes, all it takes is a look beneath the surface in order to gain a fuller perspective. I want for you to know this joy, that ***God is speaking to you!*** Enjoy!

Denny Stevens

January 1

Genesis 1:1–2:25; Matthew 1:1–2:12; Psalm 1:1–6; Proverbs 1:1–6

The Spirit Hovers

In the beginning God created the heavens and the earth. Now the earth was formless and empty, darkness was over the surface of the deep, and the Spirit of God was hovering over the waters.
    —Genesis 1:1–2

Mary was pledged to be married to Joseph, but before they came together, she was found to be with child through the Holy Spirit ... what is conceived in her is from the Holy Spirit.
    —Matthew 1:18, 20

What an awesome introduction—to see the activity of the Holy Spirit in the opening verses of both the New and Old Testaments! In the beginning of time and the ushering in of salvation, it is the Spirit who initiates God's activity among humankind.

The Spirit of God hovered over the face of the waters to bring about God's created order. Then once more to initiate a new and better covenant, it is the Spirit of God who hovers over and plants the seed of the divine into the womb of a willing, humble virgin. It was the seed of the Spirit that brought forth Immanuel —*God with us*—in human flesh. It was this Jesus, the God-man, who would bring God's redemption into full view.

Know that, as we begin a brand new year, God is a God of new beginnings. And whatever God initiates in your life will be because His Spirit is at work within you. He is hovering over you. He is establishing your course to bring about a good work!

Father in heaven, I acknowledge that all You do is initiated by Your Spirit. Wherever You are hovering, You are at work to bring about Your purpose and plan. Begin that good work in my life. I pledge my devotion to You. Create in me a heart that responds to You and the promptings of Your Spirit. Amen.

January 2

Genesis 3:1–4:26; Matthew 2:13–3:6; Psalm 2:1–12; Proverbs 1:7–9

Dreams to Joseph

An angel of the Lord appeared to Joseph in a dream.
   —Matthew 2:13

I believe that the Lord directs our steps. Don't you? If we truly desire to follow after God's will, He will make known to us the path we are to walk in and He will speak to us in a language we can understand.

Joseph was front and center as a player in God's plan to raise up the Savior, Jesus. The way that circumstances were brought about, you could imagine that Joseph might need some divine coaxing to make the situation legitimate. I mean, the woman he was pledged to marry was pregnant! How could this be? So the Lord appears to Joseph in a dream not once, but *four* times *(Matthew 1:20; 2:13,19, 22)*. In each instance, God gave divine direction to move and protect Joseph and his young family. In each case, Joseph readily understood what God was trying to convey and was then quick to respond.

Today, God still uses dreams and visions to direct and protect us. He uses many other means, as well. We have His Word. His indwelling Spirit prompts and leads us. Wise counselors, parental figures and caring pastors serve to mentor us. Yet, God will use whatever means it takes to get and keep our attention in order to steer us in the straight path—including dreams and visions.

How does God speak to you? What are the ways He uses to grab your attention? Do you recognize His voice when He calls to you? What was the last thing He impressed upon you?

Father, I thank You for Your pursuit of me. In these last days, pour out Your Spirit on all flesh. Let the older men dream dreams and the younger men see visions. Father, use whatever means it takes to keep me on the straight and narrow. I desire You and Your will. Amen.

January 3

Genesis 5:1–7:24; Matthew 3:7–4:11; Psalm 3:1–8; Proverbs 1:10–19

God's Pleasure

Enoch walked with God; then he was no more, because God took him away.
—Genesis 5:24

I sensed today the pleasure of God—the pleasure of God upon individuals who walk with God. It is God's sheer delight and glory to find that one who will commit and pattern his or her life to walk daily in the counsel and friendship of God.

Enoch was a man who walked with God for 365 years in the confines of the earth—a short life in those days. I can only imagine that his companionship was desired in closer proximity, so God said: *"Come up here a little closer!"*

In Genesis 6, the Lord saw wickedness abound to such heights that He was grieved that he had made humans. His heart was filled with pain and He determined to put an end to it. Yet, there was a man who was blameless in the midst of the corruption. That man was Noah. He was righteous, and he walked with God. God was so pleased with Noah.

In Matthew 3, another man—Jesus—had walked with God in a blameless manner for thirty years and was baptized by the prophet John. The pleasure of God was displayed. Heaven was opened, the Spirit of God descended with lightning and a voice proclaimed His pleasure.

"So we make it our goal to please Him" (2 Corinthians 5:9).

Father, guide me in the way that brings You pleasure. Give me grace to live a life of obedience. May I walk with You in the cool of the day. May our communion be sweet. I seek Your counsel and Your smile. Amen.

January 4

Genesis 8:1–10:32; Matthew 4:12–25; Psalm 4:1–8; Proverbs 1:20–23

Set Apart

Know that the Lord has set apart the godly for himself.
    —Psalm 4:3

If you had responded to my rebuke, I would have poured out my heart to you and made my thoughts known to you.
    —Proverbs 1:23

The Lord has called you to be set apart from this world unto Himself. Amidst the barrage of enticements that call us to stray, God is jealous over you and wants to be your primary affection. God is holy, and He desires you also to be holy. He is committed to that process that will bring about your sanctification. To say it simply: it is the daily embracing of what He loves and the rejection of what He hates.

Even when God must bring correction, it's because He loves us and wants to keep us from harm and pain. Responding to His rebuke is to acknowledge that He knows best and we do not.

In the precious communion that He calls us to, He longs to share His heart. In that place, He hears us when we call to Him. The light of His face shines upon us. He fills our heart with greater joy. We lie down and sleep in peace.

The key to this communion with God is how my heart responds. If I willingly desire God's activity and welcome His plans and purposes, God says He will pour out His heart to me and reveal His thoughts. *Wow…to know God's thoughts on a matter!*

Gracious Father in heaven, You do not share Your secrets with just anyone. I ask that You set me apart unto Yourself, that I might know what is on Your heart. Draw my affections away from the lifeless stuff of earth and onto the eternal pleasures of Your presence. Amen.

January 5

Genesis 11:1–13:4; Matthew 5:1–26; Psalm 5:1–12; Proverbs 1:24–28

The Beatitudes Simplified

Blessed are the poor ... those who mourn ... the meek ... those who hunger and thirst ... the merciful ...the pure in heart ... the peacemakers ... those who are persecuted ...
—Matthew 5:3–10

Jesus opens His teaching on the Sermon on the Mount with these promises, called the *Beatitudes*. These eight attitudes bring about God's blessing. It is the centerpiece of the sermon and God's premiere desire for every believer. You can be sure of one thing—that God, by His Holy Spirit, is relentless at working to bring about these beautiful flowers to bloom in your heart and in your life.

My simplified version of the Beatitudes may help to make application:

Blessed are the *poor*—those who acknowledge their spiritual poverty before a holy God. Blessed are those who *mourn*—those who grieve over their sinful inclinations and come to God in true repentance. Blessed are the *meek*—those who choose the posture of humility. Blessed are those who *hunger and thirst*—those who persist in seeking God's righteous standard on every level. Blessed are the *merciful*— those who are gracious to the undeserving, choosing not to cast judgment. Blessed are the *pure*—those who are making themselves ready as a spotless bride, untainted, with right motives and thoughts. Blessed are the *peacemakers*—those who proactively reconcile relationships. Blessed are those who are *persecuted*—those who courageously endure adversity because of unshakable convictions.

Father, thank You for disclosing Your plans and purposes for me—what You desire to bring to fruition in my heart and life. I long to adopt my worldview around these verses. I will give an account before You concerning them. Let my life reflect Your Spirit's work to bring these characteristics about. Amen.

January 6

Genesis 13:5–15:21; Matthew 5:27–48; Psalm 6:1–10; Proverbs 1:29–33

Abram Believes for the Impossible

I will make you into a great nation and I will bless you; I will make your name great, and you will be a blessing. I will bless those who bless you, and I will curse those who curse you; and all peoples on earth will be blessed through you. Abram believed the Lord, and he credited it to him as righteousness.
    —Genesis 12:2–3; 15:6

The Lord had made some outrageous promises to Abram. Following the death of his father, while in Haran, the Lord proclaimed the initial "Abrahamic blessing." Abram was seventy–five years old and the Lord was making promises that through him will come a great nation.

The Lord appeared again to Abram to confirm this promise several times *(13:14; 14:19; 15:1–6)*. One such time happened after Lot had separated company from Abram and, given the option, Lot chose to travel east. The very next words declared, *"Look north and south, east and west. It's all yours."* It wouldn't matter what direction Lot chose!

The word of the Lord once again came to Abram in a vision following a military victory over four kings. Now the interaction became increasingly personal: *"The nation I produce will be brought about through your own body."* Now, let's recall … Abram was how old?

Promises that God gives are not something that we can achieve or manufacture in our own strength. They may seem outrageous and beyond all imagination. And yet, here, Abram believed God. What is it that the Lord has promised you? Will you believe Him for it?

Father, thank You for Your great and precious promises. If You have declared such a thing so, I will trust You for it. Add to my faith. Give me grace to pursue Your will all the while as You prepare me to receive it. I believe You can do marvelous things with my life, because You do all things well. Amen.

January 7

Genesis 16:1–18:19; Matthew 6:1–24; Psalm 7:1–17; Proverbs 2:1–5

Waiting for the Promise

So after Abram had been living in Canaan ten years, Sarai took her Egyptian maidservant Hagar and gave her husband to be his wife. "Perhaps I can build a family through her."
    —Genesis 16:2–3

It is more often than not, that when we receive a word or a promise from the Lord, we are more than ready to seize it. God discloses a personal plan for me and I am ready to claim it *right now!* And if things don't unfold the way we think they should or as quickly as they ought, we make the grievous mistake to implement our own strategies to "hurry up" the process. In Abram and Sarai's case, it had been ten years! So … had God forgotten?

Sarai's plan to bring about God's promise obviously doesn't work. Plan B never does. When we think that God somehow needs our help, then an Ishmael is sure to surface. Going down that bunny trail only serves to produce heartache and grief.

Yet God, in His kindness, confirms His covenant with Abram once again. Now Abram is renamed Abraham *(father of many)*, and he is ninety–nine years of age. Sarai is also given a new name—Sarah. In essence, God was saying to Abraham: *"Nothing has changed in my mind. We're right on schedule. Next year at this time you will have a son."* Abraham and Sarah chuckle to themselves, but God proves to them one more time that nothing is too hard for the Lord.

Father, Your word says that no one who waits upon the Lord will be disappointed. You grant strength to those who wait. In my waiting, Lord, satisfy my longings even when I don't see the progress with my eyes. Don't let me do anything in my own strength to speed Your promises along. My best effort is Plan B. I desire only Your best. Amen.

January 8

Genesis 18:20–19:38; Matthew 6:25–7:14; Psalm 8:1–9; Proverbs 2:6–15

The Sin of Sodom

Then the Lord said, "The outcry against Sodom and Gomorrah is so great and their sin so grievous … the outcry has reached me."
—Genesis 18:20–21

The story of Lot and the two angels in Sodom reveals to us how the sin of a city is not brushed aside as unimportant by the Lord. Sodom's trespass gains the attention of heaven.

It would be easy to rail against the obvious. We all know from the story that homosexuality marked this city. And yes, God is reviled and grieved concerning this twisting of natural desires. (For more on this topic, refer to Leviticus 18:22, Romans 1:21-27, 1 Corinthians 6:9-11.) But there is more…

Ezekiel 16:49–50 gives us a larger view of what depicted Sodom. There were more societal breeches that led to their reputation of lewdness. Here, Sodom is said to have been arrogant, overfed and unconcerned. They did not help the poor and needy. They were haughty and did detestable things before God. *Ouch!*

The underpinnings that led to Sodom's demise were broader than we may first have thought. And what's more, it hits closer to home. I may not be entrenched in gross sin, but the attitudes that are allowed to go unchecked gain steam to become arrogance and an unconcern for the real needs around me. This self-serving attitude is an outcry that reaches heaven and it grieves the heart of God.

Father God, before I point my finger at someone else's sin, rescue me from selfish pride and self-serving ways. I repent on behalf of the sins of my city that have reached your attention. I pray for my city. Move upon us. I ask that the rain of Your Spirit will come and prepare the ground for revival. Amen!

January 9

Genesis 20:1–22:24; Matthew 7:15–29; Psalm 9:1–12; Proverbs 2:16–22

Integrity of Heart

Now Abimelech had not gone near her (Sarah), so he said…"I have done this with a clear conscience and clean hands."
—Genesis 20:4–5

In a bizarre circumstance, Abraham, for the second time, claims his wife, Sarah, to be his sister so that he would not be ill-treated by a foreign ruler. It was not unusual for kings to add beautiful women to their harem. Sarah, even at eighty–nine years young, must have been very attractive. And technically, Sarah was Abraham's half-sister! But God sternly warns Abimelech, king of Gerar, in a vivid dream that he is not to touch her.

Up until this point, Abimelech had not gone near Sarah. He responds to the Lord in his own defense, *"I have a clear conscience and clean hands" (v.5)*. This uncompromising life before God and all of mankind has a name. It is called *integrity*.

Integrity, more than anything, is the one thing God longs to produce in every one of us. It is living our life in absolute honesty before the watchful eye of God. Whether before man or in private, it is walking in the light without knowingly violating the inner umpire of my conscience. It is this wholeness of heart that allows me to sleep at night with a sense of peace and rest.

It is by integrity that His name is rightly represented in my life.

Father, if there is one thing that You desire for me, it is truth on my inward parts. May integrity and uprightness protect me, because my hope is in You. Let my actions and responses, in public or in private, be honoring to You. Amen.

January 10

Genesis 23:1–24:51; Matthew 8:1–17; Psalm 9:13–20; Proverbs 3:1–6

Words to Live by

Let love and faithfulness never leave you; bind them around your neck, write them on the tablet of your heart. Then you will win favor and a good name in the sight of God and man. Trust in the Lord with all your heart and lean not on your own understanding; in all your ways acknowledge him, and he will make your paths straight.
—Proverbs 3:3–6

Favor, a good name, and a straight path. In these familiar verses are promises that the Lord gives through the writer Solomon.

We win favor and a good name when we decide that, by our attitudes and our actions, we make love and faithfulness our banner. We make the conscious effort to keep these before us in the way we carry ourselves. As a pastor, faithfulness and loyalty were traits I valued perhaps more than anything. It looks like God values them the same. It's the trait of being steady and able to be counted upon. It's the marathon pace, not the fifty-yard dash. When our lives are marked by love and faithfulness, God says that His favor is upon us and our names are marked by integrity.

Life is seldom a straight path. That's why this second promise is important. God will make our paths straight when we trust him with all our heart. Trusting Him with all means I cannot bear all my weight upon my own conclusions. It's the easiest thing to do. But God sees ahead better than I. He can lead me around obstacles I can't foresee. So if I'll trust Him and acknowledge Him in all my ways, then He can lead me down the right path. I don't want to have to learn all of life the hard way. God says: *"Look to Me, I have your best in mind."*

Father, all Your ways are good. My life is blessed when I look to You in every situation. I ask for Your favor. Let me trust You and be found faithful. Amen.

January 11

Genesis 24:52–26:16; Matthew 8:18–34; Psalm 10:1–15; Proverbs 3:7–8

God's Prescription for Health

Do not be wise in your own eyes; fear the Lord and shun evil. This will bring health to your body and nourishment (strength) to your bones.
—Proverbs 3:7–8

I believe God's interest in you and in me extends to the whole person: body, soul and spirit. That means He is aware of our mental and psychological make-up. He understands our emotional and physical needs. God designed our total package. Salvation is God's rescue of the entire person, and healing is God's complete repair, in order that we may accomplish His will with the bodies we live in.

It is God's nature to heal. It is who He is and what He does. In Exodus 15:26, God reveals Himself as Jehovah Rophe—*I am the Lord, who heals you.*

God provides healing by the stripes that Jesus bore *(Isaiah 53:45)*. We receive healing by faith—even by the faith of friends *(Mark 2:1–12)*. The sick who pray in faith can be made well again *(James 5:15)*. One of His benefits is that He heals all our diseases *(Psalm 103:3)*. His words are health to the whole of our person *(Proverbs 4:20–22)*. God's Word penetrates even to the level of our physical body *(Hebrews 4:12)*. A reverential fear of the Lord results in nourishment *(Proverbs 3:7–8)*.

Is there a need that you have for your physician? *The Doctor is in!*

Father God, You are my primary physician. You have given me a prescription to follow. I embrace the benefits of the cross of Jesus for my body to be healed. Give me a hatred for evil so that I will shun temptation, instead of entertain it. Grant me grace to reverence Your name in every circumstance. Hallowed be Your name! Amen and amen.

January 12

Genesis 26:17–27:46; Matthew 9:1–17; Psalm 10:16–18; Proverbs 3:9–10

Then They Will Fast

John's disciples came and asked him, "How is it that we and the Pharisees fast, but your disciples do not fast?" Jesus answered, "How can the guests of the bridegroom mourn while he is with them? The time will come when the bridegroom will be taken from them; then they will fast."
—Matthew 9:14–15

Fasting, as we see here, was a common practice that identified the disciples with their faith. It was not a new concept. But the question gave Jesus the opportunity to clarify the principle of fasting.

Fasting is a way to deny the flesh of a basic creature comfort, most commonly—food. While the extent of a fast may vary, it is a deliberate act of humbling to seek the Lord in prayer. In and of itself, fasting does not make you more saintly, but it positions your heart before the Bridegroom to receive from Him and to be drawn to Him in a more consecrated way. It tenderizes your heart to hear Him more clearly.

Because Jesus was with them, He says: *"It is not necessary now to fast, because I am among you. But there will be a time that you will!"*

Jesus also addressed fasting during his sermon on the mount *(Matthew 6)*. He spoke, not *"if"*, but *"when"* you fast. The same was spoken of prayer and giving. These concepts are absolutes in the kingdom that Jesus was establishing. In our western culture today, we look upon these as "extra bonus points for the super-spiritual." Not so from Jesus. This is Christianity 101. *"Then they will fast"* is now!

Father, I desire to position myself closer to the Bridegroom—Jesus. I ask that You would give me grace to fulfill Your command to fast. I desire You more than anything, including food. Draw my heart to You in the secret place of prayer and fasting. In Jesus' name I pray, Amen.

January 13

Genesis 28:1–29:35; Matthew 9:18–38; Psalm 11:1–7; Proverbs 3:11–12

Jacob's Open Heaven

(Jacob) had a dream in which he saw a stairway resting on the earth, with its top reaching to heaven, and the angels of God were ascending and descending on it. There above it stood the Lord…
    —Genesis 28:12–13

After Jacob received his father Isaac's blessing, his brother Esau came to hold a serious grudge. Jacob came to realize that it was now high time to leave home. Can you imagine the gamut of emotions that Jacob must have felt? He was compelled to run *from* imminent danger, but he would run *toward* the safe haven of his mother's brother—uncle Laban. It was on this trek that Jacob experienced an open heaven.

An open heaven is not your everyday experience. But in the tentative position that Jacob found himself in, what he desperately needed was God's tangible presence. In this visitation, Jacob experiences God for himself. The Lord confirms His covenant with Jacob and assures him of His promise and blessing. The reality of God's presence was so vivid that Jacob made a vow to serve the Lord. He built a memorial and called the place Bethel—*the house of God.* This heavenly visitation forever left its mark upon Jacob.

There are times in our lives that only His presence will see us through.

Reiterated similarly is Psalm 11:4–5: *"The Lord is in his holy temple; the Lord is on his heavenly throne. He observes the sons of men; his eyes examine them. The Lord examines the righteous…"*

Father God, I thank You for the Bethel experiences that you give that help mark our way in our life pursuit of You. I pray that You will give me an open heaven reality of Your presence wherever I am. May I walk in the light of Your counsel and blessing, and under Your watchful eye. Amen.

January 14

Genesis 30:1–31:16; Matthew 10:1–25; Psalm 12:1–8; Proverbs 3:13–15

The Truth of Good News

I am sending you out as sheep among wolves. Therefore be as shrewd as snakes and innocent as doves.
—Matthew 10:16

One thing that raises my blood pressure are some of the comments made on the Editorial page of the newspaper. *Some people just don't get it!* Of course, these same people will say the same thing about what I think! Speaking forth the gospel is like that. You can be sure that some will oppose you.

Jesus sent out his disciples with the message that the kingdom of heaven *is near.* He gave them authority to demonstrate the power of the gospel—to heal the sick, raise the dead, cleanse the leprous and drive out demons.

You would think that people everywhere would welcome this good news. But because people don't realize their sinful condition and their absolute need for a savior, there are many who will oppose the truth. Because of pride, they are comfortable in their mess.

Therefore, be discerning, shrewd and cunning. Consider how you will present the truth in a manner they will understand. Loving them can be disarming! At the same time, be entirely innocent. Don't answer hate tactics with hate. Remember, we don't wrestle with people who oppose us, but with principalities and powers that oppose God.

Father, I thank You that the gospel is the power of God unto salvation. I thank You for the message that has delivered me from the dominion of Satan to the kingdom of Your dear Son. Give me wisdom and a heart of love that reaches out to others, so they no longer would have to walk in the bondage of sin. Amen.

January 15

Genesis 31:17–32:12; Matthew 10:26–11:6; Psalm 13:1–6; Proverbs 3:16–18

Jacob Meets His Match

Moreover, Jacob deceived Laban the Aramean by not telling him he was running away.
—Genesis 31:20

In the Old Testament, names meant something. Jacob lived up to his. While he had many strong points of character—a good businessman, determined and patient; he was also a deceiver, a *"supplanter."*

At a young age, Jacob deceived his brother Esau to gain the birthright. Then again, he stole the blessing meant for the eldest son (Esau) from his father Isaac *(Genesis.27:36)*. He fools dad with help from his mother, Rebekah. Here, a third time, Jacob begins his return journey to Canaan with Laban's daughters and no proper farewell. And what's more, Esau lies in wait for Jacob back home. After twenty years of service to Laban, still fresh in Jacob's mind is the breathing threats from Esau to end Jacob's life.. *"In great fear and distress Jacob divided the people who were with him into two groups" (Genesis 32:7)*.

As important as it was for the covenant to be passed from one generation to the next, God was equally mindful of the character that His chosen people displayed. Was it representative of the God they called upon? It all came to a climax in a place called Peniel. An angel wrestled Jacob throughout the night. The tenacity of Jacob would not let go until he received a blessing. And that he did. Jacob was renamed *Israel*, which meant "the one who struggles with God and overcomes." God had successfully dealt with his character issue. Jacob was forever changed. A limp would not ever let him forget!

Father, You know my human tendencies and weaknesses. I am, indeed, poor in spirit. I acknowledge my great need for Your intervention in my life. Deal with me in Your kindness to bring about the character of Christ. Amen.

January 16

Genesis 32:13–34:31; Matthew 11:7–30; Psalm 14:1–7; Proverbs 3:19–20

A Heart Tension

From the days of John the Baptist until now, the kingdom of heaven has been forcefully advancing, and forceful men lay hold of it.
—Matthew 11:12

Take my yoke upon you and learn from me, for I am gentle and humble in heart...
—Matthew 11:29

I see a tension in this chapter worthy of comment. Do you see it?

First, Jesus gives us the visual of what's going on in the spirit realm. Since John has come upon the scene to prepare the way for Jesus, the kingdom of heaven is *forcefully advancing,* or *is forcibly entered. Men lay hold of it by using force. They seize it for themselves.* That sounds militant! Do I need to equip myself with army boots to advance in my relationship with the Lord here?

At chapter's end, Jesus offers rest for the weary and burdened, and then He gives us the only self description of His person stated in the gospels. Jesus says: *I am gentle (meek) and humble (lowly) in heart.* Is this a soft and mild Savior?

It may appear as an oxymoron. But I think not. To be *meek* is not to be weak. It is confidence and conviction displayed through humility. *Forceful men advancing* are people of courage, passion and unwavering faith. His kingdom's rule is established within our heart—the seat of our person. We embrace His kingdom, not passively, but assertively and wholeheartedly.

Father God, Your yoke is easy and Your burden is light. You have freed me from my burdens. You have made my weary heart glad. Instill in me a tenacity to apprehend all that You have for me in a spirit of meekness. Amen.

January 17

Genesis 35:1–36:43; Matthew 12:1–21; Psalm 15:1–5; Proverbs 3:21–26

Who May Dwell with You?

Lord, who may dwell in your sanctuary? Who may live on your holy hill?
—Psalm 15:1

I must admit—there is a sentimental value attached to Psalm 15. This was Margaret Reynolds' favorite Psalm. "Grandma" Reynolds, as she became known to me, was the person who challenged me to find a personal relationship with Jesus Christ when I was being courted and convicted by the Holy Spirit. After I accepted His kind invitation for salvation, I, as a young believer in high school, would visit Grandma Reynolds for hours. I would always come away encouraged and strengthened in my faith. Her eyes glowed with God. She impacted my life. And this was her favorite Psalm.

Lord, who may dwell in your sanctuary... where You are?

It is the one who lives righteously before God in all the affairs of his or her life. It affects our actions, our speech, our relationships, our attitudes, our word and our money. This person who honors the Lord in all manner of dealings will be one whom the Lord invites to be near His holy presence. It's not automatic. And it's not to be taken for granted.

Of course, we do not have this righteousness by our own merit. It is bestowed upon those who are made righteous by faith in His dear Son. He invites us to be where He is. Will you take His invitation to draw near?

Father, thank You for Your invitation to draw near. Thank You for allowing me access into Your holy presence. I give you permission to affect my life in every way. May the manner of my life be honoring to You and give witness to Your glory. Amen.

January 18

Genesis 37:1–38:30; Matthew 12:22–45; Psalm 16:1–11; Proverbs 3:27–32

Blasphemy Against the Spirit

And so I tell you, every sin and blasphemy against the Spirit will not be forgiven. Anyone who speaks a word against the Son of Man will be forgiven, but anyone who speaks against the Holy Spirit will not be forgiven...
—Matthew 12:31–32

Blasphemy is a strong word and a stout charge. For Jesus to declare such a thing should grab our attention and pique our curiosity.

It is interesting that Jesus said: *"You can reject Me, but you can't reject the person and work of the Holy Spirit."* And they certainly did bring insult to the Savior. But it is the Holy Spirit who convicts of sin and draws us toward a relationship with God. The Holy Spirit is the One who woos us. Our spirit is made alive only when the Holy Spirit indwells us. Change is possible when the Spirit of God engages our heart.

So, a resolute and deliberate rejection of the Spirit's work is to reject the abundant life of cleansing and forgiveness that Christ came to freely give us. It is the kindness of God that leads us to repentance, and we are all given an opportunity to respond to His kind offer of mercy. Only God knows the heart, and conviction is a hard thing to gauge, but to knowingly snub the Spirit's leading and drawing is a dangerous place to be. The ongoing resistance of a calloused heart is the ultimate refusal that results in damnation.

And, oh by the way, if you have any interest at all in the things of God, don't worry. You have not blasphemed the Holy Spirit!

Father God, I thank You that You are patient toward us, not wanting any to perish, but for all to come to repentance. Keep me from offense and anything that would lend itself to a calloused heart. Instead, may I honor Your name and give place to Your Spirit's promptings always. Amen.

January 19

Genesis 39:1–41:16; Matthew 12:46–13:23; Psalm 17:1–5; Proverbs 3:33–35

My True Family

While Jesus was still talking to the crowd … Someone told him, "Your mother and brothers are standing outside, wanting to speak to you." He replied to him, "Who is my mother, and who are my brothers?" Pointing to his disciples, he said, "Here are my mother and my brothers. For whoever does the will of my Father in heaven is my brother and sister and mother."
—Matthew 12:46–50

I can imagine the shock and dismay this probably caused the immediate *biological* family of Jesus. I wish I could have been there to witness the body language and hear the intonation in the voice of the currier who made the report to Jesus. My curiosity wonders whether he was just reporting the fact, or whether he was insinuating that, *"Yes, Jesus, you are just a man of flesh, and no more!"* Either way, it was a good time to point out what real family was all about in the scope of His eternal kingdom.

Family, of course, is important to God. Family lineage and genealogies have always played an important role throughout Bible history. But here, Jesus highlights the fact that our common faith is what makes us a true family. Doing all the will of God is what marks our DNA as sons and daughters of God. Our faith in the Father unites us as one and knits us closer in spirit than we ever could on a biological level. That is why we are to value our brothers and sisters in the Lord. These are the family relationships that will endure throughout the ages and all of eternity.

Father God, I thank You that You call me one of Your own. You have placed me in Your great family alongside all those who call upon Your name. Establish righteous relationships in my life. Put godly people around me. May I be a source of blessing to each one. Amen.

January 20

Genesis 41:17–42:17; Matthew 13:24–46; Psalm 18:1–15; Proverbs 4:1–6

The Making of a Man

As soon as Joseph saw his brothers, he recognized them, but he pretended to be a stranger. .Although Joseph recognized his brothers, they did not recognize him. Then he remembered his dreams about them…
—Genesis 42:7–9

The story of Joseph's life is fascinating. You know the story. He was a favored son of Jacob's, from his wife Rachel. At a young age, Joseph had dreams where his brothers bowed down before him. However innocently his intentions may have been, they were not received well.

Yet, Joseph's dreams were from God. They were valid, legitimate, prophetic dreams. The awkward circumstances that followed were all preparatory for the assignment God had for Joseph. Rejected by his own brothers. Sold into slavery. Wrongfully accused. Innocently jailed. Overlooked for the promotion. Forgotten in a bad way. Yet, the Lord was with Joseph and showed him kindness and granted him favor in whatever he put his hand to. The obvious question in the midst of the disappointment was: *"God, are You sure You know what You're doing? Remember the dreams You gave me?"*

Among the highlights of Joseph's rise to fame concerned his integrity while in the house of Pharaoh. Looking into the face of temptation—and an alluring face it was—Joseph replies to Pharaoh's wife, *"How could I do such a wicked thing and sin against God? (39:9)"* The job that God was raising Joseph up for would require purity of heart. Joseph passed the test. He could be trusted.

Joseph, you're a man of God and a hero in my eyes!

Father, thank You for the example Joseph is. I know that with Your favor and my obedience, Your promises are Yes, and Amen. Grant unto me the wisdom, patience, perseverance and purity Joseph had to go the distance. Amen.

January 21

Genesis 42:18–43:34; Matthew 13:47–14:12; Psalm 18:16–36; Proverbs 4:7–10

My Dad is the Best.

He reached down from on high and took hold of me. He rescued me because he delighted in me. It is God who arms me with strength and makes my way perfect. You stoop down to make me great.
    —Psalm 18:16,19,32,35

Upon reading Psalm 18, I couldn't help but think of how, as a kid growing up, I was proud of my dad and would brag, *"My dad is the best dad in the whole world!"* Of course, in my eyes, that was the honest truth. I was very blessed to have such a caring father who was engaged in my upbringing. Along with my two brothers, all within two and a half years in age, my dad would still have time for us. He was the scoutmaster for our Boy Scout troop. He got me to all of my little league baseball games. What a tremendous influence he had upon my life. More than anything, I always knew that I was loved.

This Psalm makes me feel the same way about my heavenly Father.

God's heart towards me is very evident here. From His vantage point in heaven, He delights in me. He is always with me. He takes the time to train, strengthen and prepare me. He gives me the confidence I need to wage war against my enemy. He is my shield and my refuge. He protects me and sustains me. He causes me to see the light and walk in the light. He alone makes me great!

With my Divine Dad, we can conquer every foe and meet every challenge. *"For who is God besides the Lord?" (v.31).*

Father God, I am amazed at Your love for me. It is a tender, yet powerful love that comes from Your strong hand. Your way is perfect. Keep my lamp burning, I pray, for with You, I can scale a wall and bend a bow of bronze. Amen.

January 22

Genesis 44:1–45:28; Matthew 14:13–36; Psalm 18:37–50; Proverbs 4:11–13

A Solitary Place

He withdrew by boat privately to a solitary place. After he had dismissed them, he went up on a mountainside by himself to pray. When evening came, he was there alone…
—Matthew 14:13,23

It is quite obvious that Jesus drew His strength in the quiet place alone with His Father. *"I do nothing on my own but speak just what the Father has taught me" (John 8:28). "The Father told me what to say and how to say it" (John 12:49).*

With all His teachings and exploits and hours with people, Jesus had to know where His source of strength originated from. As a man, he became fatigued physically as we do. But Jesus withdrew to solitary places. He spent hours upon hours with His Father.

If the Son of God knew how to withdraw for prayer and rest, why would it be any different for us? Earlier, in Matthew 6:6, Jesus said, *"When you pray, go into your room, close the door and pray to your Father…"* This is the principle of closing the door on outward distractions in a resolute way in order to commune with our Father.

When we make this determined place in our life and in our day for Him, He is able to download wisdom and revelation in the knowledge of Him. That makes our spirit come alive! It's what our heart longs for. It's what Jesus would not deny Mary of Bethany *(Luke 10:38-42).* And it only comes while at His feet in complete abandon.

Father in heaven, thank You for the example Jesus gave us to spend time with You and to receive from You. Give me the heart of Mary, who chose to listen at Your feet in a posture of humility over much busyness, even if the busyness is about well-meaning things. Amen.

January 23

Genesis 46:1–47:31; Matthew 15:1–28; Psalm 19:1–14; Proverbs 4:14–19

God's Glory Declared

The heavens declare the glory of God; the skies proclaim the work of his hands. The ordinances of the Lord are sure and altogether righteous.
—Psalm 19:1,9

It's almost unfair to make any attempt to somehow add anything to the majesty of this writing. Perhaps it's best just to read Psalm 19 four or five times and stand back in awe by the glory of God revealed in two ways especially: in His *creation* and in His *Word*.

Who can witness the awesome colors and dramatic beauty of a sunset and deny the reality of a Creator's hand? What about the millions of galaxies and the billions of stars? The heavens declare, proclaim and pour forth speech continually the work of His hands, so that no one is without excuse. (Paul actually refers to this passage in Romans 1:19–20.) It's the quiet shout that some choose not to hear.

God's laws are not confining and constraining, as we may have once imagined. No, they are a guiding light to all that our heart truly desires. The Word of the Lord revives the soul, makes wise the simple, brings with it great reward, and gives joy to the heart and light to the eyes. His statutes are sweeter than honey and His precepts are more precious than gold. This Word is desirable. My spirit longs for this!

Poke your head outside and catch the sunrise or take a walk and enjoy His glory. Purpose now to become a student of His Word.

May the words of my mouth and the meditation of my heart be pleasing in Your sight, O Lord, my Rock and my Redeemer. Amen.

January 24

Genesis 48:1–49:33; Matthew 15:29–16:12; Psalm 20:1–9; Proverbs 4:20–27

The Prophetic Blessing of Judah

Judah, your brothers will praise you; your hand will be on the neck of your enemies; your father's sons will bow down to you. You are a lion's cub, O Judah; The scepter will not depart from Judah, nor the ruler's staff from between his feet, until he comes to whom it belongs and the obedience of the nations is his.
    —*Genesis 49:8–10*

What an awesome blessing! We know this to reference the family lineage that reaches all the way to a time in history when the Messiah Jesus would enter the scene as the Promised One. He would rule and reign as king over all nations, and would come through the ancestry of Judah. *"The scepter will not depart from Judah…"(v.10).*

Why did Judah's father Jacob pronounce this blessing over him? My mind raced back to the way Judah lived his life. Judah was the one who spearheaded Joseph's demise to be sold to the Ishmaelite traders! This evidenced Judah's leadership among his brothers. And later, realizing the impact of his father's grief over Joseph, it was Judah who guaranteed Benjamin's safe return from their trip to Egypt, mandated by the ruler Joseph *(Genesis.43:8-9).* I believe the truly contrite and earnest heart of Judah was integral in Jacob's choosing of Judah for the prophetic blessing. This type of heart pleases God.

Judah's very name means "praise." How interesting it is that his brothers would *praise* him! The language of the rest of this blessing speaks of the splendor and abundance that will mark Jesus' reign over the nations in the coming Millennium.

Father of glory, You knew from the beginning the path of the Promised Messiah. Likewise, You know my path. I pray that You would create in me a heart of humility and earnest seeking that releases Your blessing in my life. Amen.

January 25

Genesis 50:1–Exodus 2:10; Matthew 16:13–17:9; Psalm 21:1–13; Proverbs 5:1–6

Natural Thinking vs. Spiritual Thinking

Jesus replied, "Blessed are you, Simon son of Jonah, for this was not revealed to you by man, but by my Father in heaven." Jesus turned and said to Peter, "Get behind me Satan! You are a stumbling block to me; you do not have in mind the things of God, but the things of men."
—Matthew 16:17,23

What an astonishing piece of reading. Did you catch the irony of the passage as I did? One minute, Jesus is praising Peter for his insightful response, because it could only have been revealed by the Spirit of God. The next minute, Jesus is rebuking him for thinking in such natural terms, as inspired by Satan.

I am challenged by this, because I know this is likewise true of me. How is it that I can think and speak as one with the mind of Christ, and then, in the next breath, resort to what is logical and natural. Paul teaches us (in 1 Corinthians 2) that the natural mind does not understand the things of the Spirit. The best my natural reasoning can muster up has no spiritual benefit—it is actually carnal and fleshly.

Natural thinking is fine when you decide that you need to make a trip to the store to purchase a gallon of milk. But to make determinations outside the counsel of the Holy Spirit in life issues and challenges is a mistake. By going to the Lord in prayer and consulting His Word, I allow the Holy Spirit to quicken my thoughts and my actions.

Dear gracious Father, grant unto me a spirit of wisdom and revelation in the knowledge of Your Son, so that I may know Him better. I pray that the eyes of my heart may be enlightened, to know Your hope, Your riches, and Your power. Amen.

January 26

Exodus 2:11–3:22; Matthew 17:10–27; Psalm 22:1–18; Proverbs 5:7–14

Prophetic Psalm 22

My God, My God, why have you forsaken me? … my tongue sticks to the roof of my mouth … they have pierced my hands and my feet. They divide my garments among them and cast lots for my clothing.
—Psalm 22:15,16,18

There was a unique relationship between David and Jesus. The Messiah to come, after all, would be a descendant of David's. Many Psalms spoke prophetically of details of things to come. Here, for instance, David pens an amazingly accurate description of the suffering that Jesus would endure hundreds of years later. While hanging on the cross, weighted down by the sins of the world, Jesus cried out these same words as He felt the impact of the separation sin had made: *"My God, My God, why have you forsaken me?" (Matthew 27:46)*. In both instances, David and Jesus gain victory through their suffering.

In this Psalm, David describes the agony Jesus will experience on the cross *(Psalm 22:1-21; Matthew 26-27)*. Evil men cast lots for His clothes *(Psalm 22:18; Matthew 27:35)*. Jesus was thirsty while on the cross *(Psalm 22:15; John 19:28)*. Jesus would declare God's name *(Psalm 22:22; Hebrews 2:12)*. Likewise, it should be no surprise that many times throughout His life, Jesus quoted from the Psalms of David.

The Psalm and his prayer are answered, as he is able to declare to *his brothers* the praise due unto God, before the congregation. The victory deserved public testimony.

Father, thank You for the victory won at the cross—at the expense of Your dear Son. You conquered sin and death by the perfect sacrifice of a sinless life. Words do not express adequately my gratitude for the suffering Jesus bore. Let praise come forth by my manner of life offered unto You. Amen.

January 27

Exodus 4:1–5:21; Matthew 18:1–22; Psalm 22:19–31; Proverbs 5:15–21

These Little Ones

I tell you the truth, unless you change and become like little children, you will never enter the kingdom of heaven. And whoever welcomes a little child like this in my name welcomes me. See that you do not look down on one of these little ones … your Father in heaven is not willing that any of these little ones should be lost.
   —Matthew 18:3,5,10,14

Jesus makes profound points of kingdom understanding by referring to children in these four examples.

Who is the greatest in the kingdom of heaven? Greatness according to Jesus is about humility. Learn from a child. Children know they are totally dependent upon mom and dad. They are powerless in their own right. And they believe in the Lord so easily and simply.

Don't even think about making one of these to stumble and sin. As adults, we model to them what is acceptable behavior. Children are the best imitators. They are always watching and observing.

Verse 10 is a classic. The angels *(plural)* that watch over children are positioned before the Father in heaven. God *knows* when we look down upon, neglect or mistreat any of His dear ones.

Lastly, the Father is like a Shepherd. He is so interested in every soul, that He will leave the 99 to search out the one that wanders off *(v.12)*. Restoring one who stumbles is the very heart of God. Our Father's desire is that no one should be lost. That means me. That means you!

Father in heaven, thank You for searching me out and loving me the way You do. Give me a simple faith that trusts You without reservation. And let my life be a model for others to imitate. Amen.

January 28

Exodus 5:22–7:24; Matthew 18:23–19:12; Psalm 23:1–6; Proverbs 5:22–23

The Unforgiving Servant

The servant fell on his knees… "Be patient with me," he begged, "and I will pay back everything." The master took pity on him, cancelled the debt and let him go. But when that servant went out, he found one of his fellow servants who owed him a hundred denarii … and had [him] thrown into prison.
—Matthew 18:26–28,30

Sometimes, we just need to be reminded of the great mercy of God. For some reason, we have this knack for allowing little things to skew our perception. We think they are bigger than they really are. And we forget the great debt that we ourselves once owed. That debt was beyond our ability in a lifetime to repay. We had no answer. Our only hope rested on the mercy of a righteous Judge.

In this context, I learned that failure to pay a debt could bring serious consequences—up to life imprisonment for the debtor, and the lender could force the family into slavery in order to pay off the debt. It was perhaps the only recourse for the king. To recoup the overwhelming sum the servant had owed was not going to be possible. But that amplifies the mercy that the king was extending. He forgave it all!

How then, having been forgiven of such a great debt, could the same mercy not be extended to another—over far more trivial matters? The servant who is unwilling to forgive gains nothing. He is imprisoned, bound up and unfruitful. Could holding any offense be worth that?

Who, in your life, do you need to extend mercy towards and forgive?

Merciful Father, thank You for Your compassion and forgiveness in my life. I owed a debt that I could not pay, and You wiped my slate clean. May my actions and reactions reflect the mercy and patience You displayed toward me. Amen.

January 29

Exodus 7:25–9:35; Matthew 19:13–30; Psalm 24:1–10; Proverbs 6:1–5

The Rich Young Man

Now a man came up to Jesus and asked, "Teacher, what good thing must I do to get eternal life?" Jesus answered, "… go, sell your possessions and give to the poor, and you will have treasure in heaven. Then come, follow me." When the young man heard this, he went away sad, because he had great wealth.
   —Matthew 19:16, 21–22

Here, a rich young man approaches Jesus for the assurance that his works are enough for eternal life. The commandments that Jesus highlighted were all relational commandments. And as far as the young aristocrat knew, he had kept the commandments. But Jesus exposed the root weakness of his heart.

Wealth was his god. Money had become his idol, and he could not bring himself to part with it. His fists were clutched with its' power. Thus, he had violated the first and greatest commandment: *"You shall have no other gods before me"* (Deuteronomy 5:7).

Does wealth have to have such a grip on the heart that it could keep a person from eternal life? Well … pursuing wealth is one of our culture's greatest strongholds. We all want just a little more, right?

But there is a difference between *the love* of money and being faithful stewards over what God provides. Make no mistake. God wants to bless you. But what captivates your heart? Are you willing to surrender your finances to God? The man who is truly rich is the one God entrusts to fund kingdom activity. He has a treasure in heaven! With man this is impossible, but with God all things are possible.

Father, I ask, as the rich, young man asked, "What do I still lack?" Probe my heart and reveal any idol that would take prominence over Your rightful place on the throne of my heart. I submit my all to Your Lordship. Amen.

January 30

Exodus 10:1–12:13; Matthew 20:1–28; Psalm 25:1–15; Proverbs 6:6–11

The Goshen Principle

But on that day I will deal differently with the land of Goshen, where my people live; no swarms of flies will be there, so that you will know that I, the Lord, am in this land. I will make a distinction between my people and your people. No one could see anyone else ... for three days. Yet all the Israelites had light.
—Exodus 8:22–23; 10:23

I have read over the past two days about the signs and wonders that Moses performed by God's hand in judgment of Pharaoh and Egypt. Pictures of Charlton Heston come to mind! Yet one of the great miracles that occur often gets overlooked.

With swarms and swarms of flies, a deadly plague of all livestock, massively destructive hail, total darkness *that could even be felt*, and finally the death of every firstborn, the pain is felt throughout Egypt, but *not* the Israelites in Goshen! How does this happen—*or not happen?* Goshen is a suburb! From a natural perspective, there could be no way to escape the effects of this destruction. But God makes a distinction. His people are set apart. His people are protected.

I believe the Lord would have us know that amidst all the calamities of this final era of natural history, God is going to protect His people in extraordinary ways. It doesn't matter that the financial markets are dipping to scary levels. God's economy is not dependent upon ours! God's promises to provide for us are true. Let the judgments come. They are from His hand! God will prove Himself faithful again to protect and provide for those He has set apart.

Father, I thank You for Your protection and Your provision. I look to You as my source. Give me faith to trust You when circumstances look intimidating. Cause me to live as one You have set apart unto Yourself. Amen.

January 31

Exodus 12:14–13:16; Matthew.20:29–21:22; Psalm 25:16–22; Proverbs 6:12–15

The House of Prayer

Jesus entered the temple area and drove out all who were buying and selling there. He overturned the tables of the money changers and the benches of those selling doves. "It is written," he said to them, "My house will be called a house of prayer, but you are making it a den of robbers."
—Matthew 21:12–13

Anytime Jesus makes a demonstrative statement such as this, you have to pause and consider. *I mean,* Jesus had a lot of zeal and passion on this. He was not passive. Jesus displayed a holy, righteous anger to overturn tables and benches, and to drive out merchants selling!

It wasn't so much that Jesus witnessed the gross overcharging of goods. Even though it must have been convenience store pricing during a busy Passover season—still, that wasn't the main point.

What Jesus was so moved by was what the temple was being used for. Ask yourself! *What is the place of worship supposed to be for?* The reason we gather together as a people is to cultivate a life in communion with God, and then with people. Is prayer our mainstay? Do we promote and prioritize a deeper and more intimate relationship with God that only comes through prayer?

Jesus quotes Isaiah 56:7. *"My house will be a house of prayer for all nations."* No one is to be excluded. Jews and Gentiles alike share in this joy on God's holy mountain!

Father, I thank You for making prayer such a passionate topic for Jesus. It shows me the absolute prominence that prayer must take in my life and in the life of our congregations. Take me deeper in communion with you today. Amen.

February 1

Exodus 13:17–15:18; Matthew 21:23–46; Psalm 26:1–12; Proverbs 6:16–19

Praise Is First

And when the Israelites saw the great power the Lord displayed against the Egyptians, the people feared the Lord and put their trust in him. Then Moses sang this song … Then Miriam the prophetess took a tambourine and all the women followed her, with tambourines and dancing.
—Exodus 14:31; 15:1,20

I think this day in the history books for Israel was especially intense. The firstborn of every Egyptian dies in the night. Upon a quick exit, the Israelites plunder their former hosts. A couple million people take all their belongings on their backs and leave on foot, and yet, are also armed for battle. They receive divine guidance and protection. They escape successfully, only to find themselves backed up against the Red Sea. Egyptian chariots chase them down and are poised ready to exact revenge. Then God makes the water stand up as a wall, the ground is dried, and all Israel crosses over. The enemies of God are entirely covered over by water and not one survives. *Whewh!*

The power of the Lord was displayed firsthand. The deliverance of a nation was secured. And the people rightly feared a holy, righteous God. And what is the first response of Moses? Moses sings this song of deliverance. *"I will sing unto the Lord, for He is highly exalted. The horse and rider He has hurled into the sea. Who is like you—majestic in holiness, awesome in glory, working wonders?" (15:1,11).* Miriam then leads all the women in a dance of praise to express their heartfelt gratitude.

Can I ask? … When was the last time you sang to the Lord a vocal expression of thanks to celebrate the deliverance of God in your life?

Father God, You have delivered me from the domain of darkness and have translated me into the kingdom of Your dear Son. I praise You with all that I am and all that I have. May I never withhold the praise due Your name. Amen.

February 2

Exodus 15:19–17:7; Matthew 22:1–33; Psalm 27:1–6; Proverbs 6:20–26

Jehovah Rophe

He [the Lord] said, "If you listen carefully to the voice of the Lord your God and do what is right in his eyes, if you pay attention to his commands and keep all his decrees, I will not bring on you any of these diseases…I am the Lord, who heals you."
—Exodus 15:26

As you read through the Bible, the Lord unveils His character in a progressive sort of way. An example of this is found in Exodus 6:3: *"I appeared to Abraham, to Isaac, and to Jacob as God Almighty (El Shaddai), but by My name the Lord (Yahweh) I did not make Myself known to them."* You see, God revealed Himself in greater measure as time went on, building upon what was previously known. God was the same unchanging God, but revealing more as One who acts and speaks.

Here, today, God reveals Himself as *Jehovah Rophe*—the Lord who heals you. It is who He is. It is what He does. God Almighty is the Great Physician. He is the same yesterday, and will be forever. God does not change. It is the Lord's will that you be made whole.

It would be a mistake, however, not to read the entirety of the verse. *"If you listen carefully to the voice of the Lord and do what is right…If you pay attention to his commands and keep all his decrees, then …"* These are overlooked prerequisites. We want the blessing, but do we want to hear His every whisper and respond to every command?

There is joy and healing in obeying the Lord with wholeheartedness.

Father God, You are Jehovah Rophe. You are the God who heals body, soul and spirit. You heal the upright in heart. I do not deserve and cannot earn Your blessing, but You desire to make me whole. I receive Your touch in Jesus' name. Amen.

February 3

Exodus 17:8–19:15; Matthew 22:34–23:12; Psalm 27:7–14; Proverbs 6:27–35

Jehovah Nissi

Moses built an altar and called it The Lord is my Banner. He said, "For hands were lifted up to the throne of the Lord. The Lord will be at war against the Amalekites from generation to generation."
—Exodus 17:15–16

It's interesting. Just yesterday, we mentioned the progressive revealing of the Lord's name and character, and *voila*, the Lord discloses a further aspect of His nature—*Jehovah Nissi, the Lord is my Banner.*

Here, the Lord reveals Himself as the God who fights for us. The Amalekites have attacked the Israelites at Rephidim, so Moses gives Joshua charge of the army to counter their adversary. But the true difference-maker was in the hands of Moses being held up. Aaron and Hur assist. As long as Moses' hands are lifted to the Lord, Israel advances. When his hands were not lifted, the Amalekites advanced. The Israelite army won a great battle that day because Moses lifted his hands in praise and surrender to Jehovah Nissi, who warred on their behalf.

We are inadequate to match our adversary, but when we lift our hands to God and ask Him to war on our behalf, we have Jehovah Nissi to go before us. When the enemy advances to exploit you, know that the Lord your Banner encamps around you to protect you and bring the victory. It is His banner of love that covers us in the battle.

Father, I lift my hands to You now in my fight against the enemy. I declare that I am overmatched in the battles I face. I need You to exercise Your strong right hand. I thank You for raising Your Banner over me. Thank You for intervening to fight and to bring victory. I surrender to You and I praise You. Amen.

February 4

Exodus 19:16–21:21; Matthew 23:13–39; Psalm 28:1–9; Proverbs 7:1–5

A Holy Fear

When the people saw the thunder and lightning and heard the trumpet and saw the mountain in smoke, they trembled with fear. Moses said to the people, "Do not be afraid. God has come to test you, so that the fear of God will be with you to keep you from sinning."
—Exodus 20:18, 20

The Lord has revealed to all of Israel that He is mighty to deliver. They knew that reality from the plagues, from the deliverance through the walls of the Red Sea, from the provision of water and manna, and from the military victories. But the majesty of God needed to be impressed deeply into their knowledge of the Holy One. This is a beginning place in our understanding of who God is.

Imagine the scene. It's a Hollywood dream with all the props, but for real. *"Mount Sinai was covered with smoke, because the Lord descended on it in fire" (19:18).* The whole mountain trembled violently, and the sound of the trumpet grew louder and louder. No wonder even the priests trembled in fear. It would be right to say that it was a righteous terror. I would have been on my face, for sure.

This is the awesome glory of God that produces a righteous fear, a fear that keeps us from sinning. Knowing that this awesome, holy God watches over every detail of our life should lead us to honor Him in all of our choices. Not to mention that we will stand before Him one day. Fearing the Lord in this way is the beginning of wisdom. Do you have a holy reverence toward this God of incredible majesty?

Father God, may I know You in truth as You are. You are righteous and holy. You are beautiful beyond description, too marvelous for words. Stamp upon my heart the knowledge of Your majesty and awe, so that I might fear Your name and not sin against You. Amen.

February 5

Exodus 21:22–23:13; Matthew 24:1–28; Psalm 29:1–11; Proverbs 7:6–23

What Will be the Sign?

At that time many will turn away from the faith and will betray and hate each other, and many false prophets will appear and deceive many people. Because of the increase of wickedness, the love of most will grow cold, but he who stands firm to the end will be saved.
—Matthew 24:10–13

In a private conversation with his disciples about the end of the age, Jesus is asked, *"When will this happen, and what will be the sign of your coming?" (v.3).*

Wars and threats of war and natural calamities are the beginning of what Jesus calls "birth pains." Deception, betrayal and hate follow. Teachers and charismatic leaders will come slyly and convincingly in order to deceive and lead many astray. Sin and lawlessness will abound. Society will embrace sin and scoff at righteousness. Even believers will take offense at the judgments that God Himself has set in motion. *How could a loving God allow this?* And because of the wickedness that runs rampant, love that once was extended will now be withheld—hearts will harden. The truth is that the darkness will get darker and the light will, indeed, become brighter.

The purpose of this writing is to heed the warning. Argue all you want about fine points of doctrine, but Jesus gives us the heads up so that we will not be deceived; that we will not turn away from our faith; so that our love will not grow cold. It's going to happen. Now you know. Guard your heart and do whatever it takes to stay close to Jesus.

Dear heavenly Father, thank You for preparing me for what lies ahead in the days to come. I ask You to draw me ever closer to Your side. Give me a faith that will not fail and a love that will not wax cold. Let the greatest days of anointing and harvest be for those who find their hope in You. Amen.

February 6

Exodus 23:14–25:40; Matthew 24:29–51; Psalm 30:1–12; Proverbs 7:24–27

The Process of Sanctification

When Pharaoh let the people go, God did not lead them on the road through the Philistine country, though that was shorter. But I will not drive them (your enemies) out in a single year… Little by little I will drive them out before you, until you have increased enough to take possession of the land.
—Exodus 13:17; 23:29–30

When I map out a trip from point A to point B, I'm looking at the interstate travel and the quickest routes. *Seems logical for a trip!*

But when God guides and directs our life, He does not map out the quickest route. Yet He knows the best path by far for us to take. The direction He has chosen for us will lead us to the great and precious promises in a place of abundance, described as a land of milk and honey. Along the way, the Lord knows there will be battles that I will face and sins I must overcome. He knows the road and He leads me.

Just as Israel is a new nation following their deliverance from Egypt, so I am a new man delivered from the kingdom of my past darkness. So leaving Egypt behind is the first step. The second step, then, is to rid the Egypt remaining within. This is the "little by little" driving out of the old sinful life. Sanctification is what we call the process of leaving behind the familiar sins and embracing the new identity we have in Christ. Transformation continues as I renew my mind in God's Word. It's a process that you cannot hurry through, and it's not always pretty. It is a lifelong process that, over time, brings about in me His ultimate goal: conformity to the image of His Son Jesus.

Father God, I thank You for the path You have laid out for me. It is a road of holiness, and You are committed to my sanctification. Give me grace to overcome the sins that I struggle with. I pursue You and Your promises for me. Amen.

February 7

Exodus 26:1–27:21; Matthew 25:1–30; Psalm 31:1–8; Proverbs 8:1–11

Get Oil

Five of them (virgins) were foolish and five were wise. The foolish ones took their lamps but did not take any oil with them. The wise, however, took oil in jars along with their lamps ... The foolish ones said to the wise, "Give us some of your oil." "No," they replied, "go buy some for yourselves."
—Matthew 25:2–4,8–9

Personally, I think this is one of the most gripping messages in all of the Bible. It lays out the condition of the church in the last days before Jesus finally comes again to rule and reign on the earth.

First, we know they are *all* believers—they are all virgins—pure in the eyes of the Lord. The critical difference between the five who were called *wise* and the five who were called *foolish* is just one thing: *oil*.

Oil throughout the Bible is a symbol of the Holy Spirit. As we draw closer to the end of the age, more than ever, effectual ministry will require dependency upon God's Spirit. Without this determined secret life in God, leaders will run around doing ministry, but will not have the anointing to endure in hard times. They will run out of oil. They will burn out.

The point is clear. *You get oil—now!* Understand that you get oil by spending time before the Lord in prayer and worship. Someone else's experience will not do it for you. The reservoir of your spirit must be filled with the oil that comes from a life engaged with the Holy Spirit.

Give me oil in my lamp. Keep me burning, burning, burning...

Father God, I pray that You would fill me to overflowing with Your Spirit. I determine in my heart that now is the time to know and be known by You. Meet me in the quiet place. Establish my schedule around You. Amen.

February 8

Exodus 28:1–43; Matthew 25:31–26:13; Psalm 31:9–18; Proverbs 8:12–13

Extravagant Worship

While Jesus was in Bethany in the home of a man known as Simon the Leper, a woman came to him with an alabaster jar of very expensive perfume, which she poured on his head as he was reclining at the table. Jesus said, "...She has done a beautiful thing to me."
—Matthew 26:6–7,10

This has become a "life passage" for me. I could never exaggerate the impact that this passage has had upon me. Here is a woman we know as Mary of Bethany. She displays an extravagant devotion with this simple act of worship.

We first meet Mary in Luke 10:38-41, where she sits at the feet of Jesus listening and choosing to do what was better. Later, when her brother Lazarus dies, Mary again is kneeling before Jesus. Here, Mary breaks her jar to anoint Jesus with an expensive nard—a fragrant ointment imported from India with a value of more than a year's wages. This was no doubt her life savings, yet she sacrifices what was most precious to her. She ministers to Jesus in this powerful way with all that she had. Jesus affirms her thoughtful and elaborate offering. She has done a beautifully extraordinary thing.

The disciples in that very room did not understand. Jesus had been preparing them for the ultimate rejection He would endure, yet Mary is probably the only person who really understood the peril He was about to face. Her act of worship reflects her faith and His worthiness.

Know that the Lord takes notice of your devotion and is pleased.

Father, I thank You for Mary's heart of devotion. May my worship to You be pleasing in Your sight. Instill in me a heart of extravagance that gives lavishly, for You are, indeed, worthy of my best. I praise You. Amen.

February 9

Exodus 29:1–30:10; Matthew 26:14–46; Psalm 31:19–24; Proverbs 8:14–26

Willing Spirit, Weak Flesh

Watch and pray so that you will not fall into temptation. The spirit is willing, but the body is weak.
—Matthew 26:41

We find Jesus in the garden of Gethsemane. His disciples are nearby. Peter, James and John are drawn ever closer. He needs them in this urgent hour. Jesus feels the overwhelming alarm of his mission now. Hoping they will keep watch with Him, Jesus goes further to pour out His heart in prayer to His Father in heaven. When He returns, the "Big Three" are fast asleep. Not once, not twice, but three times. They are simply spent—physically and emotionally exhausted.

This exemplifies what we're really made of as human beings. We live in this frail, weak, tent of a body. There are limitations—physically, mentally and emotionally. Sometimes, we want to do more than we are capable of.

The same is true in regard to our proneness to give in to fleshly urges. We want to serve God in our mind. We know it is right, yet our follow-through is weak. We have this propensity to satisfy what our flesh craves. The flesh is very demanding and sin is captivating. The default button of an unrenewed mind most often is to give in.

So Jesus pleads: *"Watch and pray!"* You don't have to give in when the temptation comes. The spirit is willing, so encourage and strengthen your spirit man. Desire and discipline is the heart of discipleship.

Father, give me a heart that follows through in my devotion to You. May I walk in step with Your Spirit, so that I will not gratify the desires of the flesh. I pledge my body to You as an instrument of righteousness. Thank You for the grace to stand. Amen.

February 10

Exodus 30:11–31:18; Matthew 26:47–68; Psalm 32:1–11; Proverbs 8:27–32

Bezalel, Son of Uri

Then the Lord said to Moses, "See, I have chosen Bezalel son of Uri, the son of Hur, of the tribe of Judah, and I have filled him with the Spirit of God, with skill, ability and knowledge in all kinds of crafts—to make artistic designs for work in gold, silver and bronze, to cut and set stones, to work in wood, and to engage in all kinds of craftsmanship."
—Exodus 31:1–5

Hats off to Bezalel, son of Uri, the (grand)son of Hur!

It is not often when the Spirit of God is mentioned in the Old Testament. There is activity to be sure, but the references made to the Holy Spirit are predominantly found in the New Testament. And when you see the Spirit of God upon a man, you think of someone of notoriety, a patriarch or a prophet. But Bezalel? Who is Bezalel?

The reason why Bezalel strikes me as he does, is that this man of God represents so many who are led by the Spirit and filled with the Spirit and press in to God to do His will and purpose on the earth that are *not* called to lead a congregation or deliver a message. Bezalel was blue collar! He was anointed to work with his hands. What he was appointed to do was no less important than preaching to a stadium of people or laying hands on the sick to be healed.

What a powerful message that should encourage every believer: Whatever God has called you to, He will anoint you with the power of His Spirit to accomplish it.

Father God, I thank You for the calling You have placed upon my life. I pray that Your Spirit will guide and direct me to accomplish all Your purposes for me. Let what I do unto You be done with excellence and skill, for Your glory and honor. Amen.

February 11

Exodus 32:1–33:23; Matthew 26:69–27:14; Psalm 33:1–11; Proverbs 8:33–36

The Distinguishing Mark

The Lord replied, "My Presence will go with you, and I will give you rest." Then Moses said to him, "If your Presence does not go with us, do not send us up from here … How will anyone know that you are pleased with me unless you go with us? What else will distinguish me and your people from all the other people?"
—Exodus 33:14–16

It's a benchmark moment in the journey to the Promised Land.

It's time for Israel to move along, and Moses is faced with the possibility of leading the nation alone, with *just an angel*. Moses pleads his case before God face to face, as a man speaks with his friend. He reminds God: *"These are not my people, but these are Your own people!"*

What results from this conversation is as telling today as it was then. If God does not go with us, then what distinguishes us from anyone else? Is it not the very presence of God? Is it not the Holy Spirit who dwells within? Without God's presence with us and upon us, how are we any different?

And furthermore, if the presence of God is what differentiates us from those of the world, then why would we pursue any other means to succeed. My best performance without the Spirit's leading and anointing is absolutely fruitless! We don't need to offer people anything less than that which authentically changes people from the inside for real. His Spirit upon my life is what I need!

Father in heaven, I pray, as Moses, don't let me go one step outside where You are. Without You, I am nothing. My identity is found in You alone. May Your smile be upon me and Your presence more evident as I walk with You. Amen.

February 12

Exodus 34:1–35:9; Matthew 27:15–31; Psalm 33:12–22; Proverbs 9:1–6

How God Describes Himself

He passed in front of Moses, proclaiming, "The Lord, the Lord, the compassionate and gracious God, slow to anger, abounding in love and faithfulness, maintaining love to thousands, and forgiving wickedness, rebellion and sin."
—Exodus 34:6–7

If you were to describe God to someone, what would you say? … God is love? He is a stern Judge? He is a grouchy old grandpa? He is the Creator of the universe?

Here, Moses wants to know the Lord more fully. He knows the God of deliverance. He knows the God of great power, the jealous God, the One who heals and fights our battles. But Moses insists: I want to know You more! *"Show me your glory" (33:18).*

The Lord answers this bold request. He hides Moses in the cleft of the rock and passes by in all His goodness. He reveals His glory, but not in the way I expected that He would. While He passes by, He proclaims His name. He discloses to Moses a more complete composite of His true nature and identity— *"compassionate, gracious, abounding in love, slow to anger, forgiving, extending mercy to thousands…"*

Are you surprised at how God chose to reveal Himself to Moses? Are you surprised to know these *kind* aspects of God's nature? You see, God is one–hundred percent holy and just in all His ways. He is also one–hundred percent love and mercy. It is not either/or, but both/and. Do you know the God of the Bible in this way?

Dear Father, You are compassionate. You are gracious. You abound in love. You are faithful to the core. You are slow to anger, and yet holy, righteous and just. Lord, reveal to me more of Your person. I want to know You! Amen.

February 13

Exodus 35:10–36:38; Matthew 27:32–66; Psalm 34:1–10; Proverbs 9:7–8

Willing Generosity

Everyone who was willing and whose heart moved him came and brought an offering to the Lord for the work on the Tent of Meeting. All who were willing, men and women alike, came and brought gold jewelry…
—Exodus 35:21–22

The instructions for the tabernacle had been articulated by the Lord to Moses. Now it would take a concerted and united effort by the whole Israelite community to make it happen. Those who would participate would be those who were *willing*.

When you come together for a project like this, you don't want people involved who are half-hearted about it. This sanctuary of the Lord's would require detail, excellence and skill from a willing heart.

Those whose hearts were stirred gave freely of their possessions to the Lord's work. The same is true today. The level of our commitment can be gauged by our pocketbooks. People who are faithful to God are also generous people for the furthering of the gospel. It may be to support a missionary family, or perhaps an oversees child in an orphanage, or an outreach in your church. Here in Exodus, the offerings from willing men and women were more than enough to accomplish the task at hand.

Our giving record is a reflection of what is dear to our heart. What does your checkbook indicate?

Dear Father, all that I have is from Your hand. I give to You my tithes and offerings from a grateful heart. It is a privilege to sow into Your work.. I give, not grudgingly or reluctantly, but enthusiastically, for You love a cheerful giver. Amen.

February 14

Exodus 37:1–38:31; Matthew 28:1–20; Psalm 34:11–22; Proverbs 9:9–10

Learning the Fear of the Lord

Come, my children, listen to me; I will teach you the fear of the Lord.
   —Psalm 34:11

The fear of the Lord can be taught. A wise son or student will do good to listen to his elders (or parents) and learn the free and easy way. But the fear of the Lord is caught more than taught, because we usually have to see it to believe it. We learn it, but usually because we had to find it out for ourselves.

The fear of the Lord is the code of honor by which we operate because the Lord is watching. It is a healthy reverence that dictates our actions, knowing that my behavior reflects upon the Lord's reputation before men. My respect for God is revealed in my actions.

This Psalm of David has many words to the wise. He spells out the principals very succinctly, from staying away from evil and keeping a reign on your tongue, to doing the right thing and pursuing peace. But David also knew that the righteous run into trouble. And when we cry out to Him, God hears us. When we are emotionally broken or our spirit is crushed, again, it is the Lord who brings the deliverance that is needed. I think David probably knows from where he speaks.

What we want to pass on to our children is this: You don't have to learn everything the hard way. This life is hard enough—even with the Lord at our side. Learn quickly that the Lord is your best advocate in every situation. He is the King of glory and He is your closest friend. *"The fear of the Lord is the beginning of wisdom"* (Proverbs 9:10).

Father God, keep me from the sin of independence. I confess my dire need for You and Your counsel. You are generous to give me wisdom from above. Amen.

February 15

Exodus 39:1–40:38; Mark 1:1–28; Psalm 35:1–16; Proverbs 9:11–12

Jesus and the Holy Spirit

I baptize you with water, but he (Jesus) will baptize you with the Holy Spirit. As Jesus was coming out of the water, he saw… the Spirit descending on him like a dove. At once the Spirit sent him out into the desert…tempted by Satan.
—Mark 1:8,10,12

It is no secret that Mark wrote his gospel account to the Romans. It is a book of action, more given to exploits, and is rapid-fire with far fewer chapters (sixteen). It is no wonder, then, that we see the Holy Spirit in the life of Jesus three different times in six verses. The link also emphasizes the work of the Holy Spirit intertwined with Jesus in every phase of His life and ministry. Even today, the ministry of the Spirit points us to Jesus.

In verse eight, John the Baptist exclaims that it is he who baptizes with water, but there will be a day when Jesus will baptize those believers with the Holy Spirit.

In verse ten, as Jesus was being baptized in water, John witnessed heaven being opened up, the voice of the Father affirming His love and pleasure, and the Spirit descending upon Him like a dove. The Trinity was present to usher in the ministry of Jesus.

In verse twelve, *at once* the Spirit led Jesus into the desert for a period of forty days, where he was tempted by Satan. *Now there's a good one!* Would we give credit to the Holy Spirit for leading us to a place of testing? At least Jesus wasn't alone. He had the wild animals and the angels and the Holy Spirit to attend him.

Father, I thank You for the ministry of the Holy Spirit. I thank You for the power You promise from on high. I thank you for the Spirit that rests upon me. And I thank You for leading me to overcome in every test. Amen.

February 16

Leviticus 1:1–3:17; Mark 1:29–2:12; Psalm 35:17–28; Proverbs 9:13–18

Through the Roof

Some men came, bringing to him (Jesus) a paralytic, carried by four of them. Since they could not get him to Jesus because of the crowd, they made an opening in the roof above Jesus, and after digging through it, lowered the mat the paralyzed man was on. When Jesus saw their faith, he said …"your sins are forgiven."
—Mark 2:3–5

This passage has special meaning to me because my wife's eldest brother had cerebral palsy. Additionally, a ministry of our church was an outreach to people with disabilities. Not surprisingly, it was called *"Through the Roof."* There is close to twenty percent of our society that claims a form of disability, and is by far one of the most unreached and unchurched people-groups of our day … and such dear souls.

Let's notice a few things about this paralytic man. *We'll give him the name Perry.* Perry had some remarkable friends. If Perry didn't have the faith to believe for healing, his four trusty friends did. They would not let a crowd dash their hopes for Perry's healing. Now picture this. The determination of these four guys gets Perry to the top of that flat roof and then lowered down through a hole they had dug through the mud and straw. With the weight of five men on that roof, you can imagine the mess that might have been!

In the end, Jesus saw their incredible faith and brought wholeness to Perry, physically and spiritually. His body was set aright and his sins were forgiven. He was a new man. Maybe now he needs a new name!

Father, I thank You for the friends You have placed in my life, that I might be encouraged and blessed. I don't always have the faith for myself. Help my unbelief. And let me be one who befriends another with a disability in order to bring him to You. Amen.

February 17

Leviticus 4:1–5:19; Mark 2:13–3:6; Psalm 36:1–12; Proverbs 10:1–2

Lord of the Sabbath

Then he (Jesus) said to them, "The Sabbath was made for man, not man for the Sabbath. So the Son of Man is Lord even of the Sabbath."
—Mark 2:27–28

Is it me, or have you noticed that when Jesus heals someone, He seems to always do it on the Sabbath? I love this about Jesus. He leaves no guesswork to the imagination.

It is the duty of the Pharisee to point out the rules, *don't you know*—rules that you must follow to earn God's favor. The Pharisees had always seen themselves as the reliable guides to their people to adapt and interpret the Law to meet the conditions of their day. What they did, however, was to process the Law down to a set of rules, in which they calculated 248 commandments and 365 prohibitions. *Oh my!*

It is these same Pharisees that are following Jesus and his disciples through the grainfields, standing ready to accuse. But Jesus calmly catches them up on their history with David and the priest Abiathar. You see, it was David who ate consecrated bread that was only lawful for priests. *Why?* Because David and his companions were hungry!

The point is nailed down in the second incident. *"Which is lawful on the Sabbath: to do good or to do evil, to save life or to kill?" (3:4).* What is the Sabbath for? The Sabbath is not an institution we bow to. The Sabbath was designed by God for the betterment of every man to rest and to honor God. *"And on the seventh day He rested."*

Father, I thank You for the Sabbath. You blessed it and made it holy. Help me to honor the Sabbath by resting from my work and honoring You. Thank You for being the Lord of the Sabbath. Amen.

February 18

Leviticus 6:1–7:27; Mark 3:7–30; Psalm 37:1–11; Proverbs 10:3–4

Power Delegated

He (Jesus) appointed twelve—designating them apostles—that they might be with him and that he might send them out to preach and to have authority to drive out demons. —Mark 3:14–15

Jesus chose twelve disciples and gave them the authority of an apostle— 1) that they might be with him; —2) to send them out to preach, and—3) have authority to drive out demons. At it's core, an apostle was a commissioned representative. Apostles, like Paul in the New Testament, started churches, followed up with appointing elders in those churches, and oversaw their health and vitality.

The power and authority to heal sickness and disease and to drive out demons comes from the original word *exousia (ex-oo-see'-ah)*. It means having the right to act, with the ability and delegated authority, to do what Jesus did. Jesus gave his followers *exousia* to preach, to teach, to heal and to deliver; and that power is still available today. Jesus says it another way in the gospel of John: *"Greater things than these will you do, because I go to the Father" (14:12).*

I look at these twelve that Jesus chose—ordinary men from varied backgrounds, and surmise … if Jesus can use two fishermen brothers who were ambitious, Type A, short-tempered *"sons of thunder,"* then just perhaps He can use me! Of course, He can use anyone who is willing and available. There is authority in the name of Jesus!

Father, I thank You for the power and authority that You bestow upon Your followers to carry out Your plans and proclaim the good news of Jesus. Empower Your church, I pray, in these last days, to be a bold witness. Heal. Deliver. Save in Jesus' name. And use my life today for "greater things." Amen.

February 19

Leviticus 7:28–9:6; Mark 3:31–4:25; Psalm 37:12–29; Proverbs 10:5

Heart Types

A farmer went out to sow his seed. As he was scattering the seed, some fell along the path ... some fell on rocky places. Other seed fell among thorns. Still other seed fell on good soil.
  —Mark 4:3–5,7–8

Jesus is a great story teller. He speaks in a language that everyone can understand, and no one can bring the truth home like Jesus.

This simple, yet profound story speaks of the types of soil that the seed falls upon, illustrating the true condition of our heart. You've heard it before, but ask yourself: *Which soil type describes your heart?*

The first heart-type is the *path*—hardened and calloused, no place for the Word to even penetrate. You've allowed Satan to steal it away. The second heart-type is among *rocky places.* (It must be the Ozarks!) This heart receives the seed gladly enough. It was a good idea, but the Word is not given prominence. The seed is shallow and not near deep enough to make a real dent. The first real challenge sends them packing. The third heart-type is among *thorns.* This happens when we allow worldly compromise to choke our heart from the nurture that comes from singular devotion. Lesser idols make this heart unfruitful. The fourth heart-type is the *good soil.* It is the deep, dark, humus soil that is soft to the touch and receives every Word, accepts every Word and obeys every Word, to bear many multiplied times a harvest.

Simply put, your heart response is everything. Won't you plow up the hard places and prepare your heart for the seed of His Word?

Father in heaven, You are so kind to cast Your seed in my direction. May the soil of my heart be prepared to receive all You have intended for a great harvest. Amen.

February 20

Leviticus 9:7–10:20; Mark 4:26–5:20; Psalm 37:30–40; Proverbs 10:6–7

Nadab and Abihu

Aaron's sons Nadab and Abihu took their censors, put fire in them and added incense; and they offered unauthorized fire before the Lord, contrary to his command. So fire came out from the presence of the Lord and consumed them, and they died before the Lord.
   —Leviticus 10:1–2

Nadab and Abihu were eyewitnesses of the mighty power of the Lord to deliver *(Exodus 24:1,9)*. They had their dad Aaron, uncle Moses and Aunt Miriam to look to as exemplary leaders. For awhile at least, they followed God wholeheartedly *(Leviticus 8:36)*. They went through the process of cleansing, consecration and ordination as prescribed. Yet, in the service of a sacred ordinance, Nadab and Abihu offered fire from their censors that was said to be profane, strange and unauthorized.

In verses just prior, fire came down that gave God's approval over all the preparation completed that permitted the sacrifices to be offered. This second time, fire came out of the Lord's presence in judgment.

Was this a petty thing that God should overlook? The instructions given were articulate and were to be obeyed. Handling the things of God is a sacred trust. The Lord articulates in Leviticus 10:10, *"Do not treat as common the holy things of God."* It is not a casual thing to take lightly or appear indifferent toward. The principle is the same today.

Those who are drawn close to the Lord have a responsibility to bear testimony of His holiness and His glory.

Father in heaven, I bow in reverence to You. Do not let me become casual around Your presence and the holy work that You've called me to. You have anointed and consecrated Your people to represent You in truth and in holiness. Grant grace, I pray. Amen.

February 21

Leviticus 11:1–12:8; Mark 5:21–43; Psalm 38:1–22; Proverbs 10:8–9

Active Faith Twice

Then one of the synagogue rulers, named Jairus, came there. Seeing Jesus, he fell at his feet and pleaded earnestly with Him, "My little daughter is dying." A large crowd followed and pressed around him (Jesus). And a woman was there subject to bleeding for twelve years; she came up and touched his cloak.
—Mark 5:22–25,27

You have to pay attention, because one story interrupts the other. Yet both are triumphal testimonies of faith in action. Both knew that the One who could heal was none other than the Lord Jesus Christ.

Jairus is the elected ruler of the local synagogue. He no doubt knew the Pharisees well, but Jairus bows low at Jesus' feet. This is a significant act of worship! And listen: *"Come and put your hands on (my girl) so that she will be healed" (v.23).* So they travel her direction.

On the way, in a crowd, Jesus feels power that has gone out from Him. A woman's bleeding stops. He stops. He doesn't wish to scold her. It is a teaching moment. Jesus wants this woman who reached out to Him to know that her faith was the agent that released healing. Faith involves action, and faith without action is no faith at all.

Back to episode one: Jesus ignores the bad reports given of the child's death. Jesus reassures dad, *"Just believe" (v.36).* When Jesus put out all the mourners, He went in the room with only the girl's parents, and Peter, James and John. He spoke directly to her: *"Little girl, get up!" (v.41).* Immediately she gets up. Jairus' active faith was answered.

Father, You tell me to believe upon You with an active faith. When circumstances tell me to give up, You say, "Just believe." Thank You for imparting to me a measure of faith so that I may respond in an affirmative way to You. Amen.

February 22

Leviticus 13:1–59; Mark 6:1–29; Psalm 39:1–13; Proverbs 10:10

Jesus' Hometown

Jesus left there and went to his hometown, accompanied by his disciples. "Where did this man get these things?" they asked. "What's this wisdom that has been given him, that he even does miracles! Isn't this the carpenter? Isn't this Mary's son?" And they took offense at him. And he was amazed at their lack of faith.
   —Mark 6:1–3,6

I'm sure Jesus had mixed emotions about returning home. I do. It's always good to see family. Memories resurface and flashbacks of yesterday spring to mind. Here, Jesus wants to bring the light of the gospel to those whom He had grown up around. It was only right.

Yet, instead of being embraced with open arms, the folks of Nazareth could only see Him one way—through the eyes of how they knew Him—that as a son and a brother from the family down the street.

They acknowledged Jesus' wisdom. They did not deny the miracles. *"But it just cannot be! He is of the same flesh as His brothers before you."* They could not rationalize in their minds the supernatural exploits that were coming from this *man*. They took offense at Him. Their unbelief even hampered the intentions of Jesus to heal. *Only a few* of the sick were healed.

It's easy to see the wet blanket that will suffocate what God intends for a community: A lack of faith. A lack of honor. And God moving outside the box that we all had Him pegged in!

Dear Father, cause me to know Your Son for who He is. Don't let my small mind put perimeters around what You can or cannot do. Help my unbelief. Help me to discern the spirit of those who choose to take offense at You. May I honor Your name always. Amen.

February 23

Leviticus 14:1–57; Mark 6:30–56; Psalm 40:1–10; Proverbs 10:11–12

Our Testimony

I waited patiently for the Lord; he turned to me and heard my cry. He lifted me out of the slimy pit, out of the mud and mire; he set my feet on a rock and gave me a firm place to stand. He put a new song in my mouth, a hymn of praise to our God. Many will see and fear and put their trust in the Lord.
—Psalm 40:1–3

I think we are all allowed to have at least ten favorite Psalms. This would have to be one. It really states well our testimony of the Lord's intervention in our life and what a beautiful story He desires to write.

We are in a mess. We plead and plead, and wait, and plead. We press in. God hears. He knows the havoc I've created. He knows the life of sin I led was a slippery slope ready to consume me. But the Lord stepped in and delivered me. He rescued me from calamity and set my feet on a solid foundation. He cleaned me up on the outside and changed my heart on the inside. He gave me a newfound hope and a reason for being. Now I have a new melody that I must express. It is a song of praise and adoration and exaltation to the One who lifted me out of the lowest pit.

Because of the life turnaround before the eyes of my neighbors, co–workers, friends and family, many will witness the grace of God upon my life and put their trust in the Lord. That's the way it works. The gospel is the power of God displayed in my life that testifies and relates in a most effective and tangible way. What could be more impacting than your own true-life story!

Father in heaven, I thank You over and over for Your intervention in my life. It was You who picked me up out of the slimy pit and made my footsteps firm. It is You who makes my heart sing. I will ever sing Your praises for Your deliverance. Amen.

February 24

Leviticus 15:1–16:28; Mark 7:1–23; Psalm 40:11–17; Proverbs 10:13–14

The Scapegoat

He (Aaron) is to cast lots for the two goats— one lot for the Lord and the other for the scapegoat. Aaron shall bring the goat…for a sin offering. But the goat chosen by lot as the scapegoat shall be presented alive before the Lord to be used for making atonement by sending it into the desert as a scapegoat.
—Leviticus 16:8–10

You have heard this term used before—someone is a *scapegoat*. They are the lucky ones who get to take the heat and guilt for someone else. That really is the meaning behind the original *scapegoat*.

Aaron is offering two male goats as a sin offering. He does this once a year on the Day of Atonement. (He does this after an offering of a bull for his own sin and that of his family.) The goats are chosen by lot. *The first goat* is sacrificed to make atonement for the Most Holy Place, because of the uncleanness and rebellion of the Israelites. Afterwards, Aaron brings forward *the live goat*, lays both his hands on the head of the goat and confesses over it all the wickedness and rebellion of the nation. Then he sends it away, carrying all the sins into a desert place.

The two goats represent the way the Lord dealt with the sins of His people. *The first goat* made the atonement to forgive the sin. *The second goat* removed the guilt of the sin. The sin was atoned for and the guilt was removed. What a vivid illustration of the cleansing we receive.

Thank God for Jesus, who was the perfect sacrifice, once-for-all time. More elaboration on this comes in Hebrews 9-10.

Father, I thank You for showing me the very real separation that sin produces and the purity of Your dwelling place. Thank You for illustrating forgiveness in a way I can understand. I embrace Your Son, who has made atonement once-for-all. Amen.

February 25

Leviticus 16:29–18:30; Mark 7:24–8:10; Psalm 41:1–13; Proverbs 10:15–16

Regard for the Weak

Blessed is he who has regard for the weak; the Lord delivers him in times of trouble. The Lord will protect him and preserve his life; he will bless him in the land...The Lord will sustain him on his sickbed and restore him from his bed of illness.
—Psalm 41:1–3

It is a recurrent theme throughout the Bible. *Blessed is he who has regard for the weak.* Showing compassion for those in need is a big deal in the eyes of God.

It is a character trait of God our Father: *"A father to the fatherless, a defender of widows, is God in his holy dwelling. God sets the lonely in families. He leads forth the prisoners with singing"* (Psalm 68:5-6).

It is the trait of true religion defined. *"Religion that God our Father accepts as pure and faultless is this: to look after orphans and widows in their distress and to keep oneself from being polluted..."* (James 1:27).

When Peter and Paul's ministries led into a different direction and focus—Peter's with the Jews and Paul's to the Gentiles—Paul reports: *"All they asked was that we should continue to remember the poor, the very thing I was eager to do"* (Galatians 2:10).

It is a bold statement. God blesses those who have regard for the weak, the poor, the widows, the orphans, the unborn and the elderly. *What are you doing to show regard to the poor and weak around you?*

Father in heaven, thank You for Your heart toward those who are weak. In a world of take, take, take, You show us ways to give, give, give. Thank You for Your provision to me that I may share with another in need. Speak to me clearly how I might be a blessing in this. Amen.

February 26

Leviticus 19:1–20:21; Mark 8:11–38; Psalm 42:1–11; Proverbs 10:17

The Original "Duh"

The disciples had forgotten to bring bread, except for one loaf they had with them in the boat. "Be careful," Jesus warned … "Watch out for the yeast of the Pharisees and that of Herod." They said, "It is because we have no bread."
—Mark 8:14–16.

If I could have been a fly on the side of that boat! I would love to have seen the perplexity of Jesus as He attempted to warn his disciples of the Pharisees' piety and Herod's political misgivings. It had to be the classic *"duh."* But then again, I don't think I got it right away either!

Keep in mind, Jesus had just encountered the Pharisees. They tested Him by asking for a sign. So while it was all fresh on His mind, Jesus issues this warning to his disciples: Be careful of the corrupting influence of these religious types that spreads like yeast in a loaf of bread. It doesn't take much of their pervasive unbelief to work through and affect the whole. It's all so subtle. Be on your guard!

Jesus continues: It has nothing to do with bringing bread! Don't you remember the examples? Twice I multiplied the loaves to thousands. I can do it again with the one loaf we have! It's not about the bread. Are you so slow to understand? It's the sly ways of those smooth talkers you need to watch out for … *Oh.*

So if Jesus says something new to your way of thinking, and if it takes you awhile to get it, just remember his disciples were present in the flesh and they didn't get it either! *Lord, open our understanding.*

Father, Thank You for putting up with my obvious shortcomings. So many times, I don't get it. Give me eyes to see and ears to hear. Thank You for warning me against those influences that can affect my faith in You. Give me wisdom and a discerning spirit so that I may overcome. Amen.

February 27

Leviticus 20:22–22:16; Mark 9:1–29; Psalm 43:1–5; Proverbs 10:18

If You Can?

"But if you can do anything, take pity on us and help us." "If you can?" said Jesus. "Everything is possible for him who believes."
—Mark 9:22–23

After coming upon a *situation,* Jesus addresses what his disciples were unable to do. A boy possessed by an evil spirit needs deliverance. The boy's father is desperate: *"If you can do anything…"*

"If?" replies Jesus. Everything is possible … for those who believe. Of course it is possible! But then Jesus ties it to the dad's faith.

I absolutely love this dad's honest response. *"Well of course I believe."* Then wondering if he really did have enough faith for something like this, and realizing who it was he was talking to, he comes clean: *"Help me overcome my unbelief!" (v.24).* If only we could all pray this way! And Jesus honors it.

Then privately, the disciples needed to know the obvious, *"Why couldn't we do that?"* Jesus explains that some kinds of demonic bondage require more power— power that comes only by prayer (and fasting). Jesus wanted them to be prepared in their heart for this kind of engagement. The spiritual power needed emerges from strategic prayer and fasting.

Tying it all together, I surmise the weightiness of faith, honesty and earnest prayer. Everything is possible, because God can make it so!

Father, You are so awesome. Please help me in my weakness. Help me to see that You can do anything if I will trust You. Nothing is too difficult for You. Build my faith and lead me in the disciplines and passion of prayer and fasting. Amen.

February 28

Leviticus 22:17–23:44; Mark 9:30–10:12; Psalm 44:1–8; Proverbs 10:19

The Light of Your Face

With your hand you drove out the nations and planted our fathers… It was not by their sword that they won the land, nor did their arm bring them victory; it was your right hand, your arm, and the light of your face, for you loved them.
—Psalm 44:2–3

For the sons of Korah, temple assistants who penned this Psalm, things around them looked grim. They were surrounded by enemies. So they remembered back upon their history and recounted the faithfulness of God. They reflect upon the similar challenges.

All eight verses boldly proclaim that it was not of their selves that Israel drove out the nations on their way to the promised land. It was God alone. It was the strength of His right hand. It was the arm of the Lord that brought victory. It was the light of His face. *Wait! It was what?*

I can visualize the burly arm of a strapping dad who can beat up whoever … But the light of His face speaks of the pride He has over the ones He loves. It is the light of His countenance, because of His favor. Think of it. It's the favor of God that we need, nothing more.

When the situation seems hopeless all around you, remember that God beams with joy over His beloved. *That is you!* He knows what you're made of. It has nothing to do with your own strength *(or lack thereof)*. Your Father just wants to show you the love He has toward you.

Father, You are beyond amazing. You put a promise in my heart. You lead me personally. You never leave me. You never forsake me. You deliver me from the hand of my enemy. It truly is in You that I make my boast all the day long. Amen.

February 29

Luke 15:11-32

The Father's Love

But while he was still a long way off, his father saw him and was filled with compassion for him; he ran to his son, threw his arms around him and kissed him… "Let's have a feast and celebrate. For this son of mine was dead and is alive again; he was lost and is found."
—Luke 15:20,23–24

This parable is referred to as the "Prodigal Son." It's the story of the younger of two sons who demands his share of his father's estate so he can pursue his own path. *Let's call him Patrick.* We understand the younger son pretty well, because he is very typical of many young people who have life by the tail and want to taste life in ways they had been sheltered from growing up. We get that, because we all know several of them or we've been there/done that. And it's no surprise when Pat squanders it all and is left with heartache and humiliation.

Imagine now how Patrick's father must have felt. A premature settling of inheritance affairs before his own passing was callous arrogance. It probably stung … considerably. But when the famine became severe, that father knew his son was going to feel its consequences. His heart went out to young Patrick. He was, after all, his own flesh and blood.

Patrick figured his father would either be mad or sad, and as a result— unapproachable. That is the way many, many people view the Father. But there Patrick's father was, anticipating him even from a distance and moved with compassion. He runs to his approaching son and embraces Patrick with open arms. That is the God I serve. Not mad. Not sad. But glad, and very merciful. That is the heart of the Father!

Abba, I can only thank You for Your great mercy. You are the God who pursues me in my brokenness and shame. Your love changes everything. Amen.

March 1

Leviticus 24:1–25:46; Mark 10:13–31; Psalm 44:9–26; Proverbs 10:20–21

A Test of Values

Jesus looked at him and loved him. "One thing you lack," he said. "Go, sell everything you have and give to the poor, and then you will have treasure in heaven. No one who has left [all] for the gospel will fail to receive a hundred times as much in this present age and in the age to come."
—Mark 10:21,29–30

Perhaps nothing in this world defines our values any more loudly than how we handle finances. It is important to be sure. After all, we will give an account for the things we were given to steward.

To those of the world, our financial status tells of our success and influence. Our earthly values are deeply rooted in money and the increasing gain of it. It consumes a majority of us all. Money is a tool we all must manage, but it's a terrible tyrant when it manages us. Jesus presents a value system that is radically different.

The rich man who approached Jesus had, without a doubt, held his money closest to his heart. It was most dear to him. It was the god that he could not relinquish. Like any idol, the acquiring of riches is a continual lust for more, never quite enough, self-centered and diametrically opposed to a life of faith. The wealth this man knew was temporary at best and non-transferable on the day of reckoning.

Even though blinded by his pursuits, Jesus *loved* the rich man. Jesus revealed a greater, eternal treasure that would bring the completeness he longed for. What is the reward you seek?

Father, You are the Rewarder of those who earnestly seek You. With You is reward now and forevermore. You see all that we give for the sake of the gospel. May my heart be stamped with the values of Your eternal kingdom. Amen.

March 2

Leviticus 25:47–27:13; Mark 10:32–52; Psalm 45:1–17; Proverbs 10:22

Greatness

Then James and John came to him ...”Let one of us sit at your right hand and the other at your left in your glory.” “You don’t know what you are asking,” Jesus said... ”whoever wants to become great among you must be your servant.”
—Mark 10:35,37–38,43

You have to like the ambition of the brothers James and John. They weren’t the *“sons of thunder”* for nothing. It sure got the ire of the other ten disciples to bring this matter up before the One who would be King—to sit at the places of honor on either side of His throne.

However, the desire for greatness is a longing that God has placed inside every one of us. *The desire to be great is not wrong!* Did you notice that Jesus doesn’t rebuke them for broaching this topic? The problem is when we try to attain greatness by the world’s measure. It is fleeting and futile even if you are able to capture the moment.

What Jesus came to do was to serve others and give His life as a ransom for many. He led by example. He humbled Himself. He served in meekness. This is what God our Father recognizes as *greatness.*

Greatness *in God’s eyes* culminates on that day when we stand before Him and give an account of our life. He will validate our greatness by how we served others in humility. Did I give of myself for the benefit of others? Did I consider my brother before my own self-interests? It’s a value that runs counter to the self-serving way the world operates, just like everything else in His upside-down kingdom!

Father, You don’t look at the things that man looks at. You measure greatness by the size of my heart. Give me the desire to serve others with vigor as unto You. Let my heart response be great in Your eyes. Amen.

March 3

Leviticus 27:14– Numbers 1:54; Mark 11:1–25; Psalm 46:1–11; Proverbs 10:23

The Tithe

A tithe of everything from the land, whether grain from the soil or fruit from the trees, belongs to the Lord; it is holy to the Lord ... The entire tithe of the herd and the flock—will be holy to the Lord. He must not pick out the good from the bad or make any substitution.
—Leviticus 27:30,32–33

Oh yeah ... now we get to hear about *tithing!* This is good news for those who actually make this their practice, but perhaps it's stepping-on-toes for those who have been avoiding it. Maybe you just have not had the knowledge that tithing is an important aspect of God's economy to advance His kingdom.

The word *tithe* means "tenth." God says the first ten percent of your income belongs to Him. It is holy. What's more, it is a reflection of your wholehearted devotion to the Lord. It says, *"I'll trust God's way in an area that I hold very dear. I give back what is His and open myself up to receive His blessing."* Besides, I am far better off with the Lord's blessing on the ninety percent I have over the one hundred percent that I might manage without His blessing. It all came from Him anyways!

God says in Malachi 3:10, *"Test me in this, and see if I will not throw open the floodgates of heaven and pour out so much blessing that you will not have enough room for it."* That is a challenge and promise from God.

If this is new to you, or you just needed the truth to challenge you, then now is the time to write out that check to the ministry or church where you are fed the Word of God. Take part in kingdom building!

Father, I trust You with my life and my future. You are my Provider. You know what I need better than I ever could. Grant me grace to give liberally to Your kingdom to further the cause of the gospel. Amen.

March 4

Numbers 2:1–3:51; Mark 11:27–12:17; Psalm 47:1–9; Proverbs 10:24–25

Render unto God

Teacher, we know you are a man of integrity ... You teach the way of God in accordance with the truth. Is it right to pay taxes to Caesar or not? Jesus said to them, "Give to Caesar what is Caesar's and to God what is God's."
—Mark 12:14,17

Coming into this scenario, the chief priests and teachers of the law were looking for a way to trip Jesus up so they could arrest him. If they could pose questions concerning legal, political and civil issues, then they might pull him into a position they could attack.

You have to like the smooth way this guy patronizes Jesus. *"We know you are a man of integrity. You aren't swayed by men, but teach the way of God" (v.14).* Jesus' answer is equally savvy. *"Give to Caesar what is due Caesar, and give to God what is due God" (v.17).*

As believers, we ought to obey the laws of the land. Taxes are a part of how our nation funds government needs. But the larger question is, *What is it that is due God?* That is a searching question that we must all ask ourselves. I believe that it starts with *our devotion* and *our praise.* He is worthy. If we don't praise Him, the rocks will cry out!

Appropriate for today, Psalm 47 calls the nations to enthusiastic praise. *"Clap your hands, all you nations; shout to God with cries of joy. God has ascended amid shouts of joy, the Lord amid the sounding of trumpets. Sing praises unto God, sing praises" (vv.1,5–6).*

Father, I render unto You my sincere devotion and my heartfelt loyalty. You are worthy to be exalted and glorified. All I have and am is from You. You are deserving of my best, and I pledge my hands and my lips to exude praise toward Your holy throne! Amen.

March 5

Numbers 4:1–5:31; Mark 12:18–37; Psalm 48:1–14; Proverbs 10:26

The Most Important Commandment

One of the teachers of the law came and heard them debating. Noticing that Jesus had given them a good answer, he asked him, "Of all the commandments, which is the most important?"
—Mark 12:28

The religious leaders of the day would often discuss the question of which commandments were heavier and which were lighter. By this time, the Jews had accumulated hundreds of laws *(613)*, but Jesus summarized the commands in two principals from *Deuteronomy 6:5* and *Leviticus 19:18:* Love God, and love people. Love the Lord with all your heart, soul, mind and strength. And then: Love your neighbor as yourself *(vv. 30-31)*. In that order.

What is striking to me is the intimacy that God desires with each of us. *"Love Me,"* God says, *"with all that you are and all that you have, with all your faculties. Give yourself to Me wholly."*

It is only in that relationship of intimacy that we can live out the second command. Loving people is nearly impossible without God's love as the reservoir to draw from. But it is also the way we show God our love to Him—by loving those around us. Actually, it happens with little effort when our primary focus is on loving God.

So keeping the first commandment first place enables us to love, while loving others reflects our love for God in an authentic way. And yet, it all begins with God's initiative of unconditional love to *me!*

Father in heaven, thank You that You loved me first. It motivates me to love You back with all that is in me. Cause me to know that I show my love towards You every time I love my neighbor and the least of these. Help me to maintain my primary focus upon loving You. Amen.

March 6

Numbers 6:1–7:89; Mark 12:38–13:13; Psalm 49:1–20; Proverbs 10:27–28

The Priestly Blessing

Tell Aaron and his sons, "This is how you are to bless the Israelites. Say to them: 'The Lord bless you and keep you; The Lord make his face shine upon you and be gracious to you; the Lord turn his face toward you and give you peace.'" "So they will put my name on the Israelites, and I will bless them."
—Numbers 6:23–27

What an eloquent blessing! Perhaps you've heard this before and wondered where it was found in the Bible.

The power of proclamation should not be underestimated. His point here is unmistakable. The desire of the Lord is to bestow upon His people His name. The name of the Lord is tantamount to the Lord's presence dwelling among them, and therefore to enrich them in every way. The object of His affection is *His* people—the nation of Israel and all who call upon the name of the Lord.

The intention of the Lord is to *bless you*. He will *keep you* and protect your coming in and your going out. When *His face shines upon you*, He is pleased. His smile is on you. His favor rests upon you. He is so *gracious* and kind in His dealings with you. He is endless in His mercy toward you. His compassions fail not. *The Lord turns His face toward you;* His gaze and attention is upon you. There is nothing about you that He is not fully aware of. He cares and is interested in every detail of your life. He alone can *grant you peace* on the inside.

It is also how our gracious God would have us speak to others. We have the power in our words to bless and to build up, but also to demean and tear down. Let's be in agreement with our God!

Father, Your kind intentions for me are only good. I live for Your face to shine upon me. Thank You for Your protection and Your peace. Likewise, may I speak only that which brings blessing to Your people. Amen.

March 7

Numbers 8:1–9:23; Mark 13:14–37; Psalm 50:1–23; Proverbs 10:29–30

Sacrifice Thank Offerings

Sacrifice thank offerings to God, fulfill your vows to the Most High, and call upon me in the day of trouble; I will deliver you, and you will honor me. He who sacrifices thank offerings honors me, and he prepares the way so that I may show him the salvation of God.
    —Psalm 50:14–15,23

Psalm 50 details the awesomeness of God, and He who is judge. The stage is set. The heavens proclaim His righteousness. God, the Mighty One, summons the earth. Around Him is devouring fire, beauty and a raging tempest. Awe is the moment.

You think that God will now judge the heathen. *But no*, His fury is focused towards His own. Judgment begins with the family of God *(1 Peter 4:17)*. They were a people of covenant with God, but the sacrifices they made had digressed to half-hearted ritual. Their hearts were not in it. God was saying: *"Remember Who it is that You worship. I own the cattle on a thousand hills. What I want is not another calf, but an offering of thanks and humble gratitude."*

We honor the Lord when we bring Him a heart of gratitude. We are mindful of His goodness. Our heart is opened to receive that which He intends for us. He will reveal the way of salvation.

"Through Jesus, therefore, let us continually offer to God a sacrifice of praise— the fruit of lips that confess his name. And do not forget to do good and to share with others, for with such sacrifices God is pleased" (Hebrews 13:15-16).

Father in heaven, I praise You with my lips. I bring an offering of gratitude and thankfulness. You are awesome and holy. Protect my heart from apathy and ritual. Amen.

March 8

Numbers 10:1–11:23; Mark 14:1–21; Psalm 51:1–19; Proverbs 10:31–32

A Miracle Meal

The rabble with them began to crave other food, and again the Israelites started wailing. The manna was like coriander seed and looked like resin. They cooked it in a pot or made it into cakes...Now a wind drove quail in from the sea.
—Numbers 11:4,7–8,31

There are several things going on in this story. Complaining was among the biggest problems Moses was now facing. The *rabble*—the mixed company of non-Israelites among them—were reminiscing of old times in Egypt. Compared to the ample fresh foods at their disposal, the manna seemed bland and boring. Yet the manna was "bread from heaven" that showed forth God's glory every morning.

Manna means *"What is it?"* How appropriate. The Israelites were provided this miracle bread for the full forty years they traveled in the desert. It tasted like wafers made with honey and olive oil. You can imagine the multiple ways they must have created this dish to keep things interesting—manna burgers, bamanna bread or fillet-of-manna (as Keith Green used to sing). The point is, God miraculously provided for His people. When they complained for meat, even Moses doubted that God could provide for the multitude; and for a whole month! Yet it happened as the Lord promised. *Quail for everyone!*

Complaining arises when we shift our attention from what we have to what we don't have—much like what we witness in the world of advertising. Perhaps it would be best to be grateful for what God has already provided. *Count your blessings... name them one by one.*

Father, You provide for Your people in miraculous ways. It is by Your hand that we are blessed and have our being. Give me faith to trust You even for the basics. If you care for the birds of the air, You certainly will provide for me! Amen.

March 9

Numbers 11:24–13:33; Mark 14:22–52; Psalm 52:1–9; Proverbs 11:1–3

Leadership Jealousy

Miriam and Aaron began to talk against Moses because of his Cushite wife…"Has the Lord spoken only through Moses?" they asked. "Hasn't he also spoken through us?" And the Lord heard this.
—Numbers 12:1–2

Moses' elder siblings, Miriam and Aaron, had played second fiddle to Moses all the while since God delivered the Israelites from Egypt. For some reason regarding his wife, Miriam and Aaron began to talk against Moses and challenge his authority. Moses had done nothing wrong. Perhaps his new bride was a threat to Miriam somehow. But jealousy was brewing and it did not pass by the Lord's notice.

The immediacy of the Lord's intervention should tell us of the importance of God-ordained leadership. It was not an ordinary leader we are talking about, either. This man was one whom God had spoken face-to-face and revealed His glory to. Yet Miriam and Aaron were not afraid to speak against God's anointed!

I'm sure many of us have seen the travesty of what backbiting and grumbling against church leadership can do. No pastor is perfect. But to honor and pray for those who are in leadership over us is absolutely essential. We may not agree with every single aspect of their position, but God has raised them up and placed them in our lives.

"Obey your leaders and submit to their authority. They keep watch over you as men who must give an account. Obey them so that their work will be a joy, not a burden" *(Hebrews 13:17).*

Father, thank You for raising up and placing over me godly leaders. I pray that You will strengthen them in their faith and to live a blameless life. Anoint them to lead and represent You well. May Your blessing be upon them. Amen.

March 10

Numbers 14:1–15:16; Mark 14:53–72; Psalm 53:1–6; Proverbs 11:4

An Evil Report

They gave Moses this account: We went into the land to which you sent us, and it does flow with milk and honey. But the people who live there are powerful…We even saw the descendants of Anak there. (And they spread) a bad report…
—Numbers 13:28; 14:36

What a remarkable story with profound impact.

God commissioned an expedition to spy out the land of Canaan with leaders from each tribe. It's a fact–finding mission. It was already declared to be in-the-bag by the Lord Himself. *"But check it out!"*

The exploration was meant to build anticipation for a victorious conquest. They brought back huge, magnificent clusters of grapes, pomegranates and figs. Yet it was all very overwhelming when they viewed it through natural eyes. I'm not exactly sure what they were expecting to see! Everything God had claimed it to be was in tact. *"So what if there's someone in the way! No worries!"* Every promise from God comes with the grace to overcome.

Their report spread unbelief and hopelessness like gangrene throughout the camp. That's what an evil or false report will do when spewed out as if it were truth. We must remember that words are weighty, especially when they come from esteemed leaders.

Thank God for Caleb and Joshua. They were taking God at His word. Their summation works for me: *"If the Lord is pleased with us, he will lead us into that land … and will give it to us"* (14:8).

Father, cause me to know the weightiness of my words. May my words speak life and provoke men to faith. Your promises are Yes and Amen. So be it!

March 11

Numbers 15:17–16:40; Mark 15:1–47; Psalm 54:1–7; Proverbs 11:5–6

Korah's Rebellion

Korah son of Izhar ... and certain Ruebenites- Dathan and Abiram and On—became insolent and rose up against Moses. With them were 250 Israelite men, well-known community leaders who had been appointed members of the council. They came as a group to oppose Moses and Aaron ..."You have gone too far!"
—Numbers 16:1–3

It seems this has been a trying week for Moses. First, the natives are restless. Manna is not enough. Now they want meat. Then, his brother and sister take issue with Moses' wife and are jealous of his authority. Moses' expedition to the Promised Land backfires with a bad report that escalates throughout the camp. And today, Korah recruits 250 influential men to lead a rebellion against Moses and Aaron.

Korah and his cohorts, of the Levi and Rueben tribes, wanted the power of the priesthood. They were not content with the high privilege they had to serve at the tabernacle. Now they wanted more influence and political clout. Yet, as Moses points out, this was an assault upon God. The office of the priest was delegated to the family of Aaron by God Himself. Korah is meddling in a higher arena.

God wants us to value the place of ministry that He leads us in, no matter what well-meaning friends or family may think. He has a special purpose for you to fulfill—unique and needful. Desiring someone else's position or anointing is inappropriately placed ambition and greed in disguise.

Father, You have a specific plan and purpose for my life. I am glad for the successful ministries that You have raised up that further Your kingdom. May I find contentment in pursuing Your plans for me and bless those who have a role in mentoring me. My motivation is to love and serve You. Amen.

March 12

Numbers 16:41–18:32; Mark 16:1–20; Psalm 55:1–23; Proverbs 11:7

Aaron's Rod

I (God) will rid myself of this constant grumbling against you by the Israelites…The next day Moses entered the Tent of the Testimony and saw that Aaron's staff, which represented the house of Levi, had not only sprouted but had budded, blossomed and produced almonds.
—Numbers 17:5,8

Enough is enough. The whole Israelite community was grumbling against Moses and Aaron yet again. What will it take? Had God not made it plain enough to them? What a dangerous place it is to fight against God's appointed authority. After 14,700 more Israelites die from a plague, the Lord brought Moses to Himself again. *"Bring me a staff from each of the twelve tribal leaders. The one I choose will sprout!"*

What God did was to validate His ordination of Aaron and his family as priests in dramatic fashion. The evidence was irrefutable. Not only does Aaron's staff sprout, but it blossomed and produced almonds overnight!

Perhaps the most personal gesture and promise to Aaron came in the next chapter (18:20). The other tribes would have land to divide, but to the Levites it was said, *"You will have no inheritance among them; I am your share and your inheritance."* More than just receiving from the tithe as compensation, the Lord Himself would be their portion. The Lord Himself would be their fulfillment. The Levites were in a unique and special place to receive directly from the Lord His reward.

Father, thank You for speaking again and again to me. Thank You for Your patience, not wanting any to perish, but for all to come to repentance and eternal life through Your Son. Let me know You as my portion. You are more than enough, O Lord. Amen.

March 13

Numbers 19:1–20:29; Luke 1:1–25; Psalm 56:1–13; Proverbs 11:8

Moses' Mistake

Now there was no water for the community, and the people gathered in opposition to Moses and Aaron. "Speak to that rock before their eyes and it will pour out its water." Then Moses raised his arm and struck the rock twice with his staff. Water gushed out, and the community ... drank.
—Numbers 20:2,8,11

You could hardly blame Moses from a natural perspective. Every time you turn around, there is someone complaining and Moses posturing himself facedown before God. This time: no water. Big problem.

Moses was clearly fed up. His response with attitude was: *"Listen, you rebels ..."* Moses strikes the rock twice. God, in His mercy, allowed water to gush. Problem solved. Except the manner in which Moses handled it did not honor the Lord. Moses had clearly disobeyed.

Just a few chapters back, in Numbers 12, we heard God's heart as He defended Moses to Miriam and Aaron. *"He is faithful in all my house. With him I speak face to face" (vv.7-8).* However, where much is given, much is required. As leader, Moses was accountable to God in every detail of obedience. The nation was watching, and He did not honor God as holy before the Israelites.

This one act of disobedience kept Moses out of the Promised Land. We are reminded that we represent the Lord in *every* situation. God cares how His name is reflected—for His honor and glory. Do your actions and reactions give an honorable witness to God?

Father, You are holy, and there is none like You in all the earth. Help me to listen closely and obey Your every word. May I honor Your name always. Amen.

March 14

Numbers 21:1–22:20; Luke 1:26–56; Psalm 57:1–11; Proverbs 11:9–11

Mary's Response of Faith

"I am the Lord's servant," Mary answered. "May it be to me as you have said." And Mary said: "My soul glorifies the Lord and my spirit rejoices in God my Savior, for he has been mindful of the humble state of his servant."
—Luke 1:38,46–48

It is a divine exchange. Mary, a virgin pledged to be married, is visited by the angel Gabriel to deliver news of the coming Savior. Mary, most likely in her late teens, is chosen by God to bring this *Son of the Most High* into the world. But why Mary?

Mary is called *"you, who are highly favored"* twice. God, no doubt, chose the right young woman to do the job of raising His Son in our time and space of history and of mankind. Favor from God is good!

The two facets that stand out boldly to me—that marked her favor from God—is her life of *humility* and her response of *faith*.

During her visit with Elizabeth, twice Mary references the humble state that God is drawn to. Humility is that one prerequisite that God so values in choosing a servant to use. Her response to this naturally impossible feat was met with affirmation of God's promise: *"Be it unto me as you have said. OK! I'm in. May your promise come to pass!"*

The Lord observes the humble and faithful to show forth His favor.

Father God, You seek to do the impossible if I would only respond to You in faith. Help my unbelief. May You find in me a heart that values the humility that Mary walked in. I desire Your favor upon my life. Use me, O God. I pray in Jesus' name, Amen.

March 15

Numbers 22:21–23:30; Luke 1:57–80; Psalm 58:1–11; Proverbs 11:12–13

The Prophet Balaam

Balak, of Moab, sent messengers to summon Balaam. "Now come and put a curse on these people (the Israelites), because they are too powerful for me." The angel of the Lord said to Balaam, "Go… but speak only what I tell you."
—*Numbers 22:4–6,35*

Beginning in Numbers 22, we have the episode of Balaam. Balaam is a well-known prophet summoned by Balak, king of Moab, for the purpose of declaring a curse upon the Israelites. That way, Moab might defeat them, because from Balak's perspective, this people out of Egypt were too numerous and powerful.

Understand that Balaam is a sorcerer, a diviner *(See Numbers 24:1)*. He seeks the counsel of the Lord because even pagan prophets recognized the greatest affect for good or bad would come from the people's own gods. In our text today, Balaam does not see the angel of God, yet his donkey does! The angel exclaims to Balaam, *"Your path is a reckless one…Go, but speak only what I tell you"* (22:32,35).

Curses are powerful words that declare death and destruction. The Lord would not allow that to happen to His people. The adversary, then, is restricted in his activity by the oversight of the Lord. Balaam utters, *"How can I curse those whom God has not cursed? I have received a command to bless; he has blessed, and I cannot change it. The Lord their God is with them; the shout of the King is among them"* (23:8,20–21).

Think about the conversation that comes from your lips. Do you speak blessing? Do you speak what is in agreement with God?

Father, You have decreed blessing over Your people. What You have declared, let it be true and come to pass. May I walk in Your favor. Protect me from the evil one. Let the words of my mouth declare blessing upon Your people. Amen.

March 16

Numbers 24:1–25:18; Luke 2:1–35; Psalm 59:1–17; Proverbs 11:14

The Balaam Sequel

Moses was angry with the officers of the army...They (the women) were the ones who followed Balaam's advice and were the means of turning the Israelites away from the Lord in what happened at Peor... While Israel was at Shittim, the men began to indulge in sexual immorality with the Moabite women ... So they joined in worshipping the Baal of Peor.
—Numbers 31:14,16; 25:1,3

The story is not finished. And what a story it is! Balaam was unsuccessful in bringing a curse upon Israel, but his advice to the Moabite king that followed may have proved just as effective. The explanation of this action is found in Numbers 31.

If you can't bring them down one way, then try a different approach. The advice of Balaam was this: appeal to the men's sexual appetite with seductive women, who just happened to invite them to engage in the sacrifices made to their gods. If they would participate in the worship of other gods, then God would have to bring judgment upon His people in righteousness. Oh man, did the plan ever work! One named Zimri was even brazen enough to bring a Midianite woman before the eyes of Moses. *The Lord's anger burned, and 24,000 died.*

What a seductive plan it was to bring down the people of God. This teaching remains needful today. John warns the church at Pergamum, in Revelation 2, that there are some who embrace the teaching of Balaam, who are enticed to sin by committing immorality. It twists a holy act designed by God within the bonds of marriage into a selfish sin for more. *Do not be unaware of the devil's schemes.*

Father, raise up a church that will embrace purity. You are raising up a spotless bride for Your Son. Give me a keen discernment to the ploys of our enemy. You are holy and righteous in all Your ways. I embrace You. Amen.

March 17

Numbers 26:1–51; Luke 2:36–52; Psalm 60:1–12; Proverbs 11:15

Anna, the Prophetess

There was also a prophetess, Anna, the daughter of Phanuel ... she was eighty–four. She never left the temple but worshipped night and day, fasting and praying.
　—Luke 2:36–37

Three verses speak volumes to us of a life given to prayer. First of all, Anna is a prophetess. This means that she had an incredibly close walk with the Lord. She knew and spoke what was on God's heart. Here, *"she spoke about the child to all who were looking to the redemption of Jerusalem" (2:38).* Along with Simeon, these two had never lost their hope to see the promised Messiah. And now, they are among the first to bear witness of Jesus.

Anna had lived with her husband for seven years before he died, then she dedicated her life to intercession through night and day prayer in the temple. This means that Anna had focused her life for approximately sixty years unto the Lord, given to prayer and fasting. She found her place before the Lord with anointing and steadfastness. What a testimony! I wonder how many of us are the result of a praying grandmother?

I believe the Lord is raising up an end-time army of intercessors to make their appeal to God with night and day prayer. God is calling together intercessors to pray on behalf of this generation in anticipation of our coming King to rule and reign on the earth. Will you join this remnant of intercessors for the end-time harvest?

Father, I thank You for raising up Anna's all over this globe that are committed to night and day prayer. You call me to pray for our generation. You ask me to stand in the gap for a people that does not yet know You. Grace me for this task. Amen.

March 18

Numbers 26:52–28:15; Luke 3:1–22; Psalm 61:1–8; Proverbs 11:16–17

The Torch is Passed

Moses said to the Lord, "May the Lord appoint a man over this community to go out and come in before them, one who will lead them …" So the Lord said, "Take Joshua son of Nun, a man in whom is the spirit, and lay your hand on him. Give him some of your authority so the whole Israelite community will obey him."
—Numbers 27:15–18,20

The Lord was calling Moses home. He would first get to gaze upon the land that the Lord had promised the Israelites. But then, he would be gathered to his ancestors. Moses' concern was for the community he had led these many years. Without a leader, they would be sheep without a shepherd.

The obvious successor would be Joshua.

It was Joshua and Caleb who alone stood up before the masses of Israel and declared Canaan to be theirs for the taking. It was Joshua who led the Israelites as the field general in their battle over the Amalekites. Joshua was the only person allowed to accompany Moses up the mountain when Moses received the law. When God would speak with Moses at the entrance of the tent, Joshua was right there. He would not leave his side, but shadowed Moses and observed it all. He experienced firsthand the leadership and heart of Moses.

We are called to make disciples. That means we are discipled first ourselves, and then we mentor others. We give away to someone else what we have learned. Who is your Moses? And who is your Joshua?

Father, I thank You for the mentors that You have placed in my life. I thank You for the lives of those who have modeled the godly manner You call me to walk. And let my life be an example for someone else to follow. Amen.

March 19

Numbers 28:16–29:40; Luke 3:23–38; Psalm 62:1–12; Proverbs 11:18–19

Confidence in God Alone

My soul finds rest in God alone; my salvation comes from him. He alone is my rock and my salvation; he is my fortress, I will never be shaken. Trust in him at all times, O people; pour out your hearts to him, for God is our refuge.
   —Psalm 62:1–2,8

In spite of opposition, David confidently asserts his trust in God *alone*. The difference between trusting God and relying upon other mere humans is enormous.

David had known the exaltation of kingship. Yet, there were those near him who knew his vulnerabilities and would take him down from his lofty place given the opportunity. In the reality of eternity, however, these wicked enemies are but a breath.

It is in God alone that we find our rest. Within the walled fortress of His mighty strength, we are secure. And when things around us begin to waver and shake, then we tell ourselves again what we know is true—*"Find rest, O my soul, in God alone."* I defer to Him for my honor.

Outside, the circumstances may be tumultuous. Inside, emotional stress may feel overwhelming. Yet, my resolve must be to wait upon the Lord. I know the Lord to be a refuge. He has been faithful in the past. He has declared it so in His Word. So I admonish you—*pour out your heart to Him*—as David did. You can trust Him in this. It is another opportunity for God to prove Himself as a refuge and a fortress to you right now.

Father, every time I am faced with challenges and opposition, I remind myself of Your strength and Your kind intentions for me. You have delivered me in times past and You will prove faithful once again. I lean upon You alone. Amen.

March 20

Numbers 30:1–31:54; Luke 4:1–30; Psalm 63:1-11; Proverbs 11:20–21

Jesus is Tempted

Jesus, full of the Holy Spirit, returned from the Jordan and was led by the Spirit in the desert, where for forty days he was tempted by the devil. When the devil had finished all this tempting, he left him until an opportune time.
—Luke 4:1–2,13

It is somewhat ironic to me that Jesus was full of the Holy Spirit; yet it was the Spirit who was leading Jesus into the desert to be tempted. The end result, however, once the test was over, is that Jesus left the desert in the power of the Spirit. We can conclude that God's purpose in every test we engage in is to pass! What we gain from it makes us stronger in our spirit man than before our little test began.

In each instance, the devil questions Jesus in a condescending manner, "*If you are the Son of God…*" Satan pushes the limits of Jesus' humanity with the food issue while fasting forty days. He then tries to persuade Jesus to take a shortcut to receive His authority. Lastly, the devil attempts to twist the Scriptures in a way that would bring about Jesus' demise. Jesus, of course, has an answer for the devil, who will do anything to gain His worship.

Satan doesn't penetrate the Son of God this time. But he'll be back. Did you notice that he left *until an opportune time?* You never get away from the conniving adversary of our souls. He lurks and prowls, so keep your guard up and your mind renewed. Remember, the devil is a loser. In the end, he will get his due, and we win!

Father in heaven, thank You for empowering me by Your Spirit. Cause me to be renewed in my mind with the truth of Your Word. Cause me to be savvy to the wiles of the devil. Give me a keen discernment and a ready response. By Your Spirit, I shall overcome. Amen.

March 21

Numbers 32:1–33:39; Luke 4:31–5:11; Psalm 64:1–10; Proverbs 11:22

Authority and Power

Then he went down to Capernaum… and on the Sabbath began to teach the people. They were amazed at his teaching, because his message had authority. With authority and power he gives orders to evil spirits and they come out!
—Luke 4:31–32,36

When Jesus came onto the scene, there was something starkly different about Him compared to the charismatic leaders who came and went before Him. Yes, He could tell stories. Yes, He could capture their attention. But this man had something no one else would possess. Jesus had authority. He had weight in His words. He wielded power that could literally free people.

The demons knew who Jesus was. When they were confronted with the *Holy One of God,* they knew ultimate submission was to His command alone. No one else had the authority Jesus alone has.

News spread like a wildfire. The authentic does not need advertised. Every needy person wants to be whole. Jesus laid His hands on all the sick who came to Him, and He healed them. One in particular was Simon's mother-in-law, who had a fever. Jesus rebuked the fever; it leaves, and immediately she gets up and begins to wait on them.

In our era, never was there a more urgent need than that of the authentic power of God to bring deliverance from the sin–infested culture in which we live. Jesus gives us His name and His authority to set the captives free. *Speak His name!*

Father in heaven, Your Son came to set the captives free, and You give me Your power to do the same today, as your disciple. Give me compassion for the sick and the authority of Your name to bring freedom—freedom from the bondage of sin and freedom to serve You alone. In Jesus' name, Amen.

March 22

Numbers 33:40–36:13; Luke 5:12–28; Psalm 65:1–13; Proverbs 11:23

Thorns in Your Side

"When you cross the Jordan into Canaan, drive out all the inhabitants of the land before you. Destroy all their carved images. Take possession of it. But if you do not drive out the inhabitants of the land, those you allow to remain will become barbs in your eyes and thorns in your sides."
—Numbers 33:51–53,55

There is a great lesson in our reading today, but it can be tricky. The Lord had taken great care to birth a nation that would follow His ways. *They would be His people!* God was holy and righteous. He would raise up a people who were, likewise, holy and righteous. These directives were critical for Israel, so they would not compromise their ideals and become as the heathen nations they were driving out.

The Lord would say to us that we are not to compromise the values that He has so impressed upon our hearts and minds. Let the values from His Word become your *convictions.* Do not entertain or give place to that which contradicts. If you give in and justify their values, they will become a barb to your eyes and a thorn to your side. *Ouch!*

God is always looking out for us. He wants us to avoid the traps and pitfalls of the enemy. By following His Word, we walk in His covering. When we compromise, by desiring the best of both worlds, we walk outside of the protection of His umbrella. Wherever we go, wherever God leads us, there will be opportunity to compromise. Even in the name of winning the lost, we may put ourselves in a compromising position. *Take heed, where you walk …*

O You who hear prayer, Father, You love all people and desire that they be saved, and You may lead me to present Your life-giving message. But You know me better than I do. Keep me from the way of sinners and compromise. Amen.

March 23

Deuteronomy 1:1–46; Luke 5:29–6:11; Psalm 66:1–20; Proverbs 11:24–26

Levi's Banquet

Levi got up, left everything and followed him. Then Levi held a great banquet for Jesus at his house... Jesus answered them, "It is not the healthy who need a doctor, but the sick. I have not come to call the righteous, but sinners..."
—Luke 5:28–29,31–32

I cheated a little here. I stole the last two verses from yesterday's reading because the story bleeds over. But as I reflected, what actually happens today gives us the flip-side of what yesterday's study was about. While we should not sit in the seat of scoffers and put ourselves in a position of compromise, Jesus knew what He was here for. He was not about to be pulled into their sin.

Jesus loves people. He went where the people lived. These verses so aptly reveal the heart and the mission of Jesus.

Here He is calling Levi, a Jewish tax collector (also known as Matthew) and he immediately follows Jesus, leaving all his sordid past behind. And not only that, but Levi wants all of his buddies to know what has happened to him too, so he has a banquet to honor Jesus at his home.

Pharisees, as was typical, seemed to lurk and critique Jesus at his every move. They were the religious ones who wrapped their sin in respectability. They had the outward veneer of good, but were self-righteous and loved to point out the shortcomings of others.

Jesus chose to spend time with people who *knew* they were not good enough. They could repent, because they knew their sin all too well.

Father, thank You for loving me when I was unlovely. Thank you for showing me Your remedy for my sin. Impart to me the eyes that see individuals in light of your salvation. Let me love people as You love. In Jesus' name, Amen.

March 24

Deuteronomy 2:1–3:29; Luke 6:12–38; Psalm 67:1–7; Proverbs 11:27

Love Your Enemies

But I tell you who hear me: Love your enemies, do good to those who hate you, bless those who curse you, pray for those who mistreat you…Then your reward will be great, and you will be sons of the Most High, because he is kind to the ungrateful and wicked.
—Luke 6:27–28,35

Some verses you just want to skim past. *You know what I mean?* Now don't put your religious face on. This is real, nitty-gritty stuff. I don't know too many folks who like to be ridiculed and rejected. *I don't.* So let's think about this for a moment. Say it out loud… *Love your enemies.*

Just how does that work? Am I supposed to put on a fake smile when one of those enemies comes near? Emotionally, I don't want to do that either. So let's try to minimize the emotional side of it and see this the way our Father sees it. Because people are people—they are intrinsically selfish. There will always be people who aren't your fans.

This is about the nature of God, as much as anything. He is kind to the ungrateful and wicked *(v.35)*, and merciful *(v.36)*. You see, I cannot love my enemies in my own strength. I just don't have it in me. But God loves *that* person as much as He loves *me!* My version of Romans 6:12: *"We do not wrestle against people with skin, but against unseen forces of evil."* Let's see it for what it is. It's an evil spirit that perpetuates this.

My Father in heaven declares that I am the blessed one if I can resist the emotional reaction and respond with mercy and prayer.

Father in heaven. I need Your help on this one. I pray for that one who has never given me the benefit of the doubt. I ask that Your kindness well up in me. Let me act as a son of the Most High would. I ponder Your great mercy for me. Amen.

March 25

Deuteronomy 4:1–49; Luke 6:39–7:10; Psalm 68:1–18; Proverbs 11:28

A Privileged People

What other nation is so great as to have the gods near them the way the Lord our God is near us whenever we pray to him? Has any other people heard the voice of God speaking out of fire, as you have, and lived? Has any god ever tried to take for himself one nation out of another nation… by miraculous signs and wonders… like the Lord your God did for you?
—Deuteronomy 4:7,33–34

Much of Deuteronomy is Moses' final opportunity to emphasize the laws of God for his people to follow. They are words passionately spoken from a fatherly leader who knew his God. What pours forth in this passage is the emotions that God has for his people. This is a privileged people that God has chosen for Himself … *"so that you might know that the Lord is God… and no other" (v.35).*

Moses warns: Be careful. Watch yourselves. No idols, *"for the Lord your God is a jealous God" (v.24).* Have you ever thought about that? Think of a jealous God like a jealous husband who watches over his bride so that she would remain faithful. If she is violated, you sure don't want to be on the wrong end of that exchange. God's love is fervently zealous for you. He is jealous for your total devotion.

Later, he explains God's heart for you even in distress: Return, *"for the Lord your God is a merciful God. He will not abandon you" (v.31).*

Lastly, *"because He loved your forefathers … He brought you out by His Presence and His great strength" (v.37).* The Lord was *with* them. His very presence was an unfair advantage for those whom He loved so.

Father God. I now know that Your love for me is tenacious. You are not slack or ambivalent towards me. You reveal Your love for me over and over. May my response to You prove to be as a faithful bride. Amen.

March 26

Deuteronomy 5:1–6:25; Luke 7:11–35; Psalm 68:19–35; Proverbs 11:29–31

The Disciples of John

John's disciples told him about all these things (miracles). Calling two of them, he sent them to the Lord to ask, "Are you the one who was to come, or should we expect someone else?"…(Jesus) replied to the messengers, "Go back and report to John what you have seen and heard."
—Luke 7:18–19,22

Here is a curious story. John the Baptist—the one who baptized Jesus—the one who said, *"One more powerful than I will come whose sandals I am unworthy to untie;"*—the one who said, *"He must increase and I must decrease."* This same John the Baptist sends a couple of his own disciples to ask Jesus if He is the real McCoy. *"Are you the Messiah to come?"* Is John now unsure about Jesus' identity? *Really?* I think not.

I think John was preparing his own disciples for the future. He had already completed his mission to prepare the way of the Lord. John was mentoring his followers to pledge their allegiance to the One that was truly worth following—the Messiah Himself. Did John know the answer to his question? *Of course.* But by having them ask Jesus, they could be convinced in their own minds that Jesus was the Messiah.

What Jesus knew—that probably no one else could—was that John was soon to lose his life. He would be beheaded at Herod's daughter's request. The impact of that loss would be devastating and leave John's disciples scrambling. So Jesus takes full advantage in order to prepare them. What an interesting way that Jesus ends His dialogue: *"Blessed is the man who does not fall away on account of me"* *(v.23).* Jesus gives them a heads up that it will not be an easy road.

Father, thank You for the kind way that You undergird and lead me, as Your disciple. You are unmistakably the only One worthy of my life's devotion. Amen.

March 27

Deuteronomy 7:1–8:20; Luke 7:36–8:3; Psalm 69:1–18; Proverbs 12:1

The Support Team

Jesus traveled about proclaiming the good news of the kingdom of God. The Twelve were with him, and also some women who had been cured of evil spirits and diseases: Mary (called Magdalene) from whom seven demons had come out; Joanna, the manager of Herod's household; Susanna; and many others. These women were helping to support them out of their own means.
—Luke 8:1–3

There is more to ministry than just the one out front on the stage. Luke was good about bringing the equality that Jesus gave to all people: rich or poor, male or female, foreign or Jewish. Here, women who had been delivered and healed themselves by Jesus were, in turn, the ones serving behind the scenes. Much like when Jesus healed Peter's mother-in-law, *"she got up at once and began to wait on them" (Luke 4:39)*. It was a no-brainer. When we have been touched, then we want to touch others and be a blessing! It's one way to say thanks!

They helped to support the ministry with their own time and effort and money. When you support the ministry with your own means, then you are *all in*. Your pocketbook is a great reflection of where your heart truly is. When you make that investment, you have a stake in it's advancement and in it's success.

The work they did was not as visible, but just as important. There were administrative challenges and practical needs. So these women, who were many, were a real asset to the effectiveness of Jesus' ministry. And I'm just guessing they made some pretty tasty dishes. Do you take joy in serving, even when you're not in front?

Father in heaven, thank You for making a place for every believer to serve and be a blessing. Help me to find my place. I offer to you my time, my energy and my resources in order to advance Your kingdom. In Jesus' name, Amen.

March 28

Deuteronomy 9:1–10:22; Luke 8:4–21; Psalm 69:19–36; Proverbs 12:2–3

The Real Reason

Be assured today that the Lord your God is the one who goes ahead of you like a devouring fire ... It is not because of your righteousness or your integrity that you are going to take possession of their land; but on account of the wickedness of these nations, the Lord your God will drive them out before you...
—Deuteronomy 9:3,5

Wow. Sometimes the truth (put that way) hurts. But, *man-oh-man*, is it true! God, through Moses, let's us know that He's got a pretty good pulse on the situation. He knows what our contribution has been to this point: rebellion, sin, and stubbornness. He doesn't mince words when He calls Israel a *stiff-necked people.*

Such is the state of man. Jeremiah puts it like this: *"The heart is deceitful above all things and beyond cure. Who can understand it?" (Jeremiah 17:9).* Paul declares that before grace, we were dead in our trespasses and sins and without hope *(Ephesians 2).* So it's nothing of our own merit that gains us favor with God.

The dynamic that we embrace today is that it's just as much about the righteous justice of a holy God who drives out the wickedness that is before Him. So His justice *and* His mercy pair up to be quite a benefit to the people of God.

"And now, what does the Lord ask of you—but to fear the Lord, walk in His ways, love and serve Him with all your heart and soul" (10:12).

Gracious Father, You are just in Your assessment of my condition, and I stand on Your mercy alone. In Your kindness, You made a way for me through repentance to be restored to fellowship with You through Your Son, Jesus. Amen.

March 29

Deuteronomy 11:1–12:32; Luke 8:22–39; Psalm 70:1–5; Proverbs 12:4

Teach Your Children

Fix these words of mine in your hearts and minds; tie them as symbols on your hands and bind them on your foreheads. Teach them to your children, talking about them when you sit…when you walk…and when you lie down.
    —Deuteronomy 11:18–19

This is a principle you may not think about until your hair starts to grey or grandkids come along. But before you know it, you see these young kids grow to be older kids and then to be parents themselves. That's when you realize that these kids will be your leaders. It is a sober thought. Are they prepared to lead in a godly way? Have they been taught rightly? Have they had their own experience with Jesus?

The jest of today's verses are simple. Talk about God's principals whenever possible. Make daily routines into teaching moments. Keep them before you. Trip over them. Let your children see how God's Word applies to everyday life. They will observe what it means to you. By this, you will shoot these "arrows" into the world to affect good.

The *"aha"* moment for me today was bringing in the preceding verses. *"Remember that your children were not the ones who saw and experienced the discipline of the Lord…his mighty hand…the signs He performed. But it was your own eyes that saw all these great things the Lord has done" (vv.2–3,7).* Similarly, I, too, witnessed the power of the Lord on my life as a teenager and I haven't looked back. But that's *my* story. My children need to have their own story. They won't bow to my God until they have experienced God for real themselves! Parents—heed this word, and pray. They're in good hands.

Abba, this topic hits close to home. As a parent. I am comforted to know that You love my children more than I ever could and You are actively wooing them by Your Spirit. I commit them to You and thank You for them. Amen

March 30

Deuteronomy 13:1–15:23; Luke 8:40–9:6; Psalm 71:1–24; Proverbs 12:5–7

An Open Hand

If there is a poor man among your brothers in any of the towns…that the Lord Your God is giving you, do not be hardhearted or tightfisted toward your poor brother. Rather be openhanded and freely lend him whatever he needs. Give generously to him and do so without a grudging heart.
—*Deuteronomy 15:7–8,10*

On the one hand … *"there should be no poor among you" (v.4).* On the other hand …*"There will always be poor people in the land" (v.11).* Some things never change. But what should be my part in the matter?

In the last couple days, we have read over similar verses that challenge us on this topic. I know that it's close to the Lord's heart. *"He defends the cause of the fatherless and the widow, and loves the alien, giving him food and clothing…"* (Deuteronomy 10:18). *"Remember the Lord your God, for it is he who gives you the ability to produce wealth…"* (Deuteronomy 8:18).

Perhaps you have seen the beggar holding the sign at a busy intersection. Perhaps you also know those who use their food stamps to somehow purchase cigarettes. There will always be questionable situations, but this isn't about the abuses. It's about how *you* posture your heart before God. Would you allow God to use you in assisting a needy family? Could you give towards a local food kitchen?

God desires a heart that is generous and openhanded, because we have been the recipients of a great love. Our Father has provided for us generously and loves to display His love to others through us!

Father God, thank You for dealing with me ever so gently about the way I utilize the very finances that You provide. I acknowledge that You are my provider. Bless me, Lord, so that I may be an extension of Your hand to bless others. Amen.

March 31

Deuteronomy 16:1–17:20; Luke 9:7–27; Psalm 72:1–20; Proverbs 12:8–9

Kingly Advice

When he takes the throne of his kingdom, he is to write for himself on a scroll a copy of this law… It is to be with him, and he is to read it all the days of his life so that he may learn to revere the Lord his God and follow carefully all the words of this law.
—*Deuteronomy 17:18–19*

For Israel, it was advice for kings. For nations ruled as a democracy, it is advice for our national leaders and presidents. Either way, it is important that we appoint the leaders whom the Lord chooses *(v.15)*.

Does it really matter? It matters to God. *"Righteousness exalts a nation" (Proverbs 14:34)*, and a nation must be led by godly leaders in order to bring about righteousness. Can you imagine a nation whose God is the Lord and takes to heart this sound advice … reading the Word of God every day? It should also matter to us. We are seeing firsthand the collapse of a nation where righteousness is not honored anymore.

But we don't give up and give in because we see the tide turning. We give ourselves to prayer for our leaders. *"I urge that prayers and intercession be made for…kings and those in authority" (1 Timothy 2:1–2)*, Ironically, today's Psalm also concerns the king. *"May people ever pray for him…" (Psalm 72:15)*. It is a heartfelt plea from King Solomon to rule with justice and righteousness. And he looks ahead to the perfect rule that will come from the future reign of King Jesus. *"He will rule…to the ends of the earth. All nations will be blessed through him" (vv 8,17)*. Come Lord Jesus!

Father in heaven, I pray for those in positions of authority, that You would give them a revelation of who You are. Turn the tide in our nation, God. Raise up godly men and women to represent You all over the earth. In Jesus' name, Amen.

April 1

Deuteronomy 18:1–20:20; Luke 9:28–50; Psalm 73:1–28; Proverbs 12:10

Until I Entered the Sanctuary

When I tried to understand all this, it was oppressive to me till I entered the sanctuary of God; then I understood their final destiny.
—Psalm 73:16–17

Why is it that the wicked prosper? At least, it sure seems that way. I am pretty sure that we all can identify with this curiosity. Asaph is a worship leader and the writer of this Psalm, and he has some pretty strong feelings on the topic.

You look around and see your neighbors, who have absolutely no regard for the things of God, living quite well-to-do. Life seems easy for them, and their grass even looks a shade greener than yours … right? All the while, you struggle to make ends meet and the differences are starting to annoy you. *"Surely in vain have I kept my heart pure" (v.13).* Trying to understand this present disparity is oppressive.

But only when I enter the sanctuary of God, get quiet before the Lord and seek His face, can I find consolation. Only when I am able to view things from His eternal perspective can I understand where this is going. It's about the values we embrace and where it ultimately leads us. When I take on God's value system, I can say, *"earth has nothing I desire besides You" (v.25).*

"Yet I am always with You; You hold me by my right hand. You guide me with your counsel (now*) and afterward you will take me into glory* (forevermore*)" (vv.23-24).* What could be sweeter than that?

O Lord, forgive me for wanting to trade places with the heathen who flourish for just a season. Their end is ruin, but You are the strength of my heart and my portion forever. Give me eternal eyes to see the way You see. In Jesus' name, Amen.

April 2

Deuteronomy 21:1–22:30; Luke 9:51–10:12; Psalm 74:1–23; Proverbs 12:11

Seventy-two are Commissioned

The Lord appointed seventy-two… and sent them two by two ahead of him to every town where he was about to go. I am sending you out like lambs among wolves. Heal the sick and tell them, "The kingdom of God is near you."
—Luke 10:1,3,9

To begin Luke 9, Jesus commissioned the Twelve to *preach* the gospel and *practice* the gospel. Give them the good news and heal their sick. To begin Luke 10, Jesus appointed seventy–two others with the same message. He was multiplying His efforts *and* He was preparing the towns for his upcoming visit.

Jesus made it clear that this would not be a pleasure trip or a casual sending. They were to be resolute in their mission and not be distracted. They were ambassadors of a new kingdom.

With the harvest field being so vast, the need for more workers (disciples) was essential. They were to make disciples, who in turn, would be workers to make more disciples. That is the model, and it hasn't changed even to this day.

Jesus compared their sending as lambs among wolves. *Wait a minute. Don't wolves eat lambs?* I'd say that is a good reason to go in pairs! You are navigating into their world, but you'll go in His authority and zeal. His protection will be upon you. Not coincidentally, Psalm 74 echoes this thought: *"Do not hand over the life of your dove to wild beasts" (v.19). "Rise up, O God, and defend your cause" (v.22).*

Dear Lord, You have given us the task to reproduce Your kingdom. You said to ask the Lord of the harvest for workers, so I am asking. Add to the front lines so that the gospel may go forth in power and might. Make my life to be an effective witness where I live today. In Jesus' name, Amen.

April 3

Deuteronomy 23:1–25:19; Luke 10:13–37; Psalm 75:1–10; Proverbs 12:12–14

The Seventy-two Return

The seventy-two returned with joy and said, "Lord, even the demons submit to us in your name." He replied, "I saw Satan fall like lightning from heaven. I have given you authority to overcome all the power of the enemy … However, do not rejoice that the spirits submit to you, but that your names are written in heaven."
—Luke 10:17–20

The missions trip of the seventy–two was an unforgettable success. They were amazed at how the power of God was displayed through them. It was true! Jesus even gives a visual report about what was occurring in the spirit realm: *"I saw Satan fall like lightning from heaven."*

Jesus underscores the point. Yes, I have given you authority to overcome. Yes, I will protect you while you give witness of Me. But the larger reason to rejoice is that your names are written in heaven. Nothing Jesus says here minimizes their need for authority, but in the end, the reason to rejoice is that our citizenship is firmly fixed in the courts of heaven.

An adjective used several times here is a form of the word "joy." The seventy–two returned with *joy*. Don't *rejoice* that the spirits submit to you, but *rejoice* that your names are written in heaven. And Jesus, full of *joy* through the Holy Spirit, praises the Father. It is joy that the Lord floods our heart with and the fullness of His livelihood in us by the Holy Spirit. Jesus was full of joy. A full heart (of joy) overflowed to cause Him to express praise to the Father. Do you know this joy? Does joy flood your heart from a life in the Holy Spirit?

Lord of heaven and earth, I praise You from a heart made full by the Holy Spirit. May I give You thanks that my name is written in the Lamb's book of life. It is the greatest joy and privilege to serve You with my life. Amen.

April 4

Deuteronomy 26:1–27:26; Luke 10:38–11:13; Psalm 76:1–12; Proverbs 12:15–17

Mary and Martha

Martha opened her home to him (Jesus). She had a sister called Mary, who sat at the Lord's feet listening to what he said. But Martha was distracted by all the preparations to be made. "Lord, don't you care?" "Martha," the Lord answered, "you are worried about many things, but only one thing is needed. Mary has chosen what is better, and it will not be taken away from her."
—Luke 10:38–42

I confess: I am a Martha. The message of this story rings true for me every time I read it. It never gets old or out-of-date.

Martha was the older sister. She was the responsible one. She owns the house. She's the Type A personality who wants everything lined up and prepared just so. She exhibited her devotion by inviting Jesus into her home. But she was also the one who became overwhelmed by all that needed to be done. She worried too much. And she didn't like it when others *(Mary)* did not pull their weight. Martha made her case to Jesus for the obvious.

But what Jesus saw in Mary was her posture of devotion, her attentive listening and her eager desire to know Him more. Mary got it. She knew who this man was. She did not want to miss one word.

What Martha was pursuing was not intrinsically evil. Her motive was good and right. Likewise, I have pursued righteous things in my life. But sometimes our struggle is not with sin, but between what is good and what is better. Mary made the choice. What is yours?

Dear Lord, I so identify with Martha, busying myself with so many things. Sometimes I need to just take a break and sit before You and hear what You have to say to me. Forgive me for missing opportunities to be still before You. Let my devotion for You be evident. Let me hear Your voice. Amen.

April 5

Deuteronomy 28:1–68; Luke 11:14–36; Psalm 77:1–20; Proverbs 12:18

God is Bigger

But if I drive out demons by the finger of God, then the kingdom of God has come to you.
—Luke 11:20

Sometimes, we get this idea in our mind of God and Satan in a boxing ring, and they're both heavy-weights duking it out. God is supposed to win, but it might be a close call ... Well, compared to the light-weights that *we* are, yes, they are both stronger. But there is only one champion, and He is in a class of His own.

There is considerable dialogue given to the subject of demons here. That's because they are very real and they oppose the work of God. You've noticed in the gospels that demons harass and bind people with every sort of misery, but when Jesus commands them to go, they have to leave. Jesus had absolute authority, and He still does today.

In verses 24-26, where an evil spirit comes out of a man then roams around and returns with more, has always seemed ominous to me. If a demon has been cast out, then how could seven more be permitted to come back? *How does that work?* The truth is that demons will enter familiar dark places if the doors are left open and the house left vacant. "Cleaning up your act" is just not enough.

When Jesus delivers us from our life of sin, we are swept clean. But now the house is occupied by a new owner—the Spirit of the living God. Demons flee the presence of God, just as light rids the darkness. The kingdom of God has come to you. You are free from torment.

Father, thank You for Your resounding authority over every puny demon that seeks to drag me down. In the name of Jesus, I cast off every lie and thought that rivals You. May Your Spirit flood me with Your light and truth. Amen.

April 6

Deuteronomy 29:1–30:20; Luke 11:37–12:7; Psalm 78:1–31; Proverbs 12:19–20

Choose Life

This day I call heaven and earth as witnesses against you that I have set before you life and death, blessings and curses. Now choose life, so that you and your children may live and that you may love the Lord your God, listen to his voice, and hold fast to him.
—Deuteronomy 30:19–20

Moses' discourse is nearing an end. He exhorts the nation to stay true to their God. In Deuteronomy 28, Moses explained the blessings that follow obedience and the curses that follow rebellion. It all culminates here with the choices they have before them. Moses is passionate and makes his case for them to choose the life that God has designed for them. It's the same plea for a decision that He asks of us today.

What God is asking of them is not too difficult or beyond their reach. *"No, the word is very near you; it is in your mouth and in your heart so that you may obey it" (30:14)*. The response is as simple as confessing with your mouth that Jesus is Lord and believing in your heart that Jesus was raised from death to give you life.

What God has revealed to us is all we need to serve the Lord for generations to come *(29:29)*. So it's not for a lack of knowledge. No, the most difficult part of obeying God's laws is making the decision to do it. It is an act of our will. We make the conscious choice.

Moses then gave us a promise—that the Lord would consecrate our hearts so that we might love him with all our heart and with all our soul, and live. He knew that we would need the motivation *(30:6)*.

Father God, thank You for making salvation available to me. I accept Your kind gift and receive it by faith. Thank You for Your mercy and the grace that enables me to hold fast. I choose life today. I choose You. Amen.

April 7

Deuteronomy 31:1–32:27; Luke 12:8–34; Psalm 78:32–55; Proverbs 12:21–23

The Cycle of Unfaithfulness

In spite of all this, they kept on sinning. Whenever God slew them, they would seek him; they eagerly turned to him again. They remembered that God was their Rock. But then they would flatter him with their mouths...their hearts were not loyal to him, they were not faithful. Yet he was merciful.
—Psalm 78:32,34,36–38

The heart of man is exposed in our Psalm today *(78)*, as well as in Deuteronomy *(31–32)*. In it appears a cycle of unfaithfulness, a cycle that revolves around what my selfish heart craves. In it, we think that we can claim to serve God *and* make our own way independent of God. But God sees it all. He is not fooled.

In spite of God's intervention and provision; in spite of His wonders and His blessings, we sin against Him. *"Is this the way you repay the Lord? Is He not your Father, your Creator, who made you and formed you?" (32:6)*. Of His people ..."*He guarded him as the apple of his eye" (32:10)*. Moses warns Joshua of the evil his people were going to do before they did it! Not the kind of news you want to hear while accepting the post as their new leader. When God dealt justice to their sinful actions, they turned... for a moment. But their hearts were not loyal.

The key to this disturbing trend is the steadfast mercy of God. *"He was merciful; he forgave their iniquities... He remembered that they were but flesh" (78:38–39)*. An honest response to this propensity to sin is to remember where God has brought you from and repent of sin that brings separation. The cycle of unfaithfulness can be broken.

Father in heaven, we have turned our backs on Your great love. We have spurned Your Spirit and have gone our own way. I repent and turn away from my sinful ways. Forgive me and remember that I am but flesh. Build in me a loyal heart. Amen.

April 8

Deuteronomy 32:28–52; Luke 12:35–59; Psalm 78:56–64; Proverbs 12:24

Much Given, Much Required

The Lord told Moses… "There on the mountain you will die and be gathered to your people. This is because both of you broke faith with me in the presence of the Israelites… and because you did not uphold my holiness among [them]."
—Deuteronomy 32:48,50–51

This is a hard lesson to wrap your mind around. But because so many envy the place of leadership, it would be good for you to understand this key principle. And it's found in both texts again—Deuteronomy and Luke: *To much is given, much is required (Luke 12:48).*

It's hard to imagine that God would come down on Moses so hard. After all, he was leading an obstinate people who majored on complaining. But God had given Moses a direct word to "speak to the rock" in order to provide water. In Moses' frustration, he struck the rock twice. Water flowed, but Moses had dishonored the Lord. He took things into his own hands. Moses had taken advantage of the close proximity of His friendship. *"You did not trust me enough to honor me as holy in the sight of the Israelites" (Numbers 20:12).*

Leadership is not about how we look before others, but how we give witness to God in truth. We are only messengers. We speak what He speaks, nothing more. I keep myself out of the equation, except to carry the weight of rightly representing God in His holiness.

Moses knew of what he spoke when he said: *"They (His words) are not just idle words for you—they are your life. By them you will live long in the land you are crossing the Jordan to possess" (32:47).*

Father God, may I be entrusted to say what You tell me to say and represent You rightly. I lift up before You those who lead Your sheep. Protect their hearts and give them ears to hear Your words. Amen.

April 9

Deuteronomy 33:1–29; Luke 13:1–21; Psalm 78:65–72; Proverbs 12:25

Integrity and Skill

But he chose the tribe of Judah. He chose David his servant… to be the shepherd of his people Jacob, of Israel his inheritance. And David shepherded them with integrity of heart; with skillful hands he led them.
—Psalm 78:68,70–72

Fascinating verses. Ironically, as we have seen over and over, one text compliments another in the same reading. In Deuteronomy, Moses pronounces blessing over each of the tribes of Israel. And in Psalm 78, Asaph recounts history as God chose from the twelve tribes—Judah; from which comes David; from which comes the Messiah Jesus.

What was the Lord looking for in a man to shepherd His people? It should be no surprise that God's choice—David—was a shepherd of sheep. He knew what it was to care for and protect his flock. David didn't know it at the time, but it was his training ground—and it was no small matter. God saw it all. When the prophet Samuel came to call, not even his father Jesse imagined the young David to be called out to lead in such capacity. What God was looking for was more than what man looks for—the inner character of integrity *(1 Samuel 16:7).*

David shepherded Israel with integrity of heart and skillful hands. He had natural abilities that he honed and integrity to do the right thing—whether it was popular or not. Integrity is what God sees in secret. It's what allows us to have a clear conscience. In other words, with the affairs of His own people, David could be trusted.

On the integrity scale, where do you sit? Only you and God can know.

Father God, You see what I cannot. You see motives and desires. Build within me truth and honesty, excellence and righteousness. Build within me integrity of heart. Let me earn Your trust in the affairs of the kingdom. Amen.

April 10

Deuteronomy 34:1–Joshua 2:24; Luke 13:22–35; Psalm 79:1–13; Proverbs 12:26

The Transition

Now Joshua son of Nun was filled with the spirit of wisdom because Moses had laid his hands on him. After the death of Moses...the Lord said to Joshua "Be strong and courageous... for the Lord your God will be with you."
  —Deuteronomy 34:9; Joshua 1:1,9

Transitions are seldom easy and many times are not asked for, but inevitable. *How does it go ... The one constant in life is change?*

Today is the end of an era under Moses' leadership, and the beginning of a new one under Joshua.

Moses gets a personal visual tour of the promised land by the Lord Himself. He was commended as one who the Lord knew face to face, describing an intimacy between God and His friend. Moses had been His mouthpiece, but now his assignment was complete.

Joshua is the new man. He had been personally tutored by Moses and had witnessed all that God had done under his leadership. Now it was Joshua's turn. When Moses laid his hands to anoint him for his new position, Joshua was filled with the spirit of wisdom. It earned him the credibility needed to lead and be honored by all of Israel. Joshua was now set up to succeed.

The charge given to him is familiar: *"Be strong and courageous"*—three times! Obey My word. Meditate upon My word. I will be with you! This is God's prescription for success for the leader in transition. And yet, it works for whatever transition you may find yourself in.

Father God, in my world that seems to change often, You are my one constant. You never change, and I can rely upon Your faithfulness. Endow me with courage to face my new season. May I find strength in Your word. Amen.

April 11

Joshua 3:1–4:24; Luke 14:1–35; Psalm 80:1–19; Proverbs 12:27–28

Memorial Stones

When the whole nation had finished crossing the Jordan, the Lord said to Joshua, "Choose twelve men... one from each tribe, and tell them to take up twelve stones from the middle of the Jordan and put them down where you stay tonight."
—*Joshua 4:1–3*

This was a curious command of the Lord, but highly significant. What the Lord was doing was to be remembered. The fulfillment of a promise was at hand. God's mighty arm would bring Israel across the Jordan River (at flood stage) on dry ground to the side of Jericho.

At the Lord's directive, Joshua chose twelve men, one from each tribe, to take up a stone from the middle of the Jordan. These stones were to be a memorial to the people of Israel forever. It was at Gilgal where the stones were set up. *"That way, when future descendants ask, 'What do these stones mean?' tell them the Lord your God dried up the Jordan before you" (4:21,23). "He did this so that all... might know that the hand of the Lord is powerful and so that you might always fear the Lord your God" (4:24).*

Joshua had prepared them: *"... tomorrow the Lord will do amazing things among you" (3:5).* He certainly did. And He continues to do amazing things today. That is why it is important that we remember those things the Lord has done. For me, it's my salvation experience. It's God's miraculous provision when we purchased our first church building. It's God's healing touch upon my wife following cancer. These are significant God—events that need a memorial stone.

Father in heaven, I acknowledge that You have done amazing things in my life. You perform miracles today, just as You have in days gone by. Let me never forget to praise You for Your mighty works in my life. I am forever grateful. Amen.

April 12

Joshua 5:1–7:15; Luke 15:1–32; Psalm 81:1–16; Proverbs 13:1

Commander of the Lord's Army

Now when Joshua was near Jericho, he looked up and saw a man standing with a drawn sword ... and asked, "Are you for us or for our enemies?" "Neither," he replied, "but as the commander of the army of the Lord I have now come ... Take off your sandals, for the place you are standing is holy."
—Joshua 5:13–15

From one memorial stone to another! As significant as the burning bush was to Moses, so was Joshua's encounter with the commander of the Lord's army. It was one of those life experiences that marks you forever. It was God's stamp on Joshua's life and mission.

There are few examples in the Bible when the natural is visited by the supernatural in a visible manner. Elisha's servant was enabled to see God's armies surrounding Dothan *(2 Kings 6)*; King Nebuchadnezzar saw a fourth man in the fiery furnace *(Daniel 3)*. But it was not a commonplace occurrence, to say the least. This was a reassurance straight from heaven that allowed Joshua to know that he would be helped in order to fulfill his mission and conquer the promised land.

This encounter was for Joshua alone. Leading the chosen nation of Israel was an awesome and holy task. It wouldn't be so much Joshua's resources or talents to lead, but his dependence upon God. An encounter with God's holiness would establish the line of authority and the chain of command. God was leading. Joshua was obeying. Have you been impacted by the holiness of God in a personal way?

Father God, it was Your plan and Your resources that brought about the victories. You were there to lead the way. Lead me to embrace the inheritance You have for me and to conquer the enemies that stand in my way. I defer to You. Amen.

April 13

Joshua 7:16--9:2; Luke 16:1–18; Psalm 82:1–8; Proverbs 13:2–3

The Impact of Iniquity

Then Joshua said to Achan, "My son, give glory to the Lord. Tell me what you have done." Achan replied, "It is true! I have sinned against the Lord." Then all Israel stoned him, and after they...stoned the rest, they burned them.
—Joshua 7:19–20,25

What a momentum killer. As high as Israel was flying from their recent conquests over the Jordan River and of Jericho, so was the low when it was found that sin in the camp prohibited any further progress. The pendulum had swung to the opposite side.

This episode is a carry-over from yesterday's reading. Joshua was found to be on his face before the Lord when God said: *"Stand up! Israel has sinned and violated my covenant. You cannot stand against your enemies until you remove* [what has caused this]*" (7:10–11,13).* Sure enough, from the entire camp, Achan was found to have stolen plunder from the enemy. Judgment was swift and thorough.

The punishment, in anyone's mind, appears to be harsh and drastic. *Yikes!* Not only did the sentence come down upon Achan, but his sons and daughters and all of his belongings too. What God wants us to understand is the impact that sin has. Iniquity cannot be overlooked. God cannot bless sin. Sin halts any progress that God had intended.

It is a deception to believe that my sin only affects me. No, it adversely affects anyone who associates with me. And if permitted, the tolerance of sin brings shame to the whole body of Christ, because I represent His holy name. My reputation and witness, that take a lifetime to earn, can vanish in a heartbeat. Sin has a way of being exposed.

Merciful Father, You repel sin as oil repels water. They do not mix. Don't let me entertain compromise, knowing just how it affects my progress and that of the body of Christ. Shine Your light on my sin, by Your Spirit, I pray. Amen.

April 14

Joshua 9:3–10:43; Luke 16:19–17:10; Psalm 83:1–18; Proverbs 13:4

The Gibeonite Ruse

When the people of Gibeon heard what Joshua had done to Jericho and Ai, they resorted to a ruse: They went as a delegation whose donkeys were loaded with worn-out sacks and...wineskins." We have come from a distant country; make a treaty with us." The men of Israel... did not inquire of the Lord.
　　—Joshua 9:3–4,6,14

Here is a story with a Hollywood flair!

If you were one of the nations in the path of the Israelite conquest, wouldn't you have to think of something? Anything? The reports of the Lord's fame and favor upon Israel was widespread. Gibeon was one of those next nations in the path, so they schemed up a line that Joshua and his leaders swallowed hook, line and sinker. Complete with moldy bread, cracked wineskins and the tired look of a long journey. Talk about good acting!

The sad truth of this story screams loudly: *"The men of Israel sampled their provision, but did not inquire of the Lord" (9:14).* They what? They did not inquire of the Lord? *Whoooops!*

Lies can look so believable sometimes. This time it brought about a Plan B. Under the guise of paying a compliment and a feel-sorry-for-us pitch for mercy, they gained the goal of self-preservation.

What Joshua did should be an eye-opener for us all. We cannot depend upon our own understanding and keen insight. We can be swayed. We can be snookered. Inquiring of the Lord is necessary in any important decision, even the ones we think we have a handle on.

Father God, If I am left to myself, I can miss the mark so badly. I confess that I need Your counsel and Your discernment on all matters, big and small. Amen.

April 15

Joshua 11:1–12:24; Luke 17:11–37; Psalm 84:1–12; Proverbs 13:5–6

Better Is One Day

How lovely is your dwelling place, O Lord Almighty! My soul yearns, even faints, for the courts of the Lord; Better is one day in your courts than a thousand elsewhere; I would rather be a doorkeeper in the house of my God than dwell in the tents of the wicked.
—Psalm 84:1–2,10

The sons of Korah were temple assistants, and never was there a greater Psalm penned of desire for God's rich, living presence. They would know of it. The temple was where they met with God.

Many times, the pilgrimage to the temple passed through the Valley of Baca, a place of barrenness and weeping. Sometimes the path we are on takes us through a time of struggle and pain. In the end, to be enveloped in God's presence somehow makes it all worthwhile, or at least I am able to put things in proper perspective.

Anyone who has encountered the presence of God knows that it has a dramatic affect upon life as we know it. It changes everything. My soul longs for this. My heart and flesh cry out! Nothing else can truly satisfy. It doesn't have to take place in a church building, but it can and often does. For me, it is usually in the quiet of my study, reading His word and listening to worshipful, instrumental music. I sense the Spirit of God keenly. Direction comes. Peace flows. He is there!

There are too many distractions in life that pull us away from that which matters most. Here, the sons of Korah get it, and proclaim it: *"There is nothing more that I desire in life than to dwell where You are!"*

Father in heaven, I love Your presence. I do not want to live without it. I have tasted and I have seen that You are good. In the good times and the bad, may I find my refreshing in Your courts! Amen.

April 16

Joshua 13:1–14:15; Luke 18:1–17; Psalm 85:1–13; Proverbs 13:7–8

The Just and the Unjust Judge

The Jesus told his disciples a parable…"In a certain town there was a judge who neither feared God nor cared about men. And there was a widow in that town who kept coming to him…(for justice). For some time he refused. But finally he said…I will see that she gets justice, so that she won't eventually wear me out."
—Luke 18:1–5

Jesus shares a parable, and the punch line is right up front: *"to show them that they should pray and not give up" (v.1).*

Don't make the first mistake and form the mindset that God is unjust and that He tires of hearing our plea. It's a teaching moment to show us just the opposite. If you can imagine that an unjust judge can bring about justice, then how much more will God, the Just Judge? *"I tell you, he will see that they get justice, and quickly" (v.8).* When you pray and bring your requests before the Lord, know that He cares about speedy justice more than you do. His timetable is not always our timetable, but He is righteous and just in all His dealings.

The attention Jesus gives to the one who prays is equally important. Jesus refers to them as *"his chosen ones, who cry out to him day and night" (v.7).* I've heard it said (and you have too) that if you really have faith, then you only need to ask God once. But here, God says faith is linked with our perseverance. When you pray, and if it matters to you, don't stop asking. Don't stop believing God for it.

"When the Son of Man comes, will he find faith on the earth?" (v.8).

Dear Father, thank You for taking such an intense interest in my prayers and what burdens my heart. You alone make things right in the end. I trust You and will not stop asking for justice and mercy while I am on this earth. Amen.

April 17

Joshua 15:1–63; Luke 18:18–43; Psalm 86:1–17; Proverbs 13:9–10

An Undivided Heart

Teach me your way, O Lord, and I will walk in your truth; give me an undivided heart, that I may fear your name. I will praise you, O Lord my God, with all my heart; I will glorify your name forever.
—Psalm 86:11–12

David knew times of trouble. He writes and pours his heart out to the One who could deliver him. And in it, David pledges his trust anew: "*…give me an undivided heart, that I may fear your name."*

When you are backed up against a wall, in the day of trouble, when the arrogant are attacking, you want to make sure in your heart that you are not a part of the problem. A divided heart would reveal areas that are subject to the same judgment you are asking for upon your enemies! A wrong motive or vengeful spirit would not make you any different, would it?

Many today speak of following their heart, even sincerely, which is to say that the heart knows what's best. But the heart is truly fickle. Jeremiah says, *"the heart is deceitful above all things…" (Jeremiah 17:9).*

How is it that your heart may be divided? It is swayed to follow in one direction or another based on what you will to pursue. Your heart could be pledged in differing directions and be divided in loyalty. That's why David is insistent upon devoting his heart in an undivided way. *"With all my heart, I will praise you."*

Father God, in the day of trouble I will call to You, for You will answer me. There is no shadow of turning with You. Let not my heart be divided between You and any other worldly pursuit. I pledge my heart to You alone. It is in Jesus' mighty name that I pray, Amen.

April 18

Joshua 16:1–18:28; Luke 19:1–27; Psalm 87:1–7; Proverbs 13:11

Wee Zacchaeus

Zacchaeus wanted to see who Jesus was, but being a short man he could not, because of the crowd. So he ran ahead and climbed a sycamore tree … Jesus reached the spot, he looked up and said, "Zacchaeus, come down immediately. I must stay at your house … Today salvation has come to this house."
—Luke 19:2–5,9

Perhaps we know the story of Zacchaeus from the song we sang as children. But Zacchaeus was not so popular among his own people. Zacchaeus was a chief tax collector for the Roman government. That made him a traitor and a gouger, made wealthy off his fellow Jews.

Jesus was drawing quite a crowd, and Zacchaeus wanted to see who this man was, but honestly, was too short to see through the crowd. Never mind that Zacchaeus was short, or that he was unpopular, or that he made his wealth by cheating; Jesus accepted him and showed a personal interest in him. There was no barrier in Jesus' eyes. This man was a human being who needed salvation as every other man.

The response of Zacchaeus was textbook. After encountering Jesus, his life was changed, and the proof of that change was made evident. Where wealth had been his god, now it was a tool to bless the poor and repay those he cheated. His faith was proven by his actions.

What was, no doubt, a surprise for all the Jews in the crowd to hear was Jesus' declaration that this former tax collector was now a fellow son of Abraham… a fellow son by faith in the Son of God.

Father, I thank You for loving the unlovely and those deemed as untouchable. You know no barriers except unbelief. May I see my fellow man with Your eyes, as persons with value, created by You and for You. Through Jesus I pray, Amen.

April 19

Joshua 19:1–20:9; Luke 19:28–48; Ps. 88:1–18; Proverbs 13:12–14

An Emotional Savior

As he (Jesus) approached Jerusalem and saw the city, he wept over it and said, "If you... had only known on this day what would bring you peace—but now is hidden from your eyes. The days will come when your enemies will hem you in...because you did not recognize the time of God's coming to you."
—Luke 19:41–44

Jesus was on his final trip into Jerusalem. With His mission fresh in His mind, knowing well what lie ahead, Jesus is probably already stirred in His emotions. Few else knew what this week would bring. He tried to tell His disciples, and they could not grasp it. But Jesus did.

Jesus neared the city riding on a donkey—fulfilling the prophecy in Zechariah 9:9 concerning His future kingship. The bustling city was preparing for Passover and a large crowd praised Him loudly, spreading their cloaks before Him on the road by the Mount of Olives. They had witnessed the miracles. *"Blessed is the king who comes in the name of the Lord!" (v.38).* It was an emotionally-charged crowd.

And as Jesus neared Jerusalem, he wept over it. He was overcome with emotion by a people who reject His offer of salvation, by Jewish leaders who would not recognize the very God-man in the flesh. His life's purpose was to seek and save those who were lost, but His own people spurn Him. Jesus weeps over a people who are lost in their sin and cannot see it.

When is the last time you were gripped by the lost state of a loved one or by a nation who has turned it's back on God?

Father, thank You for sending Jesus to atone for our sins. Your Son showed visible compassion for a people lost in their own sin. I ask that You will give me Your heart for my family members, co-workers and the nation. Amen.

April 20

Joshua 21:1–22:20; Luke 20:1–26; Psalm 89:1–13; Proverbs 13:15–16

Promise Fulfilled

So the Lord gave Israel all the land he had sworn to give their forefathers, and they took possession of it and settled there. Not one of all the Lord's good promises to the house of Israel failed; every one was fulfilled.
—Joshua 21:43,45

The last few chapters of Joshua have been the divvying up of the land between all the tribes and the cities of refuge, and now the towns for the Levites. Even Zelophehad received her promised inheritance among those of Manasseh, with only daughters. It seems like a lot of small details to have to endure in our reading through the Bible, but aren't you glad that God is in the details? He is interested in every family and the fulfillment of every promise that He made to them.

What we are considering today is the faithfulness of God and His ability to see a promise to its' fulfillment. It didn't happen overnight. Had Israel been as faithful to respond to God, many years and a generation could have witnessed it sooner. Yet, all that had been promised, beginning way back with Abram in Genesis 12 had come to pass: *"I will make you into a great nation and I will bless you"* (v.2).

It is in God's character to bless. It is who He is. Defining faith includes believing that *"He rewards those who earnestly seek Him" (Hebrews 11:6)*. God is the originator of dreams, hopes, promises and blessing. We saw its impact yesterday in Proverbs 13:12: *"Hope deferred makes the heart sick, but a longing fulfilled is a tree of life."*

Make a list of promises and dreams that God has put in *your* heart!

Father, as I consider all that You have done in my life, I am grateful. You have truly blessed me. I know there is still more for me in Your plan, because You love to bless my faith response. You are good in all Your ways! Amen.

April 21

Joshua 22:21–23:16; Luke 20:27–47; Psalm 89:14–37; Proverbs 13:17–19

You Exalt Our Horn

Righteousness and justice are the foundation of your throne; love and faithfulness go before you. Blessed are those who have learned to acclaim you, who walk in the light of your presence. They rejoice in your name all day long. For you are their glory and strength ... by your favor you exalt our horn.
—*Psalm 89:14–17*

I was struck by these few verses today. They are so profound. Before you read further, meditate upon them again, slowly. *Pause...*

What is it that your house is built upon? A foundation, of course. It's the reason your house is secure and sound. You build upon that base. Here, the very foundation of God's value system is righteousness and justice. There are other true attributes of His nature, but it starts with these. It's what His kingdom hinges upon. It's what God is about. And His reputation precedes Him—of love and faithfulness!

With that said, we are invited to draw near and know this God of glory. *You are blessed when...* you not only know what it is to behold the rich presence of God, but you are able to walk in that light. *You are also blessed when...* you are able to learn how to acclaim Him. We're even told how to acclaim—by rejoicing in His name continually. It's easy to do that when you know where your strength comes from.

It is by the favor of God that our horn is exalted. This phrase, "our horn exalted" is used twice *(v.17, 24)* and caught my attention. Our horn is our strength, as the horn of an animal is the symbol of their strength. It's God's validation upon us—He makes us who we are.

Father, teach me how to acclaim You. Let my lips speak Your praise. Let me walk in the splendor of Your presence. I acknowledge that all I am and ever will be is because of Your favor on me. You are my glory and strength. Amen.

April 22

Joshua 24:1–33; Luke 21:1–28; Psalm 89:38–52; Proverbs 13:20–23

Make the Conscious Choice

Then you crossed the Jordan…I sent the hornet ahead of you, which drove them out before you. Now fear the Lord and serve him…but if serving the Lord seems undesirable to you, then choose for yourselves this day whom you will serve. But as for me and my household, we will serve the Lord.
—Joshua 24:11–12,14–15

Joshua is nearing the end of his life and legacy. He summons all the leaders of Israel in order to give them a final charge. It would only seem right and proper to know that all was carried out as God had planned and that the nation was set up to succeed, prior to leaving.

Joshua gives them a short history lesson to remind them how they got here, from before Abraham to the present: *"You did not do it with your own sword and bow. I sent the hornet ahead of you, which drove them out" (v.12)*. I'm sure that Joshua was persuasive in speech, but the truth was undeniable. In the light of all that God has done, it is fair and right for Joshua to press them to a point of decision. *"It's your choice, and God honors your free will, but choose this day whom you will serve. Let it be known that my choice is to serve the Lord."*

The people answered as Joshua had hoped. In essence: *"How could we forsake the Lord to serve other gods, who brought us out of Egypt and to this land?"* But Joshua knew them. He knew their tendency to stray. So Joshua led them to make a binding covenant, and he told them to do two things: Throw away the foreign gods among you, and yield your hearts to the Lord. That is wise counsel. Don't allow rival gods to captivate your heart. Instead, open wide your heart to God.

Father God, You have proven Your love and faithfulness over and over in my life. You are worthy of my undivided trust. I yield my heart and life to You. I choose to serve You this day and every day. In Jesus' name, Amen.

April 23

Judges 1:1–2:9; Luke 21:29–22:13; Psalm 90:1–91:16; Proverbs 13:24–25

Number Your Days

The length of our days is seventy years—or eighty, if we have the strength; yet their span is but trouble and sorrow. Teach us to number our days aright, that we may gain a heart of wisdom. Make us glad for as many days as you have afflicted us. May the favor of the Lord our God rest upon us.
—Psalm 90:10,12,15,17

Moses pens this Psalm, making it the oldest of all the Psalms, and he gives us much sound advice and an eternal perspective upon life.

Moses doesn't gloss over the harsh realities of life. Life is hard, and then you die. My dad has told me more than once to enjoy life while you're younger, because the golden years are not very golden. There are obvious frailties and limitations that come with age. Our bodies and our minds don't always function as efficiently as they used to.

The facts are also a promise—we're given seventy years on this earth, eighty on the top end. Do with them wisely. There you have it. Sure, there are exceptions. Some live longer; some are cut short. The point is to live every day to the fullest and walk in the blessing of God, because you just never know when that day is going to come. And it does come. What I do know is that life whizzes by. You blink and see decades slip by just like that! *Where did the time go?*

With Moses' advice, we have no excuse. What we *can* do is to number our days aright and live our days out wisely. What must I change before it's too late? What should I put my hand to in this season of my life? How can I prepare my heart now for an eternity that awaits me?

Father God, thank You for the wake-up call. I understand that my life here is but for a moment, in the light of eternity. I pray that You will help me in the later years to live a fruitful life. May Your favor rest upon me. Amen.

April 24

Judges 2:10–3:31; Luke 22:14–34; Psalm 92:1–93:5; Proverbs 14:1–2

The Saddest Verse

After that generation had been gathered to their fathers, another generation grew up, who knew neither the Lord nor what he had done for Israel.
—Judges 2:10

Of all the verses in the Bible, I'd be willing to bet that you cannot find another verse any more despairing than this one here in Judges 2.

You see, the people of Israel served the Lord while Joshua was present. The generation who witnessed the great things that the Lord had done could not deny the Lord *(2:7)*. But another generation was coming onto the scene, and they were deprived of godly leadership.

It was a new era that Israel was moving into. Moses and Joshua had provided leadership by God's voice and direction. Without them, Israel was left to their own devices. They forsook the Lord *(2:11)* and they provoked the Lord *(2:12)*. When the Lord did not bail them out, they became greatly distressed. So what the Lord did was to raise up judges in regions, periodically. The first three were Othniel, Ehud and Shamgar. It was a vicious cycle, because once the judges were gone, Israel resumed in their stubborn, evil ways in greater measure.

What might have happened if the older generation would have trained up their children to fear and honor the Lord? What if they would have taught them the law as it was handed down to them? It's the same predicament we find ourselves with in our own families. Will we love and lead them to encounter God personally like we did?

Father, it must break Your heart when people You love dearly turn their backs on You. And the ones You entrusted to pass the mantle instead drop the ball. I pray for that next generation who are taking the reins even now. They need their own encounter with You. Pursue them by Your Spirit. Amen.

April 25

Judges 4:1–5:31; Luke 22:35–53; Psalm 91:1–23; Proverbs 14:3–4

Deborah, the Prophetess

She sent for Barak. "Go, take with you ten thousand men. I will lure Sisera, the commander of Jabin's army and give him into your hands." Barak said, "If you go with me, I will go; but if you don't go with me, I won't go."
—Judges 4:6–8

The cycle continues. Israel did evil in the eyes of the Lord. So the Lord allows an enemy to oppress them. When the affliction continues, Israel cries out to the Lord for help. The Lord raises up another judge.

This time, Deborah, the wife of Lappidoth, led Israel. She was a prophetess. That means she was hearing what the Lord was saying for the nation. That's why she was holding court in the hill country of Ephraim—to hear the Lord and settle disputes that arose.

Deborah was acknowledged by all of Israel as the one who was hearing the word of the Lord. When you're in a pickle, as Israel was, you need to know what the Lord is saying. You don't haggle over the messenger who is delivering that word. The fact is, God has anointed and raised up women throughout the Scriptures. My wife loves this story. It shows how women are used by God to be effectual leaders.

Barak is the one who gets a bad rap in this story. He is painted as a weakling who won't go out to war unless Deborah accompanies him. But my hat is off to Barak. He only wanted to hear the word of the Lord and have the source of that word close by. I have to ask you: *How precious is the word of the Lord to you? Do you hold it dear?* In the end, it is Jael who is the heroin of the story. She quietly subdues the Canaanite king, Jabin, with a tent peg through his temple.

Father, thank You for raising up prophets and prophetesses who hear Your voice. Thank You for speaking to us today. Give me ears to hear. Amen.

April 26

Judges 6:1–40; Luke 22:54–23:12; Psalm 95:1–96:13; Proverbs 14:5–6

Gideon, Mighty Warrior

When the angel of the Lord appeared to Gideon, he said, "The Lord is with you, mighty warrior. Go in the strength you have and save Israel out of Midian's hand. Am I not sending you?" "But Lord," Gideon asked, "how can I save Israel? My clan is the weakest and I am the least in my family?"
—Judges 6:12,14–15

The oppressor today is Midian. The chosen deliverer is Gideon. And you have to like Gideon. He is as real as they come. To God, he asked honest questions. He asked for signs. He had natural fears.

Firstly, Gideon is approached by an angel, and the angel addresses him as a "mighty warrior." *Whoa!* Gideon did not see that coming, and he wasn't at all sure that it was appropriate. *"Who me? I'm a nobody from nowheresville!"* Gideon did not have the confidence required for an assignment like this. Gideon had no lineage to boast. But the Lord's response is priceless and equally applicable for us: Go in the strength you have. I am with you. In other words: *"I know what you're made of. You do what you are able, and I will make it happen."*

Gideon, also, is not afraid to ask the honest questions that we all think to ourselves: *"If You're with us, then why all this havoc? It looks more like You've abandoned us!"* The Lord is not afraid of our questions. He likes the honesty. It's an opportunity to show Himself strong.

What Gideon could not do in his own strength, the Lord could do. God saw Gideon as a mighty warrior long before Gideon could think it. Gideon's willingness and God's Spirit could bring the deliverance.

Father God, Your valuation of me is much higher than my own. But now I know that I am able to do whatever You ask of me when I am empowered by Your Spirit. If you can enable Gideon, You can enable me. Amen.

April 27

Judges 7:1–8:17; Luke 23:13–43; Psalm 97:1–98:9; Proverbs 14:7–8

The Exploits of Gideon

The Lord said to Gideon, "You have too many men for me to deliver Midian into their hands. In order that Israel may not boast against me that her own strength has saved her... [pare the number down].
—Judges 7:2

The title is purposely deceiving. While Gideon is the one through whom God executed His plan and strategy, the whole point of this episode is to demonstrate the Lord's might and passion for His people. Never in a million years would a military commander have come up with a plan like this one on his own!

It is the natural tendency of any man to take credit for having a part of something that succeeds victoriously. We want in on that. *"Look at me. I had a part in that!"* Yet, it is clear that this was orchestrated so that no man could get any glory unto himself. God alone is praised.

But give Gideon credit. He did go through with the plan. He sifted the initial army down from 32,000 to 10,000. He followed that up with a water drinking contest to pare them down to 300. Now to be fair, Israelites from four different tribes assisted to complete the conquest, but it required only the 300 to pull off the surprise attack. This was well less than one percent of the original size. God's strategic game-plan would involve trumpets, empty jars and torches. *Brilliant!*

When it comes to advancing His kingdom, God has a plan. It may not be conventional. You'll have to listen closely. But if you are willing, God can use you, and it will bring glory to His name.

Father, my plan may not be Your plan. I yield to Your leadership in my life so that I may be a fruitful component in Your harvest. I pray that You would receive all glory from what I engage in. Lead me by Your Spirit. Amen.

April 28

Judges 8:18–9:21; Luke 23:44–24:12; Psalm 99:1–9; Proverbs 14:9–10

Death and Resurrection

It was now about the sixth hour, and darkness came over the whole land until the ninth hour, for the sun stopped shining. And the curtain in the temple was torn in two. Jesus called out... and breathed his last. On the first day of the week, very early... the women... went to the tomb. "He is not here; he has risen!"
—Luke 23:44–46; 24:1,6

Death by crucifixion was cruel and commonplace in Roman culture, but this was no ordinary death. Jesus was no ordinary man.

As Jesus hung on the cross, in the middle of the day, the sun went dark, mourning the Son of God—who was there at creation *(John 1:3)*. The curtain in the temple that separated the Holy Place and the Most Holy Place (where the high priest atoned for sins once a year) was tore. The rending of this veil granted access into the presence of God.

The greatest miracle, and the cornerstone of our faith, is the resurrection of Jesus. Two angels in stark white announce to the women who gathered early that Sunday morning: *"He is not here; he has risen. Don't you remember how he told you he would rise?" (24:6)*.

Luke's account mentions the facts, but chooses to dwell more on the relationships of those He knew. It was the women who stood at a distance. It was the women who followed Joseph to the tomb, and later brought spices. It was they who first witnessed the empty grave. It is precisely about relationships that Jesus died on the cross.

Father in heaven, You looked down upon Your faithful Son and accepted the tremendous sacrifice He made to atone for my sin, once for all. Jesus completed His task to make salvation available to all who would call upon His name. I thank You for the love that sent Jesus to the cross in my place. Amen.

April 29

Judges 9:22–10:18; Luke 24:13–53; Psalm 100:1–5; Proverbs 14:11–12

On the Road to Emmaus

They asked each other, "Were not our hearts burning within us while he talked with us on the road and opened the Scriptures to us?"
—Luke 24:32

Jesus veils His identity and catches up with two of His own disciples on the road out of Jerusalem on the day of His resurrection. He wants to capture what they've taken from the events of the last few days. Because of the Passover, the entire Roman world was aware of the crucifixion of the "prophet" Jesus. But it appears to Jesus that to these two, it was only news. Cleopas, and the other unnamed disciple, were slow of heart in their ability to make any connection.

Jesus then takes the time to walk them through the Scriptures and enlighten them as to His role, beginning with Moses and all the prophets. Can you imagine that conversation? —the promised offspring in Genesis 3:15, the prophet likened to Moses in Deuteronomy 18:15, the suffering servant in Isaiah 53, the king on a colt in Zechariah 9:9, the one pierced in Zechariah 12:10, and the messenger of the covenant in Malachi 3:1. It was He, the Christ, who was the common thread. The entire Old Testament points to Jesus.

But it wasn't until Jesus took bread, gave thanks, and broke it for them that their eyes were opened. As soon as they recognized Him, Jesus disappeared. (Oh, to be a fly on the wall and witness that!)

The disciple's response is so appropriate: *"Did not our hearts burn within us as He spoke?"* I believe that Jesus longs to open up the Scriptures to us today, and watch our hearts come alive.

Father God, without Your Spirit, I am dull and slow of heart to perceive Your words. Quicken my mind to understand and believe. Let Your words burn within. I position myself before Your life-changing Word. Amen.

April 30

Judges 11:1–12:15; John 1:1–28; Psalm 101:1–8; Proverbs 14:13–14

Full of Grace and Truth

The Word became flesh and made his dwelling among us. We have seen his glory, the glory of the One and Only, who came from the Father, full of grace and truth.
    —John 1:14

John's introduction of Jesus gives us several names and images to relate to.

Jesus is the called *the Word*. He was the source of God's message to the world, the ultimate revelation of God. He was in the beginning with God. All things were made through Him, and yet, He clothed Himself in full humanity. Yes, He was fully God and fully man—the visible expression of God with skin.

He was *the true light*. The life in Him was the light He gave to every man. His light shines in the darkness, while not always understood.

A most interesting name given of Jesus is *the One and Only*. It clarifies that Jesus is both God and the Father's only unique Son. We have not seen God, but we have witnessed the glory of God the One and Only. He has made the Father known and sits at His side, even today.

Jesus is described as *full of grace and truth*. (Whenever a phrase is repeated, you know it's an emphasis.) Moses brought to us the law and justice of God. Grace and truth were embodied in Jesus. The gospels give witness to this. Jesus operated in truth while abundant in grace. From the overflow of this grace, we are, likewise, blessed.

Father in heaven, You gave us the finest expression of Yourself when You sent Your Son to dwell among us. He made You known to us. And by receiving and believing in His name, I am given the right to become Your child. So be it!

121

May 1

Judges 13:1–14:20; John 1:29–51; Psalm 102:1–28; Proverbs 14:15–16

Mr and Mrs Manoah

Then Manoah inquired of the angel of the Lord, "What is your name, so that we may honor you when your word comes true?" He replied, "It is beyond understanding." The woman gave birth to a boy and named him Samson.
—Judges 13:17–18,24

We have seen a limited number of times where an angelic messenger has been sent to communicate and prepare God's people for the next big thing. We saw it with Jacob. We saw it with Joshua and Gideon, with Mary and Joseph. Here again is another visitation from heaven.

As interesting as names are throughout the Bible, this angel visits the *wife* of Manoah. You would think that the one visited deserved to have her name acknowledged. Perhaps it's was Manoah's persistence to witness the angel and his conversation that was of most notable importance. Intriguing also is the fact that Manoah did not perceive that the man was an angel until he ascended in the flame of the burnt offering that he offered on the altar.

While speaking of names and their significance, Manoah inquired of the angel's name, *"so that we may honor you..."* But the heavenly man asks, *"Why?"* He infers, *"My name is beyond your scope to understand and too wonderful to imagine."* Some of the glories of heaven just cannot yet be fathomed or grasped within our limited faculties.

The fact is that God intervened in order to prepare them for their miracle child to be born. Samson would be the next deliverer of Israel.

Father in heaven, thank You for the times You have intervened in my life, whether I knew it or not. For the things that I cannot grasp, I defer to You. Amen.

May 2

Judges 15:1–16:31, John 2:1–25, Psalm 103:1–22, Proverbs 14:17–19

The Spirit upon Samson

The Spirit of the Lord came upon him (Samson) in power. Finding a fresh jawbone of a donkey, he grabbed it and struck down a thousand men … He awoke from his sleep and thought, "I'll go out as before and shake myself free." But he did not know that the Lord had left him.
—Judges 15:14–15; 16:20

Samson led Israel for twenty years in the days of the Philistines. He was the twelfth judge in this era of the judges. It's safe to say that Samson was not your run-of-the-mill prototypical leader.

Samson was raised as a Nazarite by his parents, following the angel's directives. This meant no razor was to be used on his head. He was to be set apart unto God. The unique way that the Lord used him was through his physical strength. At least three times it is stated that *"the Spirit of the Lord came upon him in power,"* and then he would pull off an extraordinary feat and kill many of the enemy Philistines.

But this mighty man of God was fickle and hard to figure at times. Samson had anger issues. He gave in to sensuality. He many times reacted in revenge. He confided in the wrong people. You get the idea that Samson could have done so much more if he would have applied himself more wisely, and set himself apart *in devotion* to God.

Samson knew what it was to have the Spirit of the Lord come upon him and use him for a righteous cause. But Samson took the Spirit of God for granted. When the Lord had left him, *he did not even know it!* The thought that I could engage the Spirit and then be so dull as to not even recognize His absence is egregious.

Father God, may I not take Your Spirit for granted. Let my spirit perceive the movements of Your Spirit. Sensitize my heart and set me apart. Amen.

May 3

Judges 17:1–18:31, John 3:1–21, Psalm 104:1–23, Proverbs 14:20–21

Nicodemus Humbly Seeking

In reply [to Nicodemus] Jesus declared, "I tell you the truth, no one can see the kingdom of God unless he is born again ... no one can enter the kingdom of God unless he is born of water and the Spirit... For God did not send his Son into the world to condemn the world, but to save the world through him."
—John 3:3,5,17

Nicodemus was more than curious. He knew that Jesus had an undeniable connection to God, but what was it? Nicodemus was himself a learned teacher, but this message was way beyond him.

Nicodemus was a Pharisee and a member of the ruling council. It was the religious Pharisees that criticized Jesus the most. But Nicodemus came humbly searching for the answers he knew not of. To withstand obvious ridicule from his own, Nicodemus approached Jesus at night.

Jesus laid out the gospel plainly. Just as you are born of water in the flesh, your spirit must also be born of the Spirit. Our spirit is dead until God's Spirit makes us alive on the inside. We cannot even perceive (see) the kingdom of God unless we are born from above.

Jesus, full of grace and truth, came into the world to save us from the condemnation that comes from unbelief. God gave us the gift of His Son that we might believe and have eternal life. And Jesus knew something of heaven. Because of love, Jesus left heaven to make salvation known and available to us all. Will you believe Him now?

Father God, thank You for loving me so much that You sent Your one and only Son to restore me back into relationship with You. Blow upon our generation, O Lord, by Your Spirit. Draw all men unto You. I embrace Your salvation through Jesus our Lord, Amen.

May 4

Judges 19:1–20:48, John 3:22–4:3, Psalm 104:24–35, Proverbs 14:22–24

A Friend of the Bridegroom

The bride belongs to the bridegroom. The friend who attends the bridegroom waits and listens for him, and is full of joy when he hears the bridegroom's voice. That joy is mine, and is now complete. He must become greater; I must become less.
—John 3:29–30

John the Baptist helps his disciples understand a transition that is going on. In the process, he brings greater clarity to the role of the One sent from above. John's role has been fulfilled. He has prepared the way of the Lord. Now comes the shift of attention and focus to the central figure, God's Son, the Messiah and Savior.

The appropriate analogy that John uses is that of the bridegroom and the friend of the bridegroom. The day belongs to the bridegroom. The story is about the bridegroom. But, oh the joy to be the one who attends the bridegroom. He had the privilege of close proximity, and to make Him known. He waited and listened for Him. He knew the joy firsthand. Now John humbly takes a place of lesser prominence.

After all, the One He announced was the One from heaven, the One sent from God and who speaks the words of God. The Father placed all authority into His hands and gave the Holy Spirit without measure in order to represent Him rightly and fully. Jesus Christ was the highest revelation of God to all of humankind. Eternal life is the prize to all who accept His testimony and believe.

Will you be a friend of the Bridegroom?

Father, thank You for sending Jesus in order that I might know who You are. You loved me through this Man and made salvation possible. I accept His testimony of You. Now let me know You as a friend of the Bridegroom. Amen.

May 5

Judges 21:1–Ruth 1:22, John 4:4–42, Psalm 105:1–15, Proverbs 14:25

The Samaritan Woman

Yet a time is coming and now has come when the true worshippers will worship the Father in spirit and truth, for they are the kind of worshippers the Father seeks. God is spirit, and his worshippers must worship in spirit and in truth.
—John 4:23–24

Traveling through Samaria, Jesus encounters a woman at Jacob's well in the town of Sychar. Jesus takes the opportunity to dialogue with this woman—*let's call her Samantha, Sam for short.*

What sort of man would give the time of day to a despised Samaritan, let alone a woman, and a woman with a sordid reputation? Sam wasn't sure exactly. She wondered if Jesus was on the par of their forefather Jacob. When Jesus read her mail, she thought Him to be a prophet. In the end, Sam embraces the fact that this man, Jesus, is indeed the Messiah. As a matter of fact, because of her testimony, many from that town came to acknowledge that He *really is the Savior of the world.* What began as a question for a drink of water became the opportunity to drink of the living water welling up to eternal life!

Why the effort over an outcast and foreigner? Because the Father seeks worshippers. Because the Father loves every individual He has ever created. He seeks the worshipper who will worship Him in spirit and in truth—in His prescribed manner—genuinely and sincerely.

Father God, I want to be a worshipper who ascribes worth to Your holy Name in an appropriate and acceptable manner. I need the help of Your Spirit to do that. Thank You for Your extreme interest in the welfare of every man, woman and child, including me. In Jesus' name I pray, Amen.

May 6

Ruth 2:1–4:22, John 4:43–54, Psalm 105:16–36, Proverbs 14:26–27

Naomi and Ruth

Boaz replied, "I've been told all about what you have done for your mother-in-law since the death of your husband. May you be richly rewarded by the Lord, the God of Israel, under whose wings you have come to take refuge. All my fellow townsmen know that you are a woman of noble character."
—Ruth 2:11–12; 3:11

The book of Ruth is really the story of Naomi and Ruth. Naomi is the Jewess who married Elimelech, of Judah. Famine forced them to move to Moab, where Naomi's two sons married Moabite women, one of which is Ruth.

The story, which began in yesterday's reading, tells of the gut-wrenching turns that happen in life that you have no answer for. Noami's husband dies. Ten years later, both sons also pass away. What deep heartbreak. It's in this season of loss and despair that Ruth pledges to walk beside her mother-in-law, as Naomi chooses to return to her homeland. *"Where you go I will go, and where you stay I will stay. Your people will be my people and your God my God" (1:16).*

In time, it's a joyous ending. Ruth meets Boaz, a relative of Naomi's husband. They marry. Their child, Obed, becomes the grandfather of David *(yes, King David)!* Truly remarkable.

But it was out of bitterness and affliction that hope sprung. It is the reputation and integrity of Ruth, her noble character and kindness, that paved the way for God's blessing and favor to follow.

Father God, we do not understand the tragedies that sometimes befall us in life. And left to ourselves, we may draw wrong conclusions. But You never leave us without hope. Enable me to trust You through it all. I take refuge under Your wings. In Your mighty name I pray, Amen.

May 7

1 Samuel 1:1–2:21, John 5:1–23, Psalm 105:37–45, Proverbs 14:28–29

Always at Work

Jesus said …"My Father is always at his work to this very day, and I, too, am working. I tell you the truth, the Son can do nothing by himself; he can only do what he sees his Father doing… Yes, to your amazement he will show him even greater things than these."
—John 5:17,19–20

Jesus had fast become the object of scrutiny with the Jewish leaders. They were intensely jealous because Jesus undermined their authority while exercising power that was genuinely authentic Himself.

Case in point: Jesus heals a man who had been disabled for thirty–eight years, at the Pool of Bethesda. What a kind act. Except Jesus heals him on a Sabbath day. That's a "no-no" to these Jews, because it breaks one of their man-made rules. So the law broken was a bigger deal to them than a poor lame man who was miraculously healed!

The question may be asked of the relevance of God resting on the Sabbath, from Genesis 2:2. Yes, this is a recommended prescription from God Himself, but that doesn't overrule the opportunity to bless and do good. It's not the same as resting from labor.

The fact remains that the Father never sleeps. He is always at work. He is not a man who tires. God knows what is going on in your life. He isn't too busy and He does not turn His head so as not to notice.

Jesus did what He saw His Father doing. Greater things will He do. Aren't you glad that God doesn't keep office hours? He is open 24/7.

Father God, You are always at work in my life. You are engaged in every detail. You know the intangibles that I do not. I trust my life, my welfare and my future into Your hands. In Jesus' name I pray, Amen.

May 8

1 Samuel 2:22–4:22, John 5:24–47, Psalm 106:1–12, Proverbs 14:30–31

Your Servant Listens

*And what happens to your two sons, Hophni and Phinehas, will be a sign to you—
they will both die on the same day. I will raise up for myself a faithful priest, who
will do according to what is in my heart and mind…*
    —1 Samuel 2:34–35

What we have here is a case of two extremes. And they are both extremely
important to grasp.

On the one hand, you have an aging priest, Eli, who is responsible for the
offerings on the altar, the incense and the ark of the covenant. Eli's two sons
were the priests who carried out the holy duties. Both were wicked, having no
regard for the Lord. They slept with women who served at the Tent of Meeting
and treated the offerings with contempt. What's worse, Eli knew of their sin and
failed to restrain them. They were going through the religious motions, but their
hearts were far from the Lord and His holy requirements.

On the other hand, you have a young man, Samuel, who was ministering before
the Lord, hearing the voice of the Lord, in a day where the word of the Lord was
rare. Eli knew it. When God called to young Samuel, his reply became, *"Speak,
Lord, for your servant is listening"* (3:10). The Lord was with Samuel, and he
became recognized as a prophet *(3:20)*, priest *(2:35)*, judge *(7:15)* and leader of
Israel *(7:6)*. At Shiloh, the Lord continued to reveal Himself to Samuel through
his word *(3:21)*.

Judgment was inevitable for the house of Eli. The future would be entrusted
where the word of the Lord was honored.

*Father, You have spoken to every generation, and You speak to us today. Give me ears
to hear what You are saying. Speak Lord. I am listening. Amen.*

May 9

1 Samuel 5:1–7:17, John 6:1–21, Psalm 106:13–31, Proverbs 14:32–33

Stand in the Breach

They forgot the God who saved them, who had done great things in Egypt, miracles in the land of Ham and awesome deeds by the Red Sea. So he said he would destroy them—had not Moses, his chosen one, stood in the breach before him to keep his wrath from destroying them.
—Psalm 106:21–23

Psalm 106 is a recollection of the miracle events that delivered Israel from Egypt and a summary of man's continued rebellion that followed. After all that the Lord had done, Israel continued in sin.

They soon forgot what He had done. They exchanged their glory for an image of a bull. They despised the pleasant land. They grumbled in their tents. They provoked the Lord to anger. Let's face it, they were bent toward sin and prone to evil. That is the plight of man to this day.

By their behavior, Israel incited the Lord to anger. But it was Moses who stood in the gap to intercede on behalf of His people. They were "His" people, Moses reminded *(Exodus 32)*. Again, when Israelite men indulged in sexual immorality with Moabite women and worshipped their god, the Lord's anger was stirred. Yet again, intervention came, this time through Phinehas the priest (not the son of Eli) who stopped the sin in it's tracks. Phinehas was zealous for God's honor and it was credited to him as righteousness *(Numbers 25)*.

In a world that has given lawlessness no bounds, God is calling intercessors to stand in the breach and for believers everywhere to resist sin and be zealous for the Lord's honor.

Father in heaven, You are merciful to a rebellious people. Raise up intercessors. Lead us to nationwide repentance. Call us to righteousness once again. Amen.

May 10

1 Samuel 8:1–9:27, John 6:22–42, Psalm 106:32–48, Proverbs 14:34–35

Father and Son

When Samuel grew old, he appointed his sons as judges for Israel. The name of his firstborn was Joel and the name of his second was Abijah, and they served at Beersheba. But his sons did not walk in his ways. They turned aside after dishonest gain and accepted bribes and perverted justice.
—1 Samuel 8:1–3

I don't understand it. I just know it's true.

How is it that a godly man can produce children that do not resemble their father in any way? How can righteous parents raise children up in the admonition of the Lord and they choose another path? It happened with Eli the priest. It happened with David. It happened here with Samuel. It happens all the time. You know parents who have grieved over the choices of their children.

You can speculate all you want about how much time the father spent with his child, or didn't. Truth be known, there are many factors in that child's psyche that influence him or her. What we can do is love and pray for our children and be ready to embrace them when they are ready for change. I believe God's promises are still true. That's why we pray with confidence Proverbs 22:6, *"Train a child in the way he should go, and when he is old he will not turn from it."*

Turning the page to John 6, Jesus honored His Father in every way and represented Him truly. He said in verse thirty-eight, *"For I have come down from heaven not to do my will but to do the will of him who sent me."* Whose will are you living for? Who influences you most?

Abba, You, too, are my Father. I accept Your profound love for me. It is my desire to know You and Your ways so that I may grow up to look just like You. My ambition in life is to do Your will on this earth. Amen.

May 11

1 Samuel 10:1–11:15, John 6:43–71, Psalm 107:1–43, Proverbs 15:1–3

A Hard Teaching

I am the living bread that came down from heaven ...Jesus said to them, "I tell you the truth, unless you eat the flesh of the Son of Man and drink his blood, you have no life in you." On hearing it, many of his disciples said, "This is a hard teaching. Who can accept it?" From this time many ... turned back.
—John 6:51,53,60,66

A crowd is following Jesus now. He has marveled the masses with miracles, but then speaks a new concept that confounds and offends.

A couple of verses help unlock this passage. First of all, Jesus begins and ends the conversation with *"no one can come to me unless the Father enables, or draws him" (6:44,65)*. Salvation begins and ends with the Father wooing us to Him by the Spirit. It has nothing to do with my good works or an adherence to a set of rules. It's all God's doing.

The second key to this seemingly difficult word is this: *"The words I have spoken to you are spirit and they are life" (6:63)*. Jesus spoke of spiritual principals using terms and language they would know of. They knew about the manna. Jesus wanted them to desire spiritual food just as they would physical food for their spiritual vitality. Jesus is no cannibal or vampire. But from Him alone comes eternal life.

Lastly, the issue at hand Jesus wants them to see is that His origin is heaven; He is from God. He is the way to eternal life. He is the bread they must partake of to live forever. This was the stumbling block. It is still today. Peter spoke for the twelve when he said, *"Lord, You have the words of eternal life... You are the Holy One of God!" (6:68-69)*.

Father, thank You for sending Jesus. You made salvation available to me through the perfect sacrifice of Your Son. Your Spirit drew me, and I said "Yes." I desire to live by every word that proceeds from Your mouth. Amen.

May 12

1 Samuel 12:1–13:22, John 7:1–29, Psalm 108:1–13, Proverbs 15:4

Samuel Commits to Prayer

You have done all this evil yet do not turn away from the Lord, but serve the Lord with all your heart... For the sake of his great name the Lord will not reject his people, because the Lord was pleased to make you his own. As for me, far be it from me that I should sin against the Lord by failing to pray for you.
—1 Samuel 12:20,22–23

Samuel has led with integrity and godly fear. But he is old, and it is time to pass the torch. Not unlike Moses and Joshua before him, Samuel has the platform to remind the nation he loves to turn away from evil and serve the Lord. Within this paragraph is an encapsulation of Samuel's heart and the Lord's character.

Samuel first reminds all Israel of their history and their propensity to sin. Most recently, it was their choice to have a king reign over them. Jesus said similarly that He *"would not entrust himself to man, for he knew all men…he knew what was in a man" (John 2:24-25).*

But the Lord is full of mercy. He will not reject His people. He stands ready to do great things, as He has, if they would only turn from their sin; if they would only fear the Lord and serve Him faithfully.

Samuel's pledge should be our pledge for the people and the nation we love. Samuel said it would be a sin against God if he did not pray for them. Prayer is the one thing we can do that can make all the difference, because only God can change a heart. Our petition to God on their behalf is the best way we can love them.

Father God, thank You for Your rich mercy. You know where I came from, and You still brought me close. I pray for those I love and the nation in which I live. Draw individuals by Your Spirit. Take away the blinders. Let them see and believe. In Jesus' name, Amen.

May 13

1 Samuel 13:23–14:52, John 7:30–53, Psalm 109:1–31, Proverbs 15:5–7

Streams Will Flow

Jesus stood and said in a loud voice, "If anyone is thirsty, let him come to me and drink. Whoever believes in me, as the Scripture has said, streams of living water will flow from within him." By this he meant the Spirit, whom those who believed in him were later to receive. Up to that time the Spirit had not been given...
—John 7:37–39

Jesus speaks in a loud voice. He gets their attention. He is adamant. *"Are you thirsty? Does your soul crave what the world can't give you?"*

The sons of Korah were temple musicians. They penned and sang Psalm 42:1–2: *"As the deer pants for streams of water, so my soul pants for you, O God. My soul thirsts for God, for the living God. Where can I go and meet with God?"* Do you sense the passion in their plea?

Jesus told the Samaritan woman, just a few chapters back in John 4, that He was the source of living water that would quench her thirst for God. He would become a fountain or a spring for her to draw from. He was the source for eternal life *(4:14)*.

Here, the living water is the Holy Spirit who will flow as a stream or a river from within believers. The source of this life flow is still Jesus. He is the giver of eternal life and He is the giver of the Holy Spirit. The Spirit came upon Jesus without limit, so the Holy Spirit will be poured out as a river upon believers. This came to fruition in Acts 2, which is past tense for you and me. If you are a believer, you may be filled with the Holy Spirit to overflowing. Now you may invite the river to flow...

Father, Jesus wanted us to know that He was the giver of eternal life and of the Holy Spirit. He knew we needed both to live an overcoming life. Lord, my soul pants after You. Let Your life flow within me as a roaring river. Amen.

May 14

1 Samuel 15:1–16:23, John 8:1–20, Psalm 110:1–7, Proverbs 15:8–10

What the Lord Sees

Bit the Lord said to Samuel, "Do not consider his appearance or his height, for I have rejected him(Eliab). The Lord does not look at the things man looks at. Man looks at the outward appearance, but the Lord looks at the heart."
—1 Samuel 16:7

Samuel had anointed the new king over Israel, but his duties by the Lord are not finished. He was still the one whom God communicated with. He was the prophet who spoke the word of the Lord.

Samuel had already spoken to Saul that because of his disobedience, the Lord had sought out a man after his own heart to lead his people. That led Samuel to the house of Jesse. One of his sons would be anointed king. Only which one?

Jesse naturally thought that his firstborn son would be that one. But the Lord spoke to Samuel: *"I don't look at the things man looks at. Man judges from outward appearances. My evaluation is based on what I see in the heart of a man."* Poor David wasn't even considered by his father as a candidate. He was the youngest, left to tend the sheep. But after seven sons were not chosen, David was called in … and anointed.

Aren't you glad that the Lord puts a higher estimation upon what's on the inside? I don't have to be a physical specimen or a beauty queen to be noticed. That allows me hope that God can use anyone—even me— in the grand scheme of His plans. If I will obey Him, I position myself to be one He can utilize. I can be one on which His Spirit rests.

Father God, You see intentions, motives and desires. You see what matters. I ask for a heart after Your own, that I may pursue the things that matter to You—righteousness, obedience, being real, genuine faith and devotion to You. Amen.

May 15

1 Samuel 17:1–18:4, John 8:21–30, Psalm 111:1–10, Proverbs 15:11

The Size of David's Heart

Your servant has killed both the lion and the bear; this uncircumcised Philistine will be like one of them, because he has defied the armies of the living God.
—1 Samuel 17:36

Well it didn't take long to find out the size of David's heart.

If it didn't matter to God how impressive we had to look on the outside, then why should any person trusting in God be afraid of *anyone* who defied the living God?

We all know the story of David and Goliath. But make it personal. Here is an intimidating giant standing between you and the victory God has promised. Does it matter how big this enemy is looming over you … making you doubt the might and legitimacy of your God?

David was young, but he was growing in his knowledge of the Lord. He knew what it was to sing worshipfully before the Lord, humming praises amidst the stars and the sheep. David knew the power of God that came upon him to protect the sheep he was responsible for. If God could enable him to kill a lion or a bear, then who is this mere Philistine to stand in the way of God's people and His promise?

You have to like David's confidence. It wasn't that he was so brave, but that He knew the God who stood before him to fight the battles. Sometimes we just need to be encouraged to know that God is bigger than any enemy that stands in the way to do what God calls us to do.

Father, thank You for showing me that I can trust You in any situation that is bigger than me. My confidence is in You alone. Develop my faith to trust You in the small issues as well as the larger issues. You fight my battles. Amen.

May 16

1 Samuel 18:5–19:24, John 8:31–59, Psalm 112:1–10, Proverbs 15:12–14

Jealousy is a Terrible Thing

Saul was very angry; this refrain galled him. "They have credited David with tens of thousands," he thought, "but me with only thousands. What more can he get but the kingdom?" And from that time on Saul kept a jealous eye on David.
—1 Samuel 18:8–9

Success is a good thing. You want success. God wants you to thrive. But if your superior is not secure in his position, then he may feel threatened by your success. (Remember Samuel's conversation with Saul—*i.e. 13:14, 15:28*). Throw in the fact that Saul's son, Jonathan, the heir to the throne, also took a liking to David.

At first, it was all good. David was successful at whatever he was assigned to. But when the accolades started coming in and the comparisons were made, Saul became angry … and jealous. Singing and dancing accompanied the newest song on the hit charts: *"Saul has slain his thousands, and David his tens of thousands "* *(18:7).*

Saul's perception of David changed everything. Instead of utilizing David to his advantage, with God's blessing upon him, now Saul is attacking what he perceives as a threat. He hurls a spear at David—twice. He reduces his rank in the army. He gives his promised daughter to another man when it came time to marry. That's what jealousy does, because jealousy is an evil spirit.

Give David credit. He did not retaliate. He honored the king … regardless.

Father in heaven, when I encounter jealousy, help me to react in the right spirit. May I have the right motive, so that I am not misinterpreted. I curse a jealous spirit that would seek to divide, in Jesus' name, Amen.

May 17

1 Samuel 20:1–21:15, John 9:1–41, Psalm 113:1–114:8, Proverbs 15:15–17

Who Sinned?

As he [Jesus] went along, he saw a man blind from birth. His disciples asked him, "Rabbi, who sinned, this man or his parents, that he was born blind?" "Neither this man nor his parents sinned," said Jesus, "but this happened so that the work of God might be displayed in his life."
—John 9:1–3

Did you catch the tone of the question? *"Who sinned…?"* It was a commonly held belief in the Jewish culture that suffering or disease or tragedy was linked to someone's sin—which is a commonly held belief in our society today. *"Why did this happen to me? What did I do wrong?"* We want to be able to point a finger as to why something isn't perfect. There must be a reason!

But we live in a fallen world. This is not an eternal state of bliss as yet. If God erased every case of suffering, we would fail to trust Him. He would become our handy Santa. Let's be honest. Innocent people sometimes suffer. Justice isn't served in fullness until the end.

The point of this word is this. There is no finger-pointing, because it was no one's fault. *"It happened so that the work of God might be displayed in his life."* That is to say that every person born on this earth has the ability to bring glory to God. Isn't that the reason why we are here? Who can measure devotion and love for God, but God alone? I know people with disabilities who love the Lord. My brother-in-law, Jonathan, was one. And those who serve them have the opportunity to show love and compassion. How is it that the work of God is being displayed in your life?

Father, You have given us the opportunity to show love and compassion to those who are in need. And You have given us all the opportunity to glorify Your name with what we have. Take what I have. I give it to You. Amen.

May 18

1 Samuel 22:1–23:29, John 10:1–21, Psalm 115:1–18, Proverbs 15:18–19

David's Rag-Tag Army

David left Gath and escaped to the cave of Adullam… All those who were in distress
or in debt or discontented gathered around him, and he became their leader. About
four hundred men were with him.
—1 Samuel 22:1–2

What a motley crew that David has attracted. I have laughed out loud at this
description. *That sounds like my church!* They are described as men in distress.
There were those who were indebted. There were many who were discontented.
Their stories are varied and severe. Life is hard. Things don't go as you hoped
they would. The one they choose to follow is himself being chased as a criminal.

You are basically talking about the outcasts of society who are attracted to a
proven leader who has been unduly shunned. They resemble David's plight and
come together with something to prove to the misguided authorities. Under
David's leadership, they can become someone significant … and that they do.
These same misfits are guided under David's tutelage to become mighty men
of valor.

Actually, we can all really identify with these guys. We know what it is to
be overlooked, or hardened by injustice or disappointment. We know missed
opportunities or unplanned setbacks. God can take our sorry situations and make
warriors of us all. *Yes He can!*

Father God, You have shown me that You can take anyone, in any situation, and
make wonderful things happen to bring glory and honor to Your name. When other
people give up on me, You never give up. You are the God of hope—not a false hope—
but of real hope for positive change. I commit all I have and am unto You. Amen.

May 19

1 Samuel 24:1–25:44, John 10:22–42, Psalm 116:1–19, Proverbs 15:20–21

Precious to God

Precious in the sight of the Lord is the death of his saints.
    —Psalm 116:15

Never has there been a greater comfort.

The topic of death is mostly avoided. We don't really want to think about it and there are such varying thoughts about what really happens after. We are certain that life after death is eternal. We will all go somewhere forever. But, as usual, the Bible is the safest place for real answers. For the believer in Christ, that eternity is with God, where He is. So there need not be any fear in death. *So we lose a failing body!* Your spirit has never been more alive. From God's perspective, it is a precious thing to gather one of His saints. It's a process we will all endure that actually draws us closer in proximity to Him. But He has planned our arrival. He knows the hour.

One of my Top Ten verses in all the Bible compliments this thought. Psalm 73:24 says, *"You guide me with your counsel, and afterward you will take me into glory."* It really is the best of both worlds. While we're here, He guides me. When I graduate, He takes me to glory!

Interestingly enough, this Psalm is almost entirely a response of gratitude for being kept from a near-death experience. It must have really made him ponder these questions of eternity. Aren't you glad that, either way, we have every reason to be thankful? Are you ready?

Father God, thank You for preparing a place in heaven for Your beloved ones. To be absent from this body is to be present with You. Thank You for taking away the doubts and fears that are tied to death. My future is entirely secure, because You said so. Guide me with Your counsel until I see You face to face. Amen.

May 20

1 Samuel 26:1–28:25, John 11:1–53, Psalm 117:1–2, Proverbs 15:22–23

The Lord's Anointed

But David said to Abishai, "Don't destroy him! Who can lay a hand on the Lord's anointed and be guiltless? As surely as the Lord lives," he said, "the Lord himself will strike him … But the Lord forbid that I should lay a hand on the Lord's anointed."
—1 Samuel 26:9–11

This is an important lesson that the church would do well to hear.

David is on the run. Saul wants David out of the picture. His band of warriors cannot match up to Saul's three thousand chosen men. But David has what Saul does not … the favor of the Lord.

This is the second opportunity that David has to take out the king. The first was in a cave, in chapter twenty-four. Here, David and Abishai enter the unsuspecting camp where Saul's army is fast asleep.

From Abishai's perspective, this was God's arrangement of justice for David to slay his enemy. But David, again, cannot partner in such a plan. It is not his place to remove the king from his position of authority. It was God who placed him there. It is God's place to remove him. The end does not justify the means.

David did not react out of vengeance. His overriding conscience kept him from taking justice into his own hands. This is God's man we're talking about! I believe this humility and the mindset of honoring those in authority is what made David's legacy great.

Father God, You appoint kings, and You remove kings. It is not my place to gossip or diminish those in authority over me. May I honor those You honor. I commit to pray on their behalf. Your justice is always right. In Jesus' name, Amen.

May 21

1 Samuel 29:1–31:13, John 11:54–12:19, Psalm 118:1–18, Proverbs 15:24–26

In David's Distress

David reached Ziklag on the third day. Now the Amalekites raided Ziklag and burned it, and had taken captive the women and all who were in it ... David was greatly distressed because the men were talking of stoning him; each bitter because of their sons and daughters. But David found strength in the Lord ...
—1 Samuel 30:1–2,6

After an odd series of choices and events, David finds himself in the land of the Philistines. Yet this time he has favor with Achish, king of Gath, and is given the town of Ziklag. David and his army (now numbering 600) are even prepared to go to war against Israel, but the Philistine commanders would not permit that. After all, this is the one who had slain *"tens of thousands [of their Philistines]"(18:7)*. So David and his men return to Ziklag, a three day's journey.

To their horror, they return home to find their town attacked and burned by the Amalekites, with all the women and children missing. They weep aloud until they have no strength left to weep. What's even worse—now they are talking about stoning David for getting them in this mess. It would be an understatement to say that David was *"greatly distressed."*

Here's the punch line. *"But David found strength in the Lord his God" (30:6)*. Can you even imagine the emotional and physical drain? They do not know if their families are dead or alive. It is in this place of catastrophic upheaval that David found strength in God. David inquired of the Lord. Deliverance did come. But David did what he knew he must. What is your first response when the unthinkable happens?

Father God, when calamity comes, for whatever reason, there is no other that I can turn to. You are my Deliverer and the Lifter of my head. Amen.

May 22

2 Samuel 1:1–2:11, John 12:20–50, Psalm 118:19–29, Proverbs 15:27–28

David, King of Judah

In the course of time, David inquired of the Lord. Then the men of Judah came to Hebron and there anointed David king over the house of Judah. Meanwhile, Abner, the commander of Saul's army, had taken Ish-Bosheth son of Saul and made him king over all Israel.
—2 Samuel 2:1,4,8–9

This is a good time to talk about David as the king.

If you were wondering why David had not yet been recognized as king over Israel, since Samuel had anointed him so, then an explanation is in order. What Samuel did was to authorize God's appointment and empower David by the Spirit to go in that direction. The whole process would have to run it's course. It's much like when God calls you to something, let's say, for example, to be a pastor. You first need God's word on the matter. That helps you to gain confidence in what God is calling you to and for you to head in that direction. Maybe it's Bible College. Maybe it's being mentored under another pastor, but you are actively pursuing that call. When you are finally appointed to a church, perhaps years later, then your call comes to fruition. The same held true with David. Now was his time to realize what God had begun many years prior.

Although, you have to feel it somewhat anticlimactic. After all that was promised and all that David went through, David is made king over one tribe. Ish-Bosheth is made king over all the rest of Israel. *What's that about?* David knew it always had to be God's timing and God's doing. David's ambition was not about striving to be king. His life pursuit was to please the Lord, and Him only. The rest is God's ...

Father, You know what's best for me and You have a great plan for my life that will bring You honor. Prepare me now for that next season. Amen.

May 23

2 Samuel 2:12–3:39, John 13:1–30, Psalm 119:1–16, Proverbs 15:29–30

The Full Extent of Love

Having loved his own who were in the world, he (Jesus) now showed them the full extent of his love. After [the meal], he poured water into a basin and began to wash the disciple's feet…"Now that I, your Lord and Teacher, have washed your feet, you should also wash one another's feet. I have set you an example…"
—John 13:1,5,14–15

The full extent of love is realized only when we receive love and then give love. Jesus exemplified this by washing the disciple's feet. You are never too important to humble yourself and serve others.

In the process, going from disciple to disciple, there is a great dialogue with Peter. Apparently, Peter didn't get it. He did not see the need for his feet to be washed. Jesus answered, *"Unless I wash you, you have no part with me" (v.8).* The light goes on! Well, in that case, Peter replies, *"not just my feet, but my hands and head as well!" (v.9).*

Jesus explains to Peter in so many words: You don't need a bath. You are already clean. By trusting in me, I have cleansed you. But I need to wash your feet because your feet get soiled by walking in this world. We are affected by the world around us. Let me sanctify you.

There is a dramatic effect when we serve each other and encourage each other in humility and love. It has a way of keeping us in His love and untainted by the world.

Father God, I thank You for showing us the full extent of Your love through Your Son Jesus. He modeled what it means to serve others. He went to the cross in selfless love. Cause me to know the cleansing effect we have on one another when we serve and prefer one another. I need Your cleansing daily. In Jesus' name, Amen.

May 24

2 Samuel 4:1–6:23, John 13:31–14:14, Psalm 119:17–32, Proverbs 15:31–32

David, King of Israel

When all the elders of Israel had come to King David at Hebron, the king made a compact with them at Hebron before the Lord, and they anointed David king over Israel… And he became more and more powerful, because the Lord God Almighty was with him … David knew the Lord established him for the sake of his people.
—2 Samuel 5:3,10,12

All in God's time, David became the king over all Israel. God had prepared David for this. David knew that it was the Lord who had placed him as king for the sake of His people Israel. It was a stewardship he received. He would shepherd the people of God with the care and integrity as he did in his younger years with sheep.

In this passage, a couple of points stand out. In the early days of his reign, you see the manner in which David is going to conduct the affairs of his kingdom. When the Philistines went up in full force to attack Israel, David inquired of the Lord. It was this fellowship with God, long established, that made David a trustworthy king.

David, also, returned the ark of God back to the City of David. The ark signified the presence of God at the center of their culture. Upon it's return, once transferred in the prescribed way, David made it quite a celebration. David himself leaped and danced before the Lord with all his might to shouts and the sound of trumpets. Even the critical spirit of his own wife, Michal, did not deter his enthusiasm. David replied to her, *"I will become even more undignified than this…"(6:22)*, to praise Him. David expressed his worship with total abandon and freedom.

Father, I will praise You. You are enthroned on the praises of Your people. May I not hold back in expressing my love for You. You are deserving of my best. May I lead a life that inquires of You. I need Your counsel daily. Amen.

May 25

2 Samuel 7:1–8:18, John 14:15–31, Psalm 119:33–48, Proverbs 15:33

Another Counselor

And I will ask the Father, and he will give you another Counselor to be with you forever—the Spirit of truth ... you know him, for he lives with you and will be in you. All this I have spoken while still with you ... the Holy Spirit will teach you all things and will remind you of everything I have said to you.
  —John 14:16–17,26

Jesus spoke words of revelation about the Holy Spirit we would do good to embrace. Jesus wanted to prepare his disciples for a transition that was coming. Actually, He would not be with them for too much longer. But the Spirit of truth would be with them forever.

In times past, the Holy Spirit had come upon prophets or leaders at sporadic times, but not often. Jesus revealed that the Spirit of God would not only be with you, now He will actually live within you. This is a new thing that God would do. So even though Jesus is leaving, you won't miss a beat. The Father will send *another* Counselor—another of the same kind—to coach us as Jesus did. This word for Counselor *(paraclete)* also carries the meaning of Comforter. So, Jesus wanted to reassure them—*"You don't have to be fearful when I am gone. The Holy Spirit will comfort you and counsel you, just as I did."*

The Holy Spirit is also a teacher. Are you ready to be taught? And He will bring to your remembrance the words that Jesus spoke. He can give you recall on the words you have laid hold of. You will become more familiar with His voice and His promptings. Even though you cannot see Him, you can know Him in a most personal way. Pentecost is coming, and Jesus said that it will change everything!

Father, I am glad to know that Jesus did not leave me to myself. You sent the Holy Spirit to reside in every believer. Your Spirit is positioned to comfort, to counsel, to teach and to remind me. I welcome You Spirit of God. Amen.

May 26

2 Samuel 9:1–11:27, John 15:1–27, Psalm 119:49–64, Proverbs 16:1–3

Devine and Debranches

I am the vine; you are the branches. If a man remains in me and I in him, he will bear much fruit; apart from me you can do nothing. This is to my Father's glory, that you bear much fruit, showing yourselves to be my disciples.
—John 15:5,8

What great imagery, and so true. Jesus is the vine. God, our Father, is the gardener. We are the branches. And we have a purpose.

God's design for you is that your life may bear fruit—much fruit *(v.5),* and fruit that will last *(v.16).* We glorify God when we do and we show ourselves to be true disciples of Jesus.

So how does this happen? It happens when we "remain" in Jesus, in His word *(v.7)* and in His love *(v.9).* We remain in Him when we consciously affirm our identity in Him every day and when we obey His commands *(v.10).* We commune and we fellowship with Him. We experience His livelihood, and we soon discover that there is no life outside that vital connection. But we do not labor. Fruit is the natural outflow of a life lived in the Spirit.

Also know that when you bear fruit, there will be pruning. Now, that doesn't sound very inviting, initially, but it's for the purpose of bearing even more fruit. You don't do anything different. You continue to remain in Him—trust Him, lean on Him. It's just that the Father knows precisely how to tweak your circumstances to give you the best opportunity for a most effective life and fruitful witness.

The icing on the cake to remaining in Christ is to be called His friend!

Father, You are the Gardener who knows the best way to grow lasting fruit. I only ask that the sap of Your Spirit would freely flow in these branches. Amen.

May 27

2 Samuel 12:1–31, John 16:1–33, Psalm 119:65–80, Proverbs 16:4–5

Putting a Finger on Sin

Nathan said to David, "You are the man! Why did you despise the word of the Lord by doing what is evil in his eyes?" Then David said to Nathan, "I have sinned against the Lord."
—2 Samuel 12:7,9,13

You know the story of David and Bathsheba. It's one glaring chink in David's armor. It's the story of how sin deceives and entices and has far-reaching ramifications. But first, it's an affront to God.

David had prophets who would speak the word of the Lord into his life. There was Samuel in his younger years. Gad was another, mostly in the later years. Here, now, is Nathan. The story he told stirred David's emotions, and the message was a dagger to his heart. He was found out. There was no hiding his sin from God.

Many attributes made David great. But none are bigger than his ability to repent. This was not remorse for getting caught. He didn't justify his actions. He owned up to the truth. Afterward, David wrote Psalm 51 and cried, *"Against you, you only, have I sinned and done what is evil in your sight..." (v.4).*

In our reading in John, Jesus explains further that the Counselor to come *"will convict the world of guilt in regard to sin and righteousness and judgment" (16:9).* Thank God for the kind way He brings us back into alignment when we stumble. The Spirit of truth convicts our heart and pricks our conscience to repent.

Father, it is Your kindness that leads me to repentance. You don't ever put Your finger on my sin to condemn me, but to restore me. I humbly bow before You and confess my iniquity. Help me to see how sin separates me from intimacy with You. I receive Your forgiveness and a clean slate. Amen.

May 28

2 Samuel 13:1–39, John 17:1–26, Psalm 119:81–96, Proverbs 16:6–7

Jesus Prays for Us

"Father, the time has come ... I have revealed you to those whom you gave me out of the world. They were yours; you gave them to me and they have obeyed your word. I pray for them. I am not praying for the world, but for those you have given me, for they are yours."
—John 17:1,6,9

The time has come. Jesus' mission is now complete, and He prays for those who accepted His message. It's a powerful prayer. It is for the benefit of you and me.

Let's look at the six requests that stand out. 1) Holy Father, protect them by the power of Your name. While they are in the world, protect them from the evil one. 2) I say these things [now] so that they may have the full measure of My joy within them. 3) Sanctify, cleanse and set them apart by the truth of Your word. 4) I lift up and pray for those who will believe in Me future-tense through their message. 5) May they be brought to complete unity so that the world will see and believe. 6) I want those You have given Me to be with Me where I am and to see My glory.

As I reflect upon this heartfelt prayer, I know that Jesus has my highest interest at heart for a fruit-filled life. He knows what I need to overcome and for His kingdom to advance on this earth.

Jesus prayed for us then, and He prays for us now. *"Christ Jesus ... is at the right hand of God and is also interceding for us" (Romans 8:34).*

Father in heaven, thank You for this prayer that Jesus uttered. I cannot say anything to add to it, but to repeat it over and over again. You have equipped and empowered me to overcome in this life. May I live in obedience to Your word. In Jesus' name I pray, Amen.

May 29

2 Samuel 14:1–15:22, John 18:1–24, Psalm 119:97–112; Proverbs 16:8–9

Your Word is a Lamp

How sweet are your words to my taste, sweeter than honey to my mouth! Your word is a lamp to my feet and a light for my path. Your statutes are my heritage forever: they are the joy of my heart.
—Psalm 119:103, 105, 111

This is an appropriate place to pause and draw attention to a Psalm where the attributes of God's word are exalted. Psalm 119 is the longest Psalm and the longest chapter in the Bible—176 verses. It was written and laid out so that it could be methodically and easily memorized. Twenty–two sections of eight verses each correspond to the next letter of the Hebrew alphabet, making it an acrostic. Every verse (except six) has His "word" mentioned in one form or another.

From these verses *(97-112)* alone, we draw so much. Let's make it personal. The Psalmist has developed a love for God's law and meditates upon it constantly, and so can I. His commands make me wiser than my enemies. I gain more insight than my teachers and more understanding than even my elders. They keep me from every evil path. They are sweet to my mouth and they are the joy of my heart. I am determined to keep His decrees to the very end.

Finally, the verse we've heard the most … *"His word is a lamp to my feet and a light for my path."* I have the assurance that God will illuminate my way and guide me, so that I will not stumble. God has committed His word and His Spirit to us, so we will never be left to our own devices.

Father God, when I meditate upon Your word, You unveil to me who You are. How can I not fall in love with Your word? They are the vitamins that keep my mind sound and my heart whole. Thank you, Father, for Your word to me. Amen.

May 30

2 Samuel 15:23–16:23; John 18:25–19:22; Psalm 119:113–128, Proverbs 16:10–11

What is Truth?

"You are a king, then!" said Pilate. Jesus answered, "You are right in saying I am a king. In fact, for this reason I was born, and for this I came into the world, to testify to the truth. Everyone on the side of truth listens to me." "What is truth?" Pilate asked.
—*John 18:37–38*

Pilate is very uncomfortable, because he knows he is caught between a rock and a hard place. He is in over his head. It is clear that he would rather see Jesus exonerated. The man is innocent. But Pilate also gives in to the people's will.

Pilate is cynical. That is why he asks, *"What is truth?"* Everyone has their own version. My truth is whatever suits me. It's relative to the situation. But his question is a response to Jesus' declaration.

Jesus came to testify to the truth of a good God who loves those He created and desires to restore a lost fellowship. We were born with a propensity to sin, and unable to free ourselves from the noose. Jesus came as heaven's representative, to live in our skin. He came to bear our yoke and provide an acceptable sacrifice as atonement for sin once for all. Truth is a person. Jesus is God's word to us. In Jesus and His Word we have the standard for truth and right behavior.

In a world that evades the truth of Jesus for it's own version, it's really, really important to ground yourself in what you can stake your life upon—the Word of God. It will survive the test of time. It's not the shifting sand of a demented society. Commit to His Word. Make a place for it every day. Trip over it. *"Your word is truth"* (John 17:17).

Father God, You have loved me. You gave me Your Son. You have established Your truth in my heart. So, let me discern truth and also choose it! I pray this in Jesus' name, Amen.

May 31

2 Samuel 17:1–29; John 19:23–42, Psalm 119:129–152; Proverbs 16:12–13

A Secret No More

Later, Joseph of Arimathea asked Pilate for the body of Jesus. Now Joseph was a disciple of Jesus but secretly because he feared the Jews. With Pilate's permission, he came and took the body ... He was accompanied by Nicodemus, the man who earlier had visited Jesus at night.
—John 19:38–39

We have seen Nicodemus before in John 3 *(May 3)*. He was the Pharisee that visited Jesus at night humbly seeking. Now Nicodemus has a partner in crime—Joseph of Arimathea.

Joseph had a kindred spirit with Nicodemus. He, too, was a disciple of Jesus, but feared what would happen if it was common knowledge among his peers. His devotion was maintained, but secretly, until now. Joseph and Nicodemus, no doubt, encouraged one another privately to trust and believe in Jesus as the Messiah. Now, they had to act. They had to demonstrate their sincere faith and loyalty. Together, they prepared Jesus' body for burial.

Preparing Jesus' body for burial was no small task. It took both of them to wrap the body with seventy-five pounds of myrrh and aloes, in strips of linen, in accordance with Jewish burial customs. It took two to carry Jesus to that final resting spot.

There was a time that required Joseph and Nicodemus to come out of hiding. No more could Jesus be their secret. Perhaps you, too, have been afraid of what friends might say if they knew you were *religious*. Perhaps now is the time to share your treasure.

Father God, I am asking for You to arrange circumstances that I might share my faith with someone today. Go before me. Pave the way. Give me a holy boldness and an effective witness I pray. Amen.

June 1

2 Samuel 18:1–19:10; John 20:1–3; Psalm 119:153–176; Proverbs 16:14–15

The Race

Then Ahimaaz ran by way of the plain and outran the Cushite.
   —2 Samuel 18:23b

So Peter and the other disciple started for the tomb. Both were running, but the other disciple outran Peter and reached the tomb first.
   —John 20:3–4

OK, I confess. I am a runner. I've run six marathons, lots of 10K's and countless 5K races. I don't rack up the miles as I once did, but I would surely notice when there are not just one, but two instances of running in the same day's reading.

There was a long distance race involved when Ahimaaz wanted to take the news of Absalom's death back to his father from the front line. The duty was given to a Cushite, but Ahimaaz pressed Joab for permission also. The race was on. It was Ahimaaz winning that one.

On the first day of the week, after Jesus' burial, Mary Magdelene had reported the empty tomb to Peter and John. In a shorter distance race, it was John ("the other disciple, the one whom Jesus loved" writing in the third person) who outran Peter. But it was Peter who ventured into the tomb first. They both witnessed that the burial cloth had been folded up and there was no Jesus to be found.

In a day of races, it was actually Mary Magdalene who was the first to the tomb. She was the early riser who went to the tomb before sunrise. She reported the empty tomb and was the first to see the risen Christ. Jesus called her by name, and she beheld Him.

Father, thank You for the life and devotion of Mary Magdalene. She was delivered from a past of oppression to follow after You. May I be found running hard after You in wholehearted devotion. Amen.

June 2

2 Samuel 19:11–20:13; John 21:1–25; Psalm 120:1–7; Proverbs 16:16–17

Peter is Back on Track

When they had finished eating, Jesus said to Simon Peter, "Simon son of John, do you truly love me more than these?" "Yes, Lord," he said, "you know that I love you." Jesus said, "Feed my lambs."
—John 21:15

There was some unfinished business … Jesus had invested a great deal into Peter's life. Peter, along with James and John, was privy to Jesus' inner circle. He did things and went places others didn't, but Peter had denied Jesus three times during His trial before Pilate. There were obvious feelings of disappointment, and he did not have an opportunity to make things right. Confused by all that had transpired, Peter defaulted back to what was familiar, back to what he did before he met Jesus—that as a fisherman. But Jesus had other plans.

First, Jesus wanted to restore Peter full circle. He asked Peter three times, the same number of times he denied the Lord, *"Do you love me?"* Three times Peter affirmed that he loved Jesus—more than his friends, more than his fish. Peter needed to acknowledge with his lips that Jesus, indeed, was his primary fascination. *"You know I love you!"*

I believe that Jesus was also directing Peter into an occupational shift. *"If you do truly love me, feed my sheep. Take care of my little lambs."* This was a personal invitation for Peter to now invest in those who would believe in Him. A great move of God is just ahead. Peter is going to be an important player in the Lord's plan. By Peter's confession, he is restored and he is back on track.

Father, You are so kind. In Your dealings with Peter, You arranged for a personal encounter, so that he might be fully restored. You helped him see that You had more in store for him to do. If I will set You as my primary fascination, will you use me? That is my desire. So be it. Amen.

June 3

2 Samuel 20:14–22:20; Acts 1:1–26; Psalm 121:1–8; Proverbs 16:18

Wait for the Gift

(Jesus) gave them this command: "Do not leave Jerusalem, but wait for the gift my Father has promised, for in a few days you will be baptized with the Holy Spirit. You will receive power when the Holy Spirit comes on you; and you will be my witnesses in Jerusalem, Judea, Samaria, and the ends of the earth."
  —*Acts 1:4–5,8*

Jesus had coached his disciples in advance. He taught them about the Holy Spirit and the place He would have upon their lives (especially in John 14-16). After his resurrection, Jesus spent forty intense days with them, giving many convincing proofs and instructing them about the kingdom of God. Now was the time for the Holy Spirit to enter. His plea is passionate: *"Wait for the gift. You're going to need the gift!"*

If the Father of Glory wants you to have a gift, wouldn't you gladly receive it? Wouldn't you be curious at what God's gift would be? If He has prepared something for you, don't you think that it would only be for your benefit? Jesus said, *"If I go, then I will send him (the Holy Spirit) to you" (16:7).*

The experience of receiving the Father's gift was identified with water baptism. *"John immersed you in water. Now I will inundate you with the Holy Spirit."* It would be unforgettable. It would mark us forever.

Jesus even gave us the purpose of this gift. It was the very last words He spoke. *"You will receive power and you will be my witnesses…"*wherever you are, near and far, across this globe. If Jesus said we would need this baptism, then I'll gladly accept. How about you?

Father, You give only good gifts. The gift You prepared meant a great deal to Jesus. He insisted that we wait and receive. I am going to need Your power to represent You. I open my heart to receive all that You have for me. Amen.

June 4

2 Samuel 22:21–23:23; Acts 2:1–47; Psalm 122:1–9; Proverbs 16:19–20

The Day of Anticipation

(Peter)…"this is what was spoken by the prophet Joel: 'In the last days, God says, I will pour out my Spirit on all people.' Exalted to the right hand of God, he [Jesus] has received from the Father the promised Holy Spirit and has poured out what you now see and hear."
—Acts 2:16–17,33

They were all together, numbering about 120, in the upper room. They were joined in constant prayer. Jesus' mother and brothers were among the followers of Jesus. They all anticipated the day of promise.

The Holy Spirit came on the day of Pentecost. This was an annual feast held fifty days after Passover, so Jews from many nations were gathered in Jerusalem. When the Holy Spirit came, it was truly unmistakable. The sound of a violent wind. Tongues of cloven fire rested over each one. They each spoke in a language they knew not of, yet was known to the many foreign contingent there. *"We hear them declaring the wonders of God in our own tongues!" (v.11).*

To bring clarity to what had just happened, Peter rose and declared: *"This is what Joel prophesied! This is what Jesus promised! And this is for you and your children and for all who are far off" (vv.33,39).* In other words, the gift is available for everyone everywhere from now on—for all who will repent and identify with Christ through baptism.

Does this sound like business as usual? *Absolutely not.* But it was the inauguration of a new era. It was genuine. There was a sense of awe. God was authenticating a new day where His Spirit was evidenced. Will you welcome the Holy Spirit to fill you to overflowing?

Father God, I invite Your Spirit to fill me. However it looks, may I be filled with power and love to do your works on the earth. In Jesus' name, Amen.

June 5

2 Samuel 23:24–24:25; Acts 3:1–26; Psalm 123:1–4; Proverbs 16:21–23

Overconfidence from David

"Go and take a census of Israel and Judah." David was conscience-stricken after he had counted the fighting men, and he said to the Lord, "I have sinned greatly in what I have done … I have done a very foolish thing."
—2 Samuel 24:1,10

David ordered that a census be taken. Why was this a bad thing? To take a census amounted to a draft of all available fighting men for David's army. Except there was no real need to expand his army. Israel was already a power. This move exposed a sin in David's heart.

Even Joab, his military commander, knew that a census was unnecessary and could only bring God's judgment. But David's word overruled. By issuing the census, David was placing confidence in his own military strength. He was feeding his pride with arrogance. David's self-sufficiency was a significant step away from trusting in God's abilities. What is wrong was David's motive.

Notice that David is conscience-stricken *after* the census was completed. This is in stark contrast to how David was conscience-stricken *before,* when he had the opportunity to take Saul's life—on two occasions. *Do you remember that?* It's funny how pride can muddy up the way we perceive things!

Give David credit for owning up to the sin. But sin has a ripple effect. The consequences of our sin affect many more than we realize. For David, where much is given, much is required. Seventy thousand die. Is your confidence in the Lord or in your own strength?

Father God, if I have won a few battles, it has been by Your hand. I do not pretend to be strong on my own. My enemy is bigger than I, but no match for You. Amen.

June 6

1 Kings 1:1–53; Acts 4:1–37; Psalm 124:1–8; Proverbs 16:24

The Courage of Peter and John

When they saw the courage of Peter and John and realized they were unschooled, ordinary men, they were astonished and they took note that these men had been with Jesus. But since they could see the man who had been healed standing there with them, there was nothing they could say.
—Acts 4:13–14

Peter and John had performed a bona fide miracle. The crippled man who was healed was over forty years old. Peter took the opportunity to explain: *"It is in Jesus' name and the faith that comes through him that has given this complete healing to him, as you can all see" (3:16)*. They were proclaiming the resurrection of Jesus. The church was gaining converts and momentum, but it clearly upset the rulers and elders.

Peter and John were jailed, and the next morning were called in before the priests and rulers to give an account. *"By what power or what name did you do this?" (4:7)*. With all boldness, filled with the Spirit, Peter responds, *"It is by the name of Jesus Christ of Nazareth, whom you crucified but whom God raised from the dead, that this man stands before you healed" (4:10)*. What could they do to rebut? No one could deny what God had done!

Two things to note ... *First,* these two guys are not Harvard graduates. They are ordinary men who had been with Jesus, and were filled with the Spirit. And what a difference! Do you think it was their Type-A personalities? No way. Courage and boldness to represent Jesus came from the Spirit of God. *Secondly,* they had the wisdom to pray and ask for more courage—to preach the gospel and perform signs and wonders through the name of Jesus! Ordinary men like you and me.

Father, I love the boldness and tenacity that Peter and John displayed. I recognize what a difference Your Spirit in my life can make. Fill me up. Amen.

June 7

1 Kings 2:1–3:3; Acts 5:1–42; Psalm 125:1–5; Proverbs 16:25

Ananias and Sapphira

Then Peter said, "Ananias, how is it that Satan has so filled your heart that you have lied to the Holy Spirit and have kept some of the money? You have not lied to men but to God."
—Acts 5:3–4

From all appearances, Ananias and his wife, Sapphira, were making a generous donation from the sale of a piece of property. What an upstanding thing to do! Except they did not deal in a truthful manner.

Now, there is nothing wrong with keeping back some of the proceeds of their sale. Making an offering of any amount is commendable. But it was the agreeing together to deceive that skewed the transaction. Peter was filled with discernment when he boldly called out Ananias. Ananias succumbed to the temptation of making himself appear more generous than he really was.

The Spirit of truth would underscore the fact that wrong motives are destructive sins that have to be dealt with. You can lie to men, but you cannot get that lie past a holy God. The Holy Spirit, here identified as God, will not allow deception and blessing to go hand in hand. What we do, whatever it may be, must be done honestly and in truth.

Dishonesty, deception, covetousness and greed are sins that will prevent a genuine move of the Holy Spirit in any church. On a personal level, it will halt my spiritual growth. God knows. We're dealing with a holy and righteous God who takes sin very seriously.

Father, You remind me how vulnerable I can be to the temptation of making myself look better before men, and how my thought-life must be held accountable before You. Your Spirit is positioned within me to counsel and teach and convict. May I live honestly and truthfully before You. Amen.

June 8

1 Kings 3:4–4:34; Acts 6:1–15; Psalm 126:1–6; Proverbs 16:26–27

The Million-Dollar Question

At Gibeon the Lord appeared to Solomon during the night in a dream, and God said, "Ask for whatever you want me to give you." (Reply:) "So give your servant a discerning heart to govern your people and to distinguish between right and wrong. For who is able to govern this great people of yours?"
—1 Kings 3:5,9

How many times have you wished that God would ask that question to you—*just once?*

You have to appreciate Solomon's heart. Solomon is new at all this leadership stuff, and he knows it, but he has observed his father David. Fortunately, his dad was a really good example for him to emulate. Solomon recognizes the blessing and favor of God, and it has been extended to him. He is grateful to God for keeping His promise to have the son of David sit on the throne over Israel.

Solomon also displays a sincere humility. He acknowledges that the task to lead God's people looks overwhelming, but he has perspective on the enormity of it all. To do the assignment justly, Solomon would need the wisdom of God. Wisdom is ascertaining God's word on a situation, but it is also following up to obey that word. You can know what God says to do, but applying that directive is what makes it wisdom. Solomon asked for a discerning heart—to distinguish between right and wrong. Sometimes, it is to distinguish between what is good and what is best. There is a huge difference.

God says that if we will ask for wisdom, He will give it to us, because that is just the kind of generous God He is *(James 1:5).*

Father, I need wisdom and discernment from above. I need more than to be savvy or street-smart. I inquire of You, because You know best. Amen.

June 9

1 Kings 5:1–6:38; Acts 7:1–29; Psalm 127:1–5; Proverbs 16:28–30

A Recollection of Moses

Pharaoh's daughter brought [Moses] up as her own son. Moses was educated in all the wisdom of the Egyptians and was powerful in speech and action.
    —Acts 7:21–22

Moses said to the Lord, "I have never been eloquent, neither in the past nor since you have spoken to your servant. I am slow of speech and tongue."
    —Exodus 4:10

I'm picking on Moses, but the story is being told by Stephen. He is giving his Jewish opponents a history lesson in their own history. What I draw attention to I chuckle at, but what Stephen is having to endure is quite serious.

Nevertheless, as Stephen reviews the life of Moses, you cannot overlook the implication that Moses was brought up in the best that Egypt had to offer in culture and education. Moses was an effective communicator and confident in the way he carried himself.

But when I read this of Moses, the alarm went off! How could this account jive with what I remember reading in Exodus, when God spoke to Moses in the burning bush? When God asked Moses to be His spokesperson before Pharaoh, to deliver Israel out of Egypt, Moses began to back-peddle. *"Who, me?"* All of a sudden, Moses is a different person. Before a holy and awesome God, Moses' confidence wanes.

We know the story. Moses went on to do great exploits as God led him, but Moses had natural fears that we all have. Despite feeling terribly inadequate, all Moses needed was the assurance that God was with him. *We can do all things through Christ who strengthens us!*

Father, I am reminded that You are more interested in my availability than in my ability. I can speak Your words when I have been in Your presence. Amen.

June 10

1 Kings 7:1–51; Acts 7:30–50; Psalm 128:1–6; Proverbs 16:31–33

The Marriage Prayer

Blessed are all who fear the Lord, who walk in his ways. Your wife will be like a fruitful vine within your house; your sons will be like olive shoots around your table. May the Lord bless you from Zion ... and may you live to see your children's children.
—Psalm 128:1,3,6

I guess when you think about what is important in life, you have to be very grateful for a family life that has stuck together and honors God.

Truly, when you are at an age where you can reflect back upon the years, the family bonds you nurtured are what sustain you through the many seasons of life. They reward you with peace and fulfillment. These relationships become the indicators of what you valued most.

I can only say that I am a blessed man. My lovely wife is a fruitful vine. She has been a steady lover of God through thick and thin. Our marriage is thirty-seven years strong and counting. *Children are indeed a blessing from the Lord.* An olive shoot was an olive tree in infancy that grew to flourish and become one of the longest living trees. I have two olive shoots that are planted near and far—one in our city and the other in Europe. Both our daughters each have daughters, so we are enjoying our children's children very much!

This Psalm was called "the marriage prayer" and was often sung at Israelite weddings. But blessed and lasting marriages don't just happen. It's in the family where you learn to trust, love, serve, pray and laugh. The Scripture is true. Peace and favor are rewards to the man who honors and reveres the Lord. *(Time for a group hug!)*

Father of glory, You have been so kind to me and my family over these many years. I can only credit Your goodness. It is a joy to serve You. Amen.

June 11

1 Kings 8:1–66; Acts 7:51–8:13; Psalm 129:1–8; Proverbs 17:1

The Legacy of Stephen

Now Stephen, a man full of God's grace and power, did great wonders and miraculous signs among the people. Opposition arose, however … These men began to argue with Stephen. (Stephen:) "You are just like your fathers: You always resist the Holy Spirit!"
  —Acts 6:8–9; 7:51

Every time Stephen is referenced, he is a man described as "full of the Spirit." He was full of faith, full of wisdom and full of God's grace. Stephen knew what it was to serve among the elderly. But as the word of God spread in the young church, Stephen was one of the tools that God used to drive the kingdom forward. He proclaimed the truth of God's word and displayed the works of God with boldness.

However exciting it was to see this rapid development, it was also an unwelcome intrusion into the comfortable confines of their religious order. This movement was a challenge to their Jewish heritage. Even with Stephen's discourse into Moses and Jewish history, the bottom line was too much for them to bear. *"You always resist the Holy Spirit!"*

It's a curious thing how some folks receive truth. Sometimes, people don't want to hear it. Even though we may speak the truth in love, our hearers instead feel threatened. Here, Stephen is stoned to death. He is the church's first martyr, but he completed his assignment with vigor. He witnessed the glory of God. He saw heaven opened.

Being full of the Holy Spirit afforded Stephen to do all the will of God. Opposition to the gospel will continue to accelerate. Will you be one who will stand up for the truth when it is not a popular message?

Father, thank You for the bright light that Stephen was. He laid his life on the line. He held nothing back. Instill a tenacity in me that will not shrink. Amen.

June 12

1 Kings 9:1–10:29; Acts 8:14–40; Psalm 130:1–8; Proverbs 17:2–3

The Holy Spirit In Samaria

When they arrived (in Samaria), they prayed for them that they might receive the Holy Spirit, because the Holy Spirit had not yet come upon any of them; they had simply been baptized into the name of Jesus Christ. Then Peter and John placed their hands on them, and they received the Holy Spirit.
  —Acts 8:15–17

When Jesus proclaimed that there would be witnesses in Jerusalem, Judea, Samaria, and then to the ends of the earth *(1:8)*, it was a game plan. To this point, the Holy Spirit had been poured out on the day of Pentecost *(2:4)* and again following Peter and John's court appearance *(4:31)*. Upon Stephen's stoning, a great persecution broke out against the church in Jerusalem, and they were scattered throughout Judea and Samaria. The persecution actually furthered the gospel in ways it wouldn't have without it—a blessing in disguise.

Here, Peter and John are sent by the apostles to pray for believers in Samaria to receive the Holy Spirit. Realize that these were believers in Jesus who had already been baptized in water. Their salvation was not in question. But they needed the same Holy Spirit experience that would infuse their witness of Jesus with power.

Peter and John placed their hands on them and they received the Holy Spirit. *What exactly happened?* Did the building shake? Did they speak in another language? It doesn't mention the details, but I'm not sure they needed to. In the next verse *(8:18)*, Simon *saw* that the Holy Spirit was given. Something visible and tangible happened. In other words, they were not left guessing whether they were filled or not. They were endued with power from on high and they knew it.

Father, You are no respecter of persons. Once despised, these Samaritans were now recipients of Your Holy Spirit gift. You desire us all to be filled. Amen!

June 13

1 Kings 11:1–12:19; Acts 9:1–25; Psalm 131:1–3; Proverbs 17:4–5

Wise Man No More

King Solomon, however, loved many foreign women besides Pharaoh's daughter …
As Solomon grew old, his wives turned his heart after other gods, and his heart was
not fully devoted to the Lord his God.
  —1 Kings 11:1,4

It's hard to conceive. The man who was heir to God's promise. The one to whom God appeared twice. The king whom the whole world sought audience just to hear his wisdom. The greatest and richest king over any other king on the earth. This man, who literally had it all, was now succumbing to the temptations that went with great power. The man who could have anything he desired did just that. He stopped at nothing. 700 wives of royal birth and 300 concubines—would there ever be enough? He opened his heart to foreign women and their gods. His wives and his lust for more led his heart astray.

How could someone who loved the Lord knowingly turn his back? What happened over the years to Solomon's sincere faith?

It's easy to think that I could never do that. I certainly don't have the clout that Solomon had. But temptations come at every level and status. Any man can be deceived. It may have started subtly, but his desire was never quenched. Sin always takes you farther than you originally intend on going. He, himself, acknowledged that the eye is never satisfied … *(Eccl. 1:8).* The wisdom that he gained from God to lead a nation was not applied to his own personal life, and it cost him dearly. His legacy has a huge asterisk left beside it. Will we ever learn?

Father, I look at the life of Solomon and realize the propensity of every man to stray. We think that we can somehow find something more satisfying outside Your boundaries. May my eyes be opened to the deceitfulness of sin. May I cultivate a holy fear and be content with all You have provided. Amen.

June 14

1 Kings 12:20–13:34; Acts 9:26–43; Psalm 132:1–18; Proverbs 17:6

Saul's Turnabout

When he (Saul) came to Jerusalem, he tried to join the disciples, but they were all afraid of him, not believing that he was really a disciple. But Barnabas took him and brought him to the apostles. He told them how Saul on his journey had seen the Lord and that the Lord had spoken to him…
—*Acts 9:26–27*

Not only can God heal bodies and make blind eyes to see. Here is the testimony of how God changed the heart of Saul, a ruthless adversary of the believers in Christ, and made him to be one of the most dynamic apostles of the early church.

Documented in yesterday's reading, Saul encountered Jesus on the road to Damascus. This was the same Saul who took responsibility for the stoning of Stephen and persecuting believers. God would take the vilest of villains known to man and fashion him to be the crown jewel of Christianity in one life-changing encounter. Talk about a 180(°)! The disciples couldn't bring themselves to believe it. But the man who had all this energy to do damage would now be the chosen instrument to bring that energy to work righteousness and advance the kingdom.

Is there a person alive beyond the scope of God's grace? *I think not.* Think of the most unlikely person you know and imagine what God could do. It is possible with any man! It happened with you and me. Let this become a driving force in your life. Let your light so shine before men. Proclaim the gospel, love and pray for them, and watch the Holy Spirit draw them to a salvation opportunity.

Father God, nothing is impossible with You. You created the heart of man, and You can change the heart of man. I pray for those whose hearts seem beyond penetrating, for those whom You love and Jesus died for. Let them know You and the freedom of forgiveness, I pray in Jesus' name, Amen.

June 15

1 Kings 14:1–15:24; Acts 10:1–23a; Psalm 133:1–3; Proverbs 17:7–8

Naturally Supernatural

One day at about three in the afternoon he (Cornelius) had a vision. He distinctly saw an angel of God, who came to him and said ... He (Peter) saw heaven opened (in a trance) ... While Peter was still thinking about the vision, the Spirit said to him ...
   —Acts 10:3,11,19

God was setting the stage for something big. Like a chess match, the right pieces had to be in the right places. And God would use angels and visions to gain the undivided attention of Cornelius and Peter.

What I am mostly struck by is the activity of the Holy Spirit that was becoming more commonplace within the community of believers. In this series of events alone, we have a vision with an angel speaking and giving directives. Peter has a vision-like trance where a voice speaks to him. Moments later, the Spirit spoke to Peter pertinent details. Supernatural manifestations were the natural order here. Today, we balk at the idea of someone "hearing the Lord speak." Outside Christian circles, you would be laughed at or admitted to a psych ward.

I'll admit that I don't see visions everyday; hardly ever in fact. But I know when the Lord is speaking to my spirit. It is unmistakable. And the training to wait and listen doesn't just happen overnight. Yet, it is very much an aspect of living a spirit-led and spirit-filled life. We should expect that God will lead us by using whatever extraordinary means is necessary. God is a speaking God!

Listen ... the Word of God shouts when the Spirit of the living God breathes on it. He dwells within every believer for this very reason.

Father, You are a speaking God. I love that about You. May I hear well. Amen

June 16

1 Kings 15:25–17:24; Acts 10:23b–48; Psalm 134:1–3; Proverbs 17:9–11

The House of Cornelius

Then Peter began to speak: "I now realize how true it is that God does not show favoritism but accepts men from every nation who fear him and do what is right." While speaking ... the Holy Spirit came on all who heard ... the gift of the Holy Spirit had been poured out even on the Gentiles.
—Acts 10:34–35,44–45

The vision that God gave Peter of the unclean animals was all new territory—alarming, but quite convincing. Three times made the point. And the timing to meet Cornelius only seemed appropriate after that.

Here Peter is, before Gentiles. Never before, but it was the Lord who had arranged it. It would begin the fulfillment of the final phase of Jesus' action plan to extend His witness to the ends of the earth. That would necessitate the inclusion all peoples—Jews and non-Jews alike.

Peter's message was complete and concise. He didn't hold anything out. Jesus was the Good News proclaimed. These eager Gentiles believed *(11:14)*, and received the Holy Spirit in the same fashion they had at Pentecost. It's interesting that, this time, the believers were baptized in water after they received the Holy Spirit. Remember back to Samaria, it was in the opposite order. The point is underscored ... the Father does not discriminate. He desires every believer to receive His gift and be an effective witness of Jesus. That is still true today.

Why is this conversation about the Holy Spirit such a point of emphasis? Because it was the major point of emphasis that Jesus made in order to prepare us for life after He was gone. Let's get comfortable talking about the Holy Spirit, and more, seeking Him.

Father, I need the anointing of Your Spirit upon me. I want to be an effective witness of Jesus. Would You come and (re)fill me to overflowing? Amen.

June 17

1 Kings 18:1–46; Acts 11:1–30; Psalm 135:1–21; Proverbs 17:12–13

Elijah's Showdown

(Elijah to King Ahab:) "Now summon the people from all over Israel to meet me on Mount Carmel. And bring the four hundred and fifty prophets of Baal and the four hundred prophets of Asherah …" Elijah went before the people and said, "How long will you waver between two opinions?"
    —1 Kings 18:19,21

It had been three years since the prophet Elijah had declared the word of the Lord to Ahab: *"There will be no rain except at my word."* Elijah had been sought after, but it wasn't until now that God led him to present himself to Ahab and press the nation to make a choice.

Ahab was an exceedingly wicked king—more evil than any king before him. He and his wife, Jezebel, worshipped Baal openly and provoked the Lord to anger. Their leadership led Israel down a wicked path. So Elijah summoned Ahab and the people of Israel to a showdown. *"You can't have it both ways! Either serve God or serve Baal."*

After preparing a sacrifice for each, *"the god who answers by fire—he is God"* *(v.24)*. Elijah jeered and taunted the prophets of Baal as they called on their god to no avail. Then, in convincing fashion, with water dripping over the sacrifice, the fire fell. God answered Elijah's prayer so that they would turn their hearts back to Him. The people cried out, *"The Lord—he is God!" (v.39)*. So ended the prophets of Baal.

You may not call on Baal, but a god is whatever captures your heart. It's also called an idol. It replaces God on the throne of your life. We are faced with this choice often … to give our continual devotion to the One who is truly worthy or to lesser gods of this world.

Father, when my heart is entertained by idols, You call me to choose. You honor my free will, but desire wholehearted devotion. I choose You. Amen!

June 18

1 Kings 19:1–21; Acts 12:1–23; Psalm 136:1–26; Proverbs 17:14–15

A Whisper to Elijah

[Elijah] replied, "The Israelites have rejected your covenant ... and put your prophets to death. I am the only one left, and now they are trying to kill me." The Lord was not in the wind ... not in the earthquake ... not in the fire. After the fire came a gentle whisper. The Lord said to him, "I have reserved seven thousand in Israel—all whose knees have not bowed down to Baal."
—1 Kings 19:10–12,18

Elijah was on the run. He was physically and emotionally drained from the events at Mount Carmel. Now he is afraid for his life by the threats of Jezebel. In his exhaustion, he is also despairing. But an angel of the Lord meets Elijah. Twice he touches and provides for Elijah food and direction. After a forty day travel of over 200 miles to Mount Horeb, the Lord meets Elijah in a cave. He is safe here. Now Elijah can unburden his mind to the Lord. *"You know I am zealous for You. But I am the only prophet left and they want to kill me" (v.10).*

The Lord wants to make a point to Elijah. So with Elijah on the mountain, God reveals His mighty power through a great wind, an earthquake, a fire and a whisper. He wanted Elijah to know that the God who can do the miraculous can also be found in the quietness of a whisper. Will you humble yourself and hear the whisper?

The Lord still has a mission for Elijah to fulfill—as He elaborates. God is not finished with Elijah. But neither is Elijah the only person left on the face of the earth to fulfill God's purposes. He is one of many thousands who have a significant role in accomplishing the will of God. *Your mission is integral, and you are not alone!*

Father, You lead me through the many seasons of my life to represent You rightly and to fulfill Your purposes on this earth. Empower me for such a task. Have me know Your voice and power in the big and small. Amen.

June 19

1 Kings 20:1–21:29; Acts 12:24–13:15; Psalm 137:1–9; Proverbs 17:16

Barnabas and Saul Sent Out

In the church at Antioch there were prophets and teachers: Barnabas, Simeon, Lucius, Manaen and Saul. While they were worshipping the Lord and fasting, the Holy Spirit said, "Set apart for me Barnabas and Saul for the work to which I have called them." So after they had fasted and prayed, they placed their hands on them and sent them off.
—Acts 13:1–3

There it is again ... *"the Holy Spirit said ..."*

The persecution scattered believers northward, and so the gospel was being established wherever they went. Antioch of Syria became a hub for kingdom advancement, among Jews and Gentiles alike. It was here that believers were first called *Christians.* It was here that the first missionaries were sent out to the ends of the earth.

Barnabas was a huge catalyst in the early church. His real name was Joseph, but was given the name Barnabas by his fellow apostles, because he was an "encourager." Barnabas was the one who would stand behind you and believe in you when others were not convinced. It was Barnabas who staked his reputation on Saul when he was first converted. Later, it was John Mark whom he nurtured and discipled.

In our verses today, Saul becomes known as Paul, and these two are prayed over and sent out by the discernment of the prophets, hearing the Holy Spirit give the commission to go. They heard the Spirit speak after they had positioned themselves before the Lord through worship and fasting. Their heart preparation gave them ears to hear.

Father in heaven, You love to speak to Your people. I position myself to hear You. What is Your next assignment? Advance Your kingdom, and use me to do it. May I be one who encourages the heart of the young believer. Amen.

June 20

1 Kings 22:1–53; Acts 13:16–41; Psalm 138:1–8; Proverbs 17:17–18

A Life Statement of David

After removing Saul, he made David their king. He testified concerning him: "I have found David son of Jesse a man after my own heart; he will do everything I want him to do." For when David had served God's purpose in his own generation, he fell asleep …
—*Acts 13:22,36*

On the missionary road, it is Paul who assumes the leadership role. It is *"Paul and his companions" (13:13),* who sail to Pamphylia. In the Pisidian city of Antioch, Paul preaches in the synagogue to devout Jews, reviewing their history to lead them to salvation through Jesus. David's place in this history was irrefutable and an obvious point of agreement. In Paul's use of David, two statements are made of his life.

In verse 22, God affirms that David is a man after His own heart. He was willing to do everything that God wanted for him to do. David was a man who was preoccupied with knowing and obeying God.

In verse 36, as a summary statement (or eulogy) of his life, Paul asserts that David served God's purpose in his own generation. *Think about that.* How many can make the boast that he (or she) fulfilled all of God's purposes for him in the generation of time and space in which he lived? That is a desire that seems too lofty to attain!

In the grand scheme of history, my life's mark may not resound to the magnitude of David's, but God wants us to know for certain that we can absolutely fulfill God's will for our life to impact the generation we live in. Are you willing? Do you know God's heart? Will you set aside your own agenda for His? What will be said of you?

Father, there was an earnest desire, a seeking to know, a humility and a zeal for Your honor that David possessed—that I want. Amen.

June 21

2 Kings 1:1–2:25; Acts 13:42–14:7; Psalm 139:1–24; Proverbs 17:19–21

One Hundred Thirty–Nine

O Lord, you have searched me and you know me. Where can I go from your Spirit? Where can I flee from your presence? I praise you because I am fearfully and wonderfully made; My frame was not hidden from you when I was made in the secret place.
—*Psalm 139:1,7,14–15*

This is the favorite passage of my wife, Alaine, and for good reason. It should be in everybody's Top Ten. Before we even attempt a look into this majestic Psalm, let's read it again *slowly* ... Let certain phrases stick. Let the Spirit whisper to you. Make it personal.

There appear to be four points of emphasis in this Psalm of David. *Verses 1-6* elaborate upon God's complete knowledge of my person. He knows everything there is to know about me, and He still loves me. *Verses 7-12* speak of God's omnipresence. He is everywhere I go or ever will go, so I will never be too far from His reach. He is with me! *Verses 13-18* give us intimate thoughts while God created every detail of each individual. He fashioned me in the secret place with utmost care. His thoughts concerning me are precious. God sees me and smiles! *Verses 19-24* step away from the lofty attributes of God to point out a hatred for the enemies of God. To have a zeal for righteousness is to hate what God hates. The balance for us in real life is to love people, resist sin and give them no reason to point their finger at us!

"Search me and know my heart; test me and know my anxious thoughts. See if there is any offensive way in me...lead me in the way everlasting" (vv.23-24).

Father God, You have taken great measures to reassure me of Your perfect love for me. You know me. You are always with me. You created me so that I might reflect Your honor and glory. Search me, Holy Spirit, that I might have right motives in my dealings with people and not offend. In Jesus' name, Amen.

June 22

2 Kings 3:1–4:17; Acts 14:8–28; Psalm 140:1–13; Proverbs 17:22

Jars of Oil

Elisha said, "Go around and ask all your neighbors for empty jars. Don't ask for just a few." They brought the jars to her and she kept pouring. When all the jars were full ... he replied, "There is not a jar left." Then the oil stopped flowing.
—*2 Kings 4:3,5–6*

The wife of one of the prophets *(let's call her Jennifer)* calls on Elijah. Her husband has died and she now is responsible for an unpaid debt. Besides the grieving of death, now the creditor wants to enslave her children as payment. This was an acceptable practice in that day, but not in God's strategy for assisting the poor. See Deuteronomy 15:1-18.

Elijah showed kindness to Jennifer and her two sons by using what she already had. The little bit of oil she possessed was more than enough as long as she kept pouring into the jars that were brought to her. As long as the jars kept coming, the oil kept flowing. God's provision was as large as their faith was to provide the jars.

Throughout the Scriptures, oil is used to represent the Holy Spirit. More often than we care to admit, we don't think that we have anything to offer, but the life of the Spirit that is poured out from our lives is a never-ending flow. The oil of the Spirit is life-giving. It will meet the need of the moment. We don't realize that the perimeters of the Spirit are boundless. The pouring out of what we have is the key. We give away what God has freely given us, and it will always be enough. *"Give and it will be given unto you ..." (Luke 6:38).*

What you have within you is a precious thing. Now give it away.

Father, what You have freely given to me is meant to be passed on to others. Cause me to know the joy of being poured out. What I have, I give. Amen.

June 23

2 Kings 4:18–5:27; Acts 15:1–35; Psalm 141:1–10; Proverbs 17:23

It Seemed Good

Some men came down from Judea to Antioch and were teaching the brothers: "Unless you are circumcised ... you cannot be saved." This brought Paul and Barnabas into sharp dispute with them. So [they] were appointed to go up to Jerusalem and see the apostles and elders about this question. "It seemed good to the Holy Spirit and to us not to burden you ..."
—Acts 15:1–2,28

While in Antioch, some men came down from Judea and taught that in order to be saved, you would have to be circumcised as the law dictated. This caught the ire of Paul and Barnabas. An added yoke to Gentile believers was not going to fly. To deal with this heresy properly, a meeting of the minds would be needed to settle this issue right now—at the mother church in Jerusalem.

The apostles and the elders met to consider the question. Peter recalled his experience with the household of Cornelius. The Spirit had been given to the Gentile believers in the same manner as with the Jews. Barnabas and Paul testified to the many miraculous signs among the Gentiles. Even James spoke up to mention the prophecy of Amos 9:11-12, that the Gentiles would also bear His name. From the body of work presented, they were able to ascertain a judgment.

The phrase that caught my attention was in verse 28: *"It seemed good to the Holy Spirit and to us not to burden you with ... [unreasonable requirements]."* They perceived together what the Holy Spirit was saying to the situation. It's easy to rely upon our own rationale, but the Spirit was speaking. They learned to ask and listen for His answer.

Father in heaven, You are a speaking God, and whether it is a major decision or a small detail, You have an opinion that matters to me. Your way is always best, so I lean upon Your understanding and inquire of You. Amen.

June 24

2 Kings 6:1–7:20; Acts 15:36–16:15; Psalm 142:1–7; Proverbs 17:24–25

A Sharp Disagreement

Barnabas wanted to take John, also called Mark, with them, but Paul did not think it wise to take him, because he had deserted them in Pamphylia and had not continued with them in the work. They had such a sharp disagreement that they parted company. Barnabas took Mark and sailed for Cyprus …
  —Acts 15:37–39

Can this happen in the church? *Really?* You may have had to read this more than once just to be sure that you read it correctly. Did Barnabas and Paul really have a heated argument? *You bet they did.*

The reaction stemmed from an incident on their first missionary journey together. John Mark came along to assist Paul and Barnabas, but he returned to Jerusalem midstream. Paul's version of the event asserts that John deserted them. This issue with John Mark surfaces when they are considering another missionary journey. Barnabas wants him to go along. Paul begs to differ.

The real reason for the differences can be seen in their gift mixes. Paul is a prophet, and prophets see things black and white. John cannot be trusted. It would not be wise to overwhelm him again. Barnabas, on the other hand, is more pastoral. He wants to take the opportunity to disciple John Mark and give him another try. It is this same Barnabas who was patient with young Paul after his conversion.

Was one right and the other wrong? Not really. It was just clear that Paul would not have the patience to work with John. They agreed to disagree, so they departed, and their efforts were multiplied. Paul chose Silas, and Barnabas took John, but both parties were blessed.

Father, You have wired me to see things a certain way. Thank You for that, but give me grace to allow others the space to grow how You deem best. Amen.

June 25

2 Kings 8:1–9:13; Acts 16:16–40; Psalm 143:1–12; Proverbs 17:26

In a Philippian Jail

About midnight Paul and Silas were praying and singing hymns to God, and the other prisoners were listening to them. Suddenly there was such a violent earthquake that the foundations of the prison were shaken. At once, all the prison doors flew open ... The jailer woke up, and he drew his sword to kill himself. But Paul shouted, "Don't harm yourself! We are all here!"
—Acts 16:25–28

The travels of Paul and Silas brought them to the city of Philippi. Here, the gospel was met with hostile resistance after Paul cast the demon from a fortune-teller. She was freed from bondage, but her business owner was incensed. Paul and Silas were dragged before the city magistrates and were stripped, beaten, severely flogged, then imprisoned. You know it's bad when your feet are fastened to the stocks of an inner cell. But such was a day in the life of an apostle.

Paul and Silas would not be discouraged. They considered it an honor to suffer for Christ. Around midnight, things were just getting started. Paul and Silas were praying out loud and singing hymns to God while the other prisoners listened in. Suddenly, an earthquake shook the prisoners free. The jailer responsible for the two missionaries woke up and suspected the worst. If they escape, he will die. So Paul quickly assures him that all was intact. This jailer knows now that Paul and his friend are the real deal. Their lives line up with their message. He wastes no time to ask, *"What must I do to be saved?" (v.30).*

Before the sun rises, the jailer and his entire family believe on the Lord Jesus Christ and are baptized. Joy in believing filled their hearts.

Father, thank You for advancing the kingdom even in the darkest places. You also showed me the importance of baptism and being identified with Jesus. It's not a casual thing, but a needed aspect of the salvation experience. Amen.

June 26

2 Kings 9:14–10:31; Acts 17:1–34; Psalm 144:1–15; Proverbs 17:27–28

The Bereans

Now the Bereans were of more noble character than the Thessalonians, for they received the message with great eagerness and examined the Scriptures every day to see if what Paul said was true.
—Acts 17:11

What a blessing it must have been... for Paul and Silas (and now Timothy) to come to a town where they actually valued the Scriptures.

The church here in Berea models to us how central the Scriptures are to be in our discernment of truth. The Scriptures are the standard by which we judge a man's words. For me, knowing that my listeners are verifying my use of Bible references accurately in a message thrills me. Every pastor, teacher and public speaker should welcome the thought process that challenges us all to go deeper in the knowledge of the Lord. We should be asking questions. We should understand the context. We should know how it applies to my life right now. We ought to have our feet held to the fire in order to show ourselves approved, *"a workman who does not need to be ashamed and who correctly handles the word of truth"* (2 Timothy 2:15).

The Bereans were of more noble character because they were people of the Word. It brought transformation from the inside out that was evident in their behavior. That's what the Word does—it shapes our heart and transforms our mind to look and think and feel like the Lord Himself. The Word of God affects us for good. It anchors us.

This devotion to the Scriptures was not a rigid ritual. *"They received the message with great eagerness."* Their hearts were made to come alive by the Word as it was illuminated by the Spirit of God.

Father, let my love for You be evidenced by my love for Your Word. Amen.

June 27

2 Kings 10:32–12:21; Acts 18:1–22; Psalm 145:1–21; Proverbs 18:1

Jehoida and Joash

Joash was seven years old when he began to reign (as king of Israel). Joash did what was right in the eyes of the Lord all the years Jehoida the priest instructed him.
—*2 Kings 11:21; 12:3*

This account coupled with 2 Chronicles 24 gives us the most complete view of the story. Jehoida was the priest who was responsible for crowning Joash as king, replacing the evil Athaliah. Young Joash was just seven years old when he began his reign over Judah.

Under his rule, Joash restored the temple of the Lord. But the most telling statement that can be made of Joash was that he did what was right in the eyes of the Lord all the years of Jehoida the priest. Jehoida was a godly influence upon Joash, and God's blessing followed. Jehoida lived to be one hundred thirty. But once Jehoida was gone, Joash began to listen to the other officials' advice and abandoned the God of their fathers. Even though the Lord sent prophets to stir them back, he would not listen. A similar thing occurred when Rehoboam became king after Solomon. He took the advice of his contemporaries over the wisdom of the seasoned leaders. In both instances, the pressure to conform to the "idol of the day" was overwhelming.

Joash had not cultivated godly convictions of his own. In our ever-shifting culture, we are faced with similar pressures to be tolerant and accepting of what God calls sin. If we are not grounded in the truth of God's Word, we are vulnerable to the same deception.

Father, I am grateful for the godly people you have placed in my life. Let me learn from their example and form convictions of what I know is truth. Let them guide me all the days of my life to overcome the pressures of this world. Amen.

June 28

2 Kings 13:1–14:29; Acts 18:23–19:12; Psalm 146:1–10; Proverbs 18:2–3

Priscilla and Aquila

Meanwhile a Jew named Apollos came to Ephesus. He was a learned man, with a thorough knowledge of the Scriptures. He spoke with great fervor and taught about Jesus accurately, though he only knew about the baptism of John. When Priscilla and Aquila heard him, they invited him to their home and explained the way of God more adequately.
—Acts 18:24–26

Priscilla and Aquila are two of my favorite people in the Bible. They have always been a model of a healthy marriage for my wife and I. They complemented each other in ministry. It is even very likely that Priscilla was the more recognized leader of the two, having her name mentioned first in five of the seven times they are referenced.

Priscilla and Aquila came on the scene when they met Paul in Corinth. The three worked together as tentmakers, and then as a ministry team. They supported Paul in establishing the church in Corinth. A year and a half later, they all sailed to Ephesus, where Paul left them. It is here, in Ephesus, that Priscilla and Aquila meet Apollos.

Apollos was an effective speaker with a good handle of the Scriptures. After hearing Apollos, Priscilla and Aquila took him under their wing to explain further the aspects of baptism and the Holy Spirit that he had not yet known. He was not in need of any rebuke, only a fuller explanation of the whole story. After all, we can only walk in the light of the revelation we are given. The manner of gentleness by Priscilla and Aquila show us a proper way to bring loving correction. And credit Apollos for having such a teachable spirit.

Father, thank You for the example of Priscilla and Aquila as a married couple dedicated to ministry. Use my wife and I as a team to bless other couples. And let my home be a haven of love and edification. I pray in Jesus' name, Amen.

June 29

2 Kings 15:1–16:20; Acts 19:13–41; Psalm 147:1–20; Proverbs 18:4–5

Establishing Ephesus

Many of those (in Ephesus) who believed now came and openly confessed their evil deeds. A number who had practiced sorcery brought their scrolls together and burned them publicly ….In this way the word of the Lord spread widely and grew in power.
—*Acts 19:18–20*

It started in yesterday's reading. Priscilla and Aquila ministered in Ephesus. Paul joined them there and introduced the Holy Spirit baptism to a group of about a dozen men. They had never heard of the Holy Spirit—only the baptism of John. Paul enunciated the difference and led them into an encounter with the Holy Spirit.

Ephesus became a hub for ministry, as Paul taught daily in the hall of Tyrannus. Through this discipleship school, all who lived in the province of Asia heard the word of the Lord. Sharing this Good News was their passion and priority. They had their dissenters, but God did extraordinary miracles and healings. Evil spirits were cast out.

Freeing people of demons is not something you can manufacture in a copy-cat manner. In a specific incident, seven sons of a priest named Sceva went around imitating the method Paul was using. But because evil spirits are real, they were not swayed by the verbiage. Demons knew Jesus and Paul by name, but these boys had no authority. They were overwhelmed and beaten. A holy fear swept over the area.

Another true response to the gospel is repentance. It is the turning away from the old life of sin to walk in the newness of a transformed life. Scrolls of sorcery were burned publicly, leaving behind the past.

Father, thank You for pouring out Your Spirit to establish Your kingdom in my heart. Bring deliverance and healing and repentance to my city. Amen.

June 30

2 Kings 17:1–18:12; Acts 20:1–38; Psalm 148:1–14; Proverbs 18:6–7

A Stop-Off at Miletus

When they arrived, he said …" You know how I lived the whole time I was with you. I have not hesitated to proclaim to you the whole will of God. Now I commit you to God and to the word of his grace, which can build you up …"
—Acts 20:18,27,32

Paul was on his way back to Jerusalem, but he longed to spend a few precious moments with the elders of Ephesus, where he had spent three years of his life pouring into them. He knew if he went to Ephesus, he could very well get delayed, having had so many dear friendships. So instead, Paul called for them to make the short journey to Miletus for a proper farewell. And a tearful farewell it was.

His speech summarized … *"You know me. You know how I lived my life. I served the Lord with earnest diligence. I was badgered and ridiculed by the Jews, yet I declared this saving message to all men. I held nothing back. I took every opportunity to proclaim to you the whole counsel of God. Now I want only to finish well my assignment—to make this grace known."*

With the personal reflections came also a warning. In short … *"Take great care over the dear ones you've been given to shepherd. Be on guard for yourselves. Insolent brutes will come into your congregations in order to distort the truth and deceive."*

Lastly, Paul commits them to God and the word of his grace. Paul gives his baby—the church at Ephesus—to God the way parents have to surrender their children to the Lord. It is the Word of God that keeps them on the straight path. It is the Word of His grace that builds up the church. *"I give you to God. I commend you to His grace."*

Father, we do all that we can do for each assignment You give. In the end, we release our work and relationships to Your hands. Bring lasting fruit. Amen.

July 1

2 Kings 18:13–19:37; Acts 21:1–16; Psalm 149:1–9; Proverbs 18:8

Conflicting Reports

Hezekiah prayed to the Lord: "O Lord, God of Israel, enthroned between the cherubim, you alone are God over all the kingdoms of the earth. Give ear, O Lord. Listen to the words Sennacherib has sent to insult the living God." Then Isaiah ... sent a message to Hezekiah, "This is what the Lord says ..."
—2 Kings 19:15–16,20

Hezekiah was a righteous king (over Judah), just as his forefather David. He trusted in the Lord and the Lord was with him. But all was not well. Assyria had already captured Samaria and deported Israel (2 Kings 18). Now, Assyria was knocking on Judah's door.

Sennacherib was the king of Assyria. He sent his field commander with an army to issue threats against Judah. Brash words were used to intimidate the people and undermine the king. The aim was to cast fear and trepidation into their hearts and weaken their resolve.

What Hezekiah did was to seek out the word of the Lord. Twice the threats of the enemy came. Twice Hezekiah sought the Lord. The prophet Isaiah had the word of the Lord for Hezekiah. Both times, the Lord's report was true. Once you have God's authority on a matter, it is settled. You can take it to the bank. There is no need to despair.

The same is true of your adversary. When the devil spews forth lies to scare you into defeat, know what the Lord says. Satan wants you to doubt the very faith you hold dear. But the word of the Lord is the only word that matters. God is for you and not against you.

That night the angel of the Lord put to death 185,000 Assyrians.

You who are enthroned between the cherubim, You alone are God. Speak forth Your word to my heart that I might trust and not be afraid. Amen.

July 2

2 Kings 20:1–22:2; Acts 21:17–36; Psalm 150:1–6; Proverbs 18:9–10

Hezekiah's Prayer

Hezekiah prayed to the Lord, "Remember how I walked before you faithfully..."
Before Isaiah had left the middle court, the word of the Lord came to him: "This is
what the Lord says: I have heard your prayer and seen your tears; I will heal you ...
I will add fifteen years to your life."
—2 Kings 20:3–5

To fill in the blanks, the prophet Isaiah had just delivered the word of the Lord to Hezekiah—that he was to put his house in order, for he was going to die. It was King Hezekiah's response to pray, remind God of his faithful devotion and to weep.

There are several aspects of this story to like. When the prophet heard the word of the Lord, he did what he was suppose to do—he spoke it. Isaiah was the delivery person. He had been God's mouthpiece many times to Hezekiah. Good or bad, Isaiah spoke the word that God gave him to speak. In fact, later in this same chapter, Isaiah must speak the word of the Lord again to Hezekiah to pronounce a judgment.

Here, God heard Hezekiah's prayer and saw his tears in the present tense. *Immediately,* Isaiah sensed the word of the Lord and reported the news. Hezekiah's prayer moved the heart of God. So much so, that He added fifteen years to Hezekiah's life. It may have been desperate, but it was also earnest. God hears and answers prayer. God is a healing God. God is a speaking God. God remembers our life of righteous choices. He remembered David's life, and it brought deliverance to a nation *(v.6).*

Father God, thank You for hearing my every prayer and knowing my present tense
situation. Nothing escapes Your eye. I am confident that You will work all things
together for my good. May my prayers release Your will and move Your heart, for I
pray in Jesus' name, Amen.

July 3

2 Kings 22:3–23:30; Acts 21:37–22:16; Psalm 1:1–6; Proverbs 18:11–12

Josiah's Heart Response

"Because your heart was responsive and you humbled yourself before the Lord when you heard what I have spoken against this place and it's people and because you tore your robes and wept in my presence, I have heard you," declares the Lord. "… your eyes will not see the disaster I am going to bring."
—2 Kings 22:19–20

During the reign of King Josiah came a remarkable find. Hilkiah the high priest found the Book of the Law in the temple. My initial question was, *"Why wouldn't it be in the temple? Where did it go?"* Because of a long line of evil kings, the copies of the Pentateuch had been discarded. God's laws were lost. Can you imagine for one minute not having a copy of God's Word?

Josiah's story is most interesting. He was just eight years old when he succeeded his father Amon on the throne of Judah. He was twenty–six when he gave the orders for temple repairs. That's when Hilkiah found the Book. Shaphan the secretary read from it before Josiah. Josiah's response was one of alarm and grief—he tore his robes! God's judgments would be upon the people who did not walk in His ways.

Josiah had his leadership team to inquire of the Lord. In other words, in light of this revelation: *What do we do now?* The one entrusted with the word of the Lord at this time was the prophetess Huldah. Her word: Yes, disaster would come, but not in Josiah's lifetime.

Why? Because Josiah's heart was responsive. He humbled himself. He expressed his anguish over sin. He wept before the Lord. The Word impacted him. Have you felt the conviction that precipitates change?

Father, You were clearly moved by Josiah's heart response. Impact my heart with Your Word. I embrace Your Spirit to bring about needed change. Amen.

July 4

2 Kings 23:31–25:30; Acts 22:17–23:10; Psalm 2:1–12; Proverbs 18:13

Inevitable Judgment

The Lord sent raiders…to destroy Judah, in accordance with the word of the Lord proclaimed by his servants the prophets. Surely these things happened to Judah according to the Lord's command, in order to remove them from his presence because of the sins of Manasseh and all he had done.
  —2 Kings 24:2–3

The northern kingdom of Israel had already been taken captive to Assyria. 110 years later, the Babylonians overthrow Assyria and are the new world bullies. After Josiah, the southern kingdom of Judah deteriorated rapidly into sin and judgment became inevitable. God's only recourse was severe: removal of His very presence.

It's hard to grasp this judgment of God's own, but the Lord gave Judah every possible opportunity to repent. Prophets, including Isaiah, were sent to call them on their sin. Manasseh, especially, is called out for the massive bloodshed he was responsible for. He led the nation away from God. He desecrated the temple with idols. Manasseh even sacrificed his own sons in the fire to pagan gods. He was utterly evil.

What do we take from this? God, at the core, is holy and righteous. He cannot dwell with sin and cannot bless rebellion. Leaders are held accountable for how they lead—what they tolerate and give license to. If God says He cannot turn His head on the shedding of innocent blood, then where do we stand when governments encourage the abortion of innocent babies? … I would say on shaky ground. God is raising up a bold and powerful remnant to war against unrighteousness. Will you be a witness to God's holy standard?

Father, to be removed from Your presence is not an option. I want to be zealous for the things You are zealous for and hate the things You hate. Amen.

July 5

1 Chronicles 1:1–2:17; Acts 23:11–35; Psalm 3:1–8; Proverbs 18:14–15

A Man's Spirit

A man's spirit sustains him in sickness, but a crushed spirit who can bear?
—Proverbs 18:14

What we're talking about here is hope and the strength of a man's spirit. When my health has changed my circumstances, it is being able to endure a season that is laced with uncertainty. And because my spirit has been touched by the Spirit of God, hope can find an end and a purpose, because God is in it. He is there. I understand that my body will ultimately fail, but my God will either heal and sustain me, or take me to glory, because my hope rests in Him and His promises.

A crushed spirit is the abandonment that any hope exists, that my circumstance cannot change and that there is no redeemable purpose in it whatsoever. God, if He exists at all, has turned His back.

I have seen the fight and the grit of a man's spirit to sustain him in sickness. I have seen it in my wife when she battled through cancer—twice. I've seen it in my father-in-law when his aging heart was failing. You have seen it too. It is God who gives us hope to persevere.

The story of Viktor Frankl is a poignant one. He is a man who endured four Nazi concentration camps between 1942–1945. His family died. The suffering he witnessed was unthinkable, yet he observed how choosing your attitude in the circumstance sets in motion your future. The prisoner who had lost his faith in the future was doomed. Many believed their real opportunity in life had passed, and so gave up. Viktor believed in turning challenges into triumph. Who holds the keys to your future? Where does your hope lie?

Father, Your Word says that "a cheerful heart is good medicine, but a crushed spirit dries up the bones" (Proverbs 17:22). Give me Your joy today. Amen.

July 6

1 Chronicles 2:18–4:4; Acts 24:1–27; Psalm 4:1–8; Proverbs 18:16–18

When It's Convenient

Felix came with his wife Drusilla, who was a Jewess. He sent for Paul and listened to him. As Paul discoursed on righteousness, self-control and the judgment to come, Felix was afraid and said, "That is enough for now! You may leave. When I find it convenient, I will send for you."
—*Acts 24:24–25*

After a miraculous exit from Jerusalem, Paul is in Caesarea to be tried before Governor Felix. Ananias the high priest and his lawyer, Tertullus, made their case. Paul defended himself. Once the proceedings were adjourned, Felix deferred the decision until Lysias could come. In the meantime, Paul was held under guard loosely.

Felix was curious enough. He was well acquainted with the Way— what the group of believers were called then *(v.22)*. His wife was a Jewess *(v.24)*, so there was some intrigue there. When Felix inquired of Paul, he held nothing back. Paul spoke boldly about his faith to Felix and the practicalities of believing. Felix hoped that Paul might slip up and offer a bribe, but Paul was uncompromising in his message. Nothing in his presentation brought any undo attention to himself. Paul's life and message were consistent.

The gospel, when declared, brings you to a point of decision. It is not enough to listen and agree without bowing the knee in repentance. The gospel is confrontational like that. Felix was uncomfortable with the convicting power of the Holy Spirit. "Convenience" for Felix was only an excuse to delay the decision not to believe. *"Choose this day whom you will serve. As for me ... [I] will serve the Lord" (Joshua 24:15).*

Father, thank You for the kind way You drew me by Your Spirit to believe. When I understood the great lengths You took to provide salvation, there was only one acceptable response—to repent of my sin and believe. Amen.

July 7

1 Chronicles 4:5–5:17; Acts 25:1–27; Psalm 5:1–12; Proverbs 18:19

In the Morning

Give ear to my words, O Lord, consider my sighing. Listen to my cry for help, my King and my God, for to you I pray. In the morning O Lord, you hear my voice; in the morning I lay my requests before you and wait in expectation.
—Psalm 5:1–3

I cannot read this Psalm without singing it. It's in a different version, of course, but it's a wonderful way to pray the Scriptures—even today.

David is juxtaposing his devotion to God with the godlessness that is all around him. These deceitful men tell lies and cannot be trusted. David even calls on God to bring them down. *"Destroy them! Banish them!"* Haven't you felt like praying that way? I love David's honesty.

David's prayer is a cry for help in the midst of these lie-hounds: *"Hear me God. Consider the things that grieve me. Lead me, O Lord, in your righteousness because of my enemies. Make the path straight for me."*

The takeaway verse for me is verse three ... *"In the morning I lay my requests before you."* Twice David explains it this way for emphasis, because the morning is the first and the best part of our day, before we get other distractions to crowd our mind. In the morning, our mind is the freshest. We can think clearly. We can commit the new day to God. There is no better way I can think of to commune with God than to set aside time to pray, read and meditate in the Bible, engage in worshipful music and follow along in a helpful devotional. Every morning is a scheduled appointment with God. But, it's not just for our benefit. It's also His time to be with us!

Father in heaven, I ask that You help me to be diligent in my devotion to You. I give you the first moments of each day. I pray that my communion with You would be sweeter and sweeter. I give You my first and my best. Amen.

July 8

1 Chronicles.5:18–6:81; Acts 26:1–32; Psalm 6:1–10; Proverbs 18:20–21

Paul Before Kings

[Jesus to Paul] "I am sending you to open their eyes and turn them from darkness to light, and from the power of Satan to God, so that they may receive forgiveness of sins and a place among those who are sanctified…" [Paul:] "King Agrippa, do you believe the prophets? I know you do."
—Acts 26:17,27

It was back in Acts 9 when Saul (Paul) saw the vision of Jesus that changed his life forever. The Lord spoke to Ananias that this chosen instrument would go before Israel, the Gentiles and their kings. We have seen this come to pass especially in the last few chapters with Felix, Festus, and now Agrippa. Before kings he gave his testimony.

Agrippa was of Jewish descent and had authority over the temple and the high priest. He was familiar with these matters. That is why Paul asked, *"King Agrippa, do you believe the prophets? I know you do."*

Paul was faithful to the heavenly vision to declare the gospel first to the Jews and also to the Gentiles. He proclaimed what the prophets and Moses proclaimed— that Christ would suffer and rise from the dead. He was not partial. Paul replied to Agrippa: *"I pray God that not only you but all who are listening to me today may become what I am" (v.29).* He wanted small and great alike to repent and turn to the Lord.

When Paul was given this opportunity to speak before Agrippa, like the others, he began by sharing his personal testimony—what God had done in his life. This is where we all begin. We may not have had a light-from-heaven experience, but it was life-changing just the same. Your testimony is your most effective message, because it happened to you. And you just never know who will hear it and believe.

Father, thank You for opening my eyes and forgiving me of my sins. Give me boldness and opportunity to tell my story. To You be all the glory. Amen.

July 9

1 Chronicles 7:1–8:40; Acts 27:1–20; Psalm 7:1–17; Proverbs 18:22

A Wife is Good

He who finds a wife finds what is good and receives favor from the Lord.
—Proverbs 18:22

I am a blessed man. I know that. The Scriptures are true. I have received favor from the Lord. I have found what is good.

God knew we needed help. He said it was not good that a man be alone in this life. He created the woman to be a helper suitable for him. So marriage was God's idea from the beginning. So, in principle we probably all agree that God knew what He was doing. But a successful marriage doesn't just happen. The actual working out of this unity is forged. It requires determined, selfless effort. Two people coming together have different upbringings, different perspectives and different *everything*. And that is why two are better than one. The Lord knew what you needed to complete you.

Alaine is my bride of 37 years and brings tremendous balance to our marriage. She has a perspective I need. She has a sensibility I value. She is relational and thoughtful. Her inner beauty matches her outer beauty. Most importantly, she loves the Lord. And God uses her to hone me, that is to help conform me to the image and likeness of Christ. That's part of the deal. I cannot hide anything from her. She knows me through and through. And she continues to love me.

To be sure, we have endured our share of hardships and stress, but we have life experiences together that come only through remaining faithful for the duration. God is faithful. He does all things well!

Father in heaven, thank You for my wife. You have indeed blessed me. I pray that I will be for her what she needs in a husband. We understand that only You can satisfy the longings of our heart. We commit our way to You. Amen

July 10

1 Chronicles 9:1–10:14; Acts 27:21–44; Psalm 8:1–9; Proverbs 18:23–24

What is Man?

O Lord... how majestic is your name in all the earth! From the lips of children and infants you have ordained praise. When I consider your heavens, the work of your fingers, the moon and the stars, which you have set in place, what is man that you are mindful of him, the son of man that you care for him?
—Psalm 8:1–4

I am a sucker for coneflowers and carnations. And what majesty there is in the mountains and the streams. The most memorable Fourth of July display ever for me was the fingers of lightning racing and weaving across the sky, one after another after another. The sheer beauty of a sunrise always makes me linger in the moment. Staring at a sea of stars and finding the Big Dipper helps me to put life in better perspective. There are millions of stars, and then there is little-ole-me. But it's not about me as much as it is about the majesty of our God. It's way beyond *"wow."* The word I am looking for is *"awe."*

"When I consider your heavens and the work of your fingers ... what is man that you are mindful of him?" David rightly concluded that man is highly valuable. When God saw all that He had made (man), He proclaimed it was *very* good *(Genesis 1:31)*. We were made in His image. We bear the stamp of our Maker. We carry His name.

With this in mind, it would only seem right to praise Him with the wonder of a child, with sincerity and without reservation. Praise was ordained for the one who is not afraid to express his childlike faith with youthful exuberance. *"O Lord, how majestic is Your name!"*

Father of glory, You are worthy of all praise and honor. My lips will praise You. When I see the work of Your hands, I stand in awe. It reflects Your greatness and beauty. Let my expression of praise move Your heart. In Jesus' name I pray, Amen

July 11

1 Chronicles 11:1–12:18; Acts 28:1–31; Psalm 9:1–12; Proverbs 19:1–3

David's Mighty Men

These were the men who came to David at Ziklag … Then the Spirit came upon Amasai, chief of the Thirty, and he said: "We are yours, O David! We are with you, O son of Jesse! Success, success to you, and success to those who help you, for your God will help you."
—1 Chronicles 12:1,18

Every excellent leader has valiant qualities. One of those qualities is that he attracts valiant followers. David surrounded himself with quality people. These mighty men became a supporting cast who stood by David and behind his leadership.

1 Chronicles 11-12 list some of David's mighty men and their exploits. It's exciting to read their stories. There were the Thirty chiefs, known as "the Thirty." They were the highest ranking officers in David's army. They weren't people who were given a title, but earned their place by doing. They were courageous and distinguished. Each were ambidextrous, skilled warriors. They risked their lives to see David succeed as king over all Israel. Their allegiance was unquestioned. *"David became more and more powerful, because the Lord Almighty was with him" (11:9).* These men knew God's favor was upon David.

Here, also, the Spirit of God came upon Amasai, chief of the Thirty. The Holy Spirit empowered David's mighty men to do great exploits. In the church of Jesus Christ, there are mighty men of faith who earn their stripes every day. They do battle against the wiles of the enemy with eyes wide open. They are empowered by the Spirit and walk in God's favor. These are the ones that inspire me to fight the good fight.

Father, thank You for those mighty men of faith who serve You today. Enable me to be mighty for Your cause. Unite believers everywhere to join in the battle. Empower Your remnant, the church, in these last days. Amen.

July 12

1 Chronicles 12:19–14:17; Romans 1:1–17; Psalm 9:13–20; Proverbs 19:4–5

The Power of God

I am not ashamed of the gospel, because it is the power of God for the salvation of everyone who believes: first for the Jew, then for the Gentile. For in the gospel a righteousness from God is revealed, a righteousness that is by faith from first to last, just as it is written, "The righteous will live by faith."
—Romans 1:16–17

Paul hasn't been to Rome yet, but he intends to. From where he is in Corinth, he has heard of the faith of the believers there and proceeds to articulate his case for the gospel as clear as any that has been told.

Paul's apostolic heart longs to establish these believers on a bedrock of truth. He wants to impart to them a spiritual gift to make them strong. He prays for them continuously, at all times.

The gospel Paul proclaims hinges upon Christ Jesus, the one promised by the prophets and declared to be the Son of God through the Spirit with power by his resurrection. Paul was eager to share this news.

This message is the power of God for the salvation of everyone who will believe, a life-changing power to set free and pardon. No other gospel can impart a righteousness to cleanse and forgive. This right-standing before God is received by all who will simply believe.

Faith in Christ is the gospel. It has the power to change you from the inside out. It is no more difficult than that. There are no extra hoops to jump through. It's accepting what Jesus did for you. You are among those He has called. Will you simply believe and trust Jesus now?

Father God, thank You for sending us Your Son, so that we might be forever changed. I receive Your free gift of salvation by faith in Jesus alone. Now help me to live this life every day by faith and trust and believing. Amen.

July 13

1 Chronicles 15:1–16:36; Romans 1:18–32; Psalm 10:1–15; Proverbs 19:6–7

We are Without Excuse

For since the creation of the world God's invisible qualities—his eternal power and divine nature—have been clearly seen, being understood from what has been made, so that men are without excuse.
—Romans 1:20

The bedrock of truth that Paul must begin with is the very fact that all men are without excuse. There is a basic knowledge and instinct of God built into what we all are witness to—there is an intelligent design to this created order. Look around. Someone higher is responsible. The majesty of creation shouts the glory of it's Creator.

The problem is that man has chosen to suppress the truth by their wickedness. They initially like their sin and the freedom to sin, and are deceived by it. They don't want someone else bringing the truth to bear. Suppressing the truth leads to darkened hearts and futile thinking. This cycle leads to God giving them over to shameful lusts and a depraved mind. The expression of this indulgence is every imaginable sin. They exchange the truth of God for a lie. The end result is that they not only tolerate wickedness, but they invent new ways to express sin and they approve of those who participate. The list of sins in this chapter is numerous. God's name for them is *fool*.

The appropriate response is to marvel at His handiwork and give glory to God, to thank Him for His power displayed and retain the knowledge of God. To respond with what knowledge that you have is all that you can do. And that is enough, until God unveils more.

Father in heaven, You have displayed Your glory in the creation You have made. It leads me to inquire of You and to desire to know You more. Reveal Yourself in ever-increasing ways, I pray. Amen.

July 14

1 Chronicles 16:37–18:17; Romans 2:1–24; Psalm 10:16–18; Proverbs 19:8–9

God's Kindness

Do you show contempt for the riches of his kindness, tolerance and patience, not realizing that God's kindness leads you toward repentance? To those who by persistence in doing good seek glory, honor and immortality, he will give eternal life. But for those who follow evil ... there will be wrath and anger.
—Romans 2:4,7–8

God's judgment is the major theme here (vv.3,5–6,16). On that day, God's righteous judgment will be revealed. He will give to each person according to what he has done. It is a blessing for the people of God—glory, honor and peace (v.10). But for the self-seeking and stubborn, wrath and anger await (v.8).

Left to ourselves, we have no leg to stand on regarding righteousness. We are on the wrong side of a great gulf between a holy God and lost humanity. *But enter the kindness of God.* Paul explains God's move to bring us closer together as the riches of His kindness and His tolerance and His patience. You see, God initiated the move. In His kindness, He made a way for us to be restored—through repentance.

Repentance reflects God's brilliance. How wise it is for God to reveal our true condition and then give us an out. Repentance simply acknowledges my lost condition and chooses to agree with God's viewpoint. I become grieved over my sin because it has separated me from God. I acknowledge my sin and I recognize my need for a Savior. Repentance is the decision of humbling myself before God so that I may receive His kind gift of salvation through Jesus. His love and persistence has wooed me to this place. I am forever grateful!

Father, You have enlightened me to see my true condition and still yet provide forgiveness of sins. You have displayed great patience in Your dealings with me. May I be as persistent in doing good for Your name. Amen.

July 15

1 Chronicles 19:1–21:30; Romans 2:25–3:8; Psalm 11:1–7; Proverbs 19:10–12

Overlooking an Offense

A man's wisdom gives him patience; it is to his glory to overlook an offense.
—*Proverbs 19:11*

We have all been offended by something that was said or what someone inferred. An offense can become personal real quick. Words spoken cannot be erased. But I also know that some people are easily offended. I have learned that if I take offense, then I have pride issues of my own to deal with. I don't need to get my flesh stirred up to respond back in a combative manner. The truth is that if I take offense, then I am allowing a wall to be built, a wall that separates even the closest of friends. If I overlook the offense, I give the offender an opportunity to rebound. I give him the benefit of the doubt. Perhaps there are circumstances beneath the surface that provoked the response. Perhaps there was an element of truth that I need to consider. And sometimes, you just need to extend some mercy.

Now, I am not saying that you should turn your back on sins that need to be confronted. But the Holy Spirit will deal with the offender. He will choose whom He will use to bring correction. For that person, to speak the truth in love in a timely manner can bring healing.

Just yesterday, we noted the patience and tolerance of God linked with His kindness. God has every right to pull the plug and execute judgment. We are worthy of that. But He is patient towards us. Aren't you glad? That is the same patience we need in our dealings with fallen humanity. *"He is patient with you, not wanting anyone to perish, but everyone to come to repentance"* (2 Peter 3:9).

Father God, I have been quick to judge at times in my life, but I thank You for not giving up on me. You have extended mercy to me time and time again. I ask that You continue to conform me to the image of Your Son. Amen.

July 16

1 Chronicles 22:1–23:32; Romans 3:9–31; Psalm 12:1–8; Proverbs 19:13–14

Knowing My Condition

As it is written: "There is no one righteous, not even one ..." But now a righteousness from God has been made known. This righteousness from God comes through faith in Jesus Christ to all who believe.
—Romans 3:10, 21–22

A central truth to salvation, before we can appreciate it's value, is the understanding that no one is righteous before God on his or her own merits. Jew and Gentile alike are all under sin. It's a disease we are born into and affected by. Paul echoes the sentiment of Psalm 14: No one is innocent. We are all guilty. We have together become corrupt.

Many falsely believe that we are not so bad. *I'm a pretty good person!* After all, we have been made in God's image. He has tied a great worth to us and His love towards us is immeasurable. While these statements are true, we don't have a right standing before God based on our own good behavior. Paul states that we have all sinned. Adam and Eve began the downward spiral, but I have continued the trend pretty well. Resident in me is sin and a sinful tendency that leaves me guilty before a holy God. I have fallen short of His glory. I am in need of God's remedy. Acknowledging my true condition is a prerequisite. If I don't see my sin as an issue, then Jesus' sacrifice was needless.

When I see that my sin is a big deal, then I can marvel at the love that God extends to me through the sending of His Son Jesus. I was deserving of judgment, but He took the punishment in my place. His sacrifice atoned for my sin. I was declared "not guilty" by placing my trust in Christ. I was *justified.* That means that God now sees me as *"just-as-if-I'd"* never sinned. My sins were wiped from the record.

Father, I acknowledge my great need for You. Thank You for loving me enough to send Jesus. I receive forgiveness as a benefit of the cross. Amen.

July 17

1 Chronicles 24:1–26:11; Romans 4:1–12; Psalm 13:1–6; Proverbs 19:15–16

The Ministry of Prophesying

David, together with the commanders of the army, set apart some of the sons of Asaph, Heman and Jeduthun for the ministry of prophesying, accompanied by harps, lyres and cymbals.
—1 Chronicles 25:1

Reread the first seven verses. Try to imagine the worship in the temple with the many varied elements involved. Skilled musicians are playing guitars and harps unto the Lord. The music stirs the heart to worship. The presence of the Lord is keenly felt. Worship leaders proclaim the word of the Lord in a melody. It's a vibrant atmosphere that feeds your spirit. The congregation is edified.

This scene is not unlike the worship we long for in our gatherings today. What matters is that God is exalted and His presence is manifest. But, just as with David, what we do for the Lord should be done with skill and integrity. If it's worth doing, it's worth doing well. This was not a concert. This was about presenting a precious offering.

It is in the worship of the Lord, many times, when God will speak a word to strengthen, encourage and comfort *(1 Corinthians 14:3)*. This is called prophecy. A person who is hearing God speak is used as a mouthpiece to speak God's heart to that body of believers.

Here, sons were being raised up by their fathers to hear the word of the Lord. They were trained to listen. They were accountable for their words. Twenty-four teams of twelve were developed and honed to make worship the centerpiece of their culture. Are you active in the worship of our God? Have you heard Him speak to you?

God of glory, I want my worship to honor You. I want to offer You a sacrifice of praise that is a fragrant offering. Stir my spirit. Speak to me. Amen.

July 18

1 Chronicles 26:12–27:34; Romans 4:13–5:5; Psalm 14:1–7; Proverbs 19:17

Access to Grace

Therefore, since we have been justified through faith, we have peace with God through our Lord Jesus Christ, through whom we have gained access by faith into this grace in which we now stand.
—Romans 5:1–2

Don't you love the way Paul writes? He lays out monumental thoughts with a small amount of words. Consider his first full sentence …

Therefore, because Abraham was fully persuaded that God would keep His promise, we are likewise credited with righteousness for believing in the One who raised Jesus from the dead. We are justified—made righteous—through this 'believing' in God. Because we have been given right standing, we have peace with God. This peace was granted because the Lord Jesus removed our sins. Through Jesus, also, we gain access into His grace when we trust Him. It is in His grace that we find our identity. We stand in the realm of God's acceptance, a favor that we do not deserve. *That is just the first sentence.*

We can also rejoice in hope. When life throws us a curve ball, we can rejoice because God doesn't waste an opportunity to build us up. Hope in God never disappoints. God has poured out His love into our hearts by the Holy Spirit, who dwells within us. We are never alone.

Think about the divine exchange we have encountered. I had nothing to offer God except my wretchedness. All I do is say 'Yes' to God, and He forgives the sin and floods me with righteousness, peace, love, acceptance, favor, hope and the Holy Spirit. *What an incredible deal!*

God of hope, when I consider my options, I am a fool not to accept Your kind gift. Your Son provides right standing and Your Spirit resides within. Amen.

July 19

1 Chronicles 28:1–29:30; Romans 5:6–21; Psalm 15:1–5; Proverbs 19:18–19

David's Final Charge

"Now, who is willing to consecrate himself today to the Lord? I know, my God, that you test the heart and are pleased with integrity. All these things have I given willingly and with honest intent. O Lord ... keep this desire in the hearts of your people forever, and keep their hearts loyal to you.
—1 Chronicles 29:5,17–18

David gathers all the officials, commanders and warriors of Israel together to formally converge the kingdom onto his son Solomon. One major point of unresolved business, as far as David is concerned, is the building of the Temple for the Lord. The Lord had put it in David's heart to build, but it would be carried out by his son Solomon. David wanted the leaders of Israel to become as passionate about the building of the Temple as he was, and he took up an offering. *"Who is willing to consecrate himself today to the Lord and this cause?"*

The people gave willingly and wholeheartedly to the Lord. The response was especially gratifying to David. He embraced the moment and praised the Lord before them. *"We have only given what comes from Your hand anyways" (v.14).* Yet God loves a willing heart.

There are Kodak moments of consecration that we have in life that we will never forget. This was one. If we could hold onto this moment forever! That is precisely why David prayed, *"Keep this desire in the hearts of your people forever, and keep their hearts loyal to you."* After the moment is gone, let loyalty become the reality of their consecration. That is my prayer today—that I will continue to serve the Lord with desire, with integrity and with loyalty.

Father in heaven, I consecrate my life to You. Let me serve You in good times and bad with desire and passion. When my heart is tested, let me be found faithful. Yours is the greatness and the power and the glory forever. Amen.

July 20

Know—Count—Offer

For we know that our old self was crucified with him so that ... we should no longer be slaves to sin. In the same way, count yourselves dead to sin but alive to God in Christ Jesus. Do not offer the parts of your body to sin, as instruments of wickedness, but rather to God as instruments of righteousness.
—Romans 6:6,11,13

This is Christianity 101. Paul reveals to us how we must deal with the old desires of the flesh. If you haven't noticed, we are often lured to abandon our new identity and settle for what we always knew. Paul knows the condition well—we are weak in our natural selves.

First, *know.* I recall to mind what I know is true of me. I am united with Christ, so my old self was crucified with Him. I am no longer a slave to sin, as I once was. I've been freed from that stranglehold. We have died to sin, so we are not obligated to live in it any longer.

Then, *count.* This step puts feet to what you know. Now you consider it so. I like the New King James rendition: reckon it so. It's your judgment and determination to employ this decision. We know it's true. Now we employ the truth in our mind. We are dead to sin, therefore I will not bow to those evil desires.

Lastly, *offer.* We have also been united with Christ in His resurrection. Now I can offer every part of my body to him as instruments of righteousness. I have made the determination. Now I offer myself to God for His glory. This offering leads to holiness. It doesn't happen overnight. But it does happen. You'll find that what you once used to love, now you hate and what you once used to hate, now you love.

Father, thank You for transformation. Help me to recall daily that You have called me to life, so I will leave my old self behind. My body is Yours. Amen.

July 21

2 Chronicles 4:1–6:11; Romans 7:1–13; Psalm 17:1–15; Proverbs 19:22–23

God's Prescribed Worship

All the Levites who were musicians—Asaph, Heman, Jeduthun and their sons and relatives—stood ... dressed in fine linen and playing cymbals, harps and lyres. The trumpeters and singers joined in unison, as with one voice, to give praise and thanks to the Lord and sang: "He is good; his love endures forever."
—2 Chronicles 5:12–13

This was a holy moment to be sure. The temple of the Lord was now complete and the ark of the Lord's covenant was placed in the inner sanctuary, the Most Holy Place. It was time to worship.

The appropriate worship model was established by David. We read of it in 1 Chronicles 23. Of the Levites, four thousand were separated to praise the Lord with the musical instruments. We saw the importance of music in worship, also, in 1 Chronicles 25. Today, we see the fruit of David's order. The musicians—with many types of instruments—and singers joined in unison, with one voice, to give praise and thanks to God. The song they raised their voices to was the most sung phrase in all the Bible: *"He is good; his love endures forever."*

The elements of skilled instrumentation, vocal singers praising and giving thanks in unity to worship the Lord of glory are all essential aspects of worship—none of which should be diminished. There is something holy about worship offered up in His prescribed way. The result was the glory of the Lord in a visible cloud filling the temple.

The heart was created to worship, and the Lord is worthy of all honor and glory that we may proclaim. He actually seeks worshippers who will worship in spirit and truth. What offering will you bring today?

Father of glory, You are good and Your love endures forever. You are worthy of all honor. With my voice, I offer a sacrifice of praise to You. Amen.

July 22

2 Chronicles 6:12–8:10; Romans 7:14–8:8; Psalm 18:1–15; Proverbs 19:24–25

Two Laws at Work

Through Christ Jesus the law of the Spirit of life set me free from the law of sin and death. Those who live according to the sinful nature have their minds set on what that nature desires; but those who live in accordance with the Spirit have their minds on what the Spirit desires. The mind of sinful man is death, but the mind controlled by the Spirit is life and peace;
—Romans 8:2,5–6

We know the tension all too well. We want to follow wholeheartedly after God. We actually delight in God's law. But there is another law that assaults my mind. It wants to make me a prisoner of the sin I was prone to. *Who will rescue me from this body of sin?*

The good news is that through the sacrifice of Jesus, we are no more obligated to the bondage of sin. It's a strong pull, just as the law of gravity is a strong pull. It's very real. But a new law comes into play that releases me from it's grip. It's called living according to the Spirit.

Now the law of sin and death does not go away. The pull is still there, but now I have an out. When I choose to set my mind on what the Spirit desires—when I surrender control to the Spirit of God—then life and peace result. Gravity is strong. That law does not go away. But the law of aerodynamics is stronger, and I am able to fly unencumbered. I am able to overcome the sinful inclinations by the Spirit of God.

We have been freed from a bondage that has always enslaved us. Praise God, there is no more condemnation. Christ Jesus has declared us "not guilty." We are freed from sin and empowered to do His will.

Father God, I rejoice in the power of the cross to set me free from sin's hold. I rejoice, also, in the power of the Spirit that enables me to live above the pull of sin. I pledge my mind to what the Spirit desires. In Jesus' name, Amen.

July 23

2 Chronicles 8:11–10:19; Romans 8:9–21; Psalm 18:16–36; Proverbs 19:26

Led by the Spirit

You, however, are controlled not by the sinful nature, but by the Spirit, if the Spirit of God lives in you. And if the Spirit of him who raised Jesus from the dead is living in you, he will also give life to your mortal bodies through his Spirit, who lives in you. Those who are led by the Spirit ... are sons of God.
   —*Romans 8:9,11,14*

Please embrace this truth: *The Spirit of God lives within you.* Understand also the difference between my spirit (little "s") and the Spirit of God (big "S"). We, as human beings, are each created with a spirit. Until we come to faith in Christ, our spirit is dead. When we say "Yes" to Jesus, our spirit is made alive by the Holy Spirit, who comes to reside within us. It's a remarkable truth. It changes everything.

Look at what Paul declares since the Spirit has come to dwell within. When the Spirit lives in you, you turn over the reins of control—from the sinful nature to that of the Spirit. My spirit is alive because of righteousness. He is the same Spirit who raised Jesus from the dead. Because the Spirit dwells within me, He will give life to my mortal body. When I live according to the Spirit of God, I am enabled to put to death the misdeeds of the body. When I do, I truly live as He intended. Because I am led by the Spirit of God, I am declared to be a son of God. I have received the Spirit of sonship. God's Spirit has united with my spirit to give witness that I am indeed a child of God. The Spirit of the living God is uniquely positioned within me to make all the difference in my life.

There is a lot to grasp in this text. Meditate upon it and allow your mind to embrace more. But true life is realized when the Spirit leads.

Abba, You have made me to be Your son. I am what I am because Your Spirit has come to reside in my heart. I give You full rein of my life. Amen.

July 24

2 Chronicles 11:1–13:22; Romans 8:22–39; Psalm 18:37–50; Proverbs 19:27–29

Prayer Support

The Spirit helps us in our weakness. We do not know what we ought to pray for, but the Spirit himself intercedes for us with groans that words cannot express ... the Spirit intercedes for the saints in accordance with God's will. Christ Jesus ... is at the right hand of God and is also interceding for us.
—Romans 8:26–27,34

There are some magnificent promises in this writing. It seems a shame to pick on only a few. But I am struck with what God has purposed me to be, and He gives me what I need to own it. All three members of the Godhead are involved in making me to be more than a conqueror.

God knows my weakness. I do not even, in myself, realize the power that my prayers to God have! So the Spirit of God helps me in my weakness. I do not always know how or what to pray for, but the Spirit does. Imagine that ... the Holy Spirit intercedes on my behalf in accordance with God's will. He takes my feeble, yet earnest prayer, and brings it before the Father in a passionate way, beyond words. I am comforted by that and now have an increased confidence in my prayer life. But there's more ...

Jesus—who died and was raised to life—is at the right hand of the Father also interceding for me. *Are you kidding me?* I am set up to win. Absolutely nothing can separate us from the love of God that is in Christ Jesus our Lord. I know that God is for me, and prayer is my communication line to the Father. I have all the help I need to win the battles and challenges that I will face in this life.

Father God, You do all things well. You have a plan for me to become conformed to the image of Your Son and You have given me the tools to accomplish Your will in this life. Thank You for the active support of Your Spirit and Your Son. Amen.

July 25

2 Chronicles 14:1–16:14; Romans 9:1–21; Psalm 19:1–14; Proverbs 20:1

The Eyes of the Lord

For the eyes of the Lord range throughout the earth to strengthen those whose hearts are fully committed to him.
—2 Chronicles 16:9

King Asa led Judah for forty–one years. It was said of him that his heart was fully committed to the Lord all his life—at least until then. After the first ten years of his rule, Zerah the Cushite marched out against Asa and his army. Asa was clearly overmatched, but he called on the Lord, and He answered in a big way. He struck down the Cushites, a benchmark event in Asa's reign. In his zeal to seek the Lord, Asa is given rest from his enemies until the thirty-sixth year.

Then again, a foe encroaches upon Judah. This time it is Baasha, king of Israel. But instead of relying upon the Lord as he had done before, Asa sought a treaty with Ben-Hadad, king of Aram, for assistance. Win or lose was not the issue. Asa had sought a human solution rather than from God. Hanani is the prophet who confronted Asa:

My paraphrase would go something like this: *"You used to rely upon the Lord. You, of all people, know the delivering power of the Lord. The eyes of the Lord search the world over to show Himself strong to those whose hearts are loyal to Him. That was you, Asa, at one time!"*

Over the span of Asa's life, he was fully committed, and then he wasn't. Somewhere along the line his vibrant faith faded. He knew the power of God, but he did not continue seeking. He did not keep his hand to the plow. I've seen it before—and it scares me—as we age we somehow think we can shift into neutral and coast on past glories.

Father, You are there in every season of my life to show Yourself strong with every act of faith. May I be found loyal for the duration and finish well. Amen.

July 26

2 Chronicles 17:1–18:34; Romans 9:22–10:13; Psalm 20:1–9; Proverbs 20:2–3

Confess and Believe

But what does it say? "The word is near you; it is in your mouth and in your heart," that is, the word of faith we are proclaiming: That if you confess with your mouth, "Jesus is Lord," and believe in your heart that God raised him from the dead, you shall be saved. For it is with your heart that you believe and are justified, and it is with your mouth that you confess and are saved.
  —*Romans 10:8–10*

If there was ever a passage to spell it all out, here Paul makes plain the steps to receive salvation. Paul addresses salvation for the Jews *and* for the Gentiles— obtaining a righteousness that is by faith. Paul's desire is for his fellow Jews. They are zealous for God, but they have not submitted to God's righteousness through Christ. They had sought to establish their own righteousness through laws and traditions.

Paul references Moses *(Deuteronomy 30:11-14)* to bring home his point about Christ. This is my paraphrase: *"What I am asking of you today is not difficult or beyond you. God's salvation has been made available and is within your grasp. God has drawn you to this point. The word is near you— it is in your mouth and in your heart. The faith I am speaking of comes by confessing with your tongue that Christ is Lord and believing in your heart that God raised Him from the dead. There are no hoops to jump through. It is no more complicated than that."*

Jesus is the object of our salvation. We cannot know God apart from Christ. He fulfilled the law and accomplished what the law could not.

I am also impressed with the protocol to believe and confess. They are both so essential. But no one knows you believe if you don't confess it and proclaim it. Proclamation, by nature, is very powerful.

Father God, I believe you raised Jesus and I confess it from the rooftops! Amen.

July 27

2 Chronicles 19:1–20:37; Romans 10:14–11:12; Psalm 21:1–13; Proverbs 20:4–6

Not My Battle

Then the Spirit of the Lord came upon Jahaziel … He said, "Listen, King Jehoshaphat … This is what the Lord says: 'Do not be afraid or discouraged because of this vast army. For the battle is not yours, but God's … Take your positions; stand firm and see the deliverance the Lord will give you…'"
—2 Chronicles 20:14–15,17

Sometimes we face struggles that are clearly bigger than we are. We didn't invite it or deserve it. We're just minding our own business, but there it is before us anyways. This was Jehoshaphat's dilemma.

The Moabites, Ammonites and Meunites combine to make war on Jehoshaphat. The king is alarmed and quickly resolves to inquire of the Lord and calls a fast for all of Judah. His prayer is earnest. He reminds God of His promises and His past deliverance. But the king is up against a wall here. He is at a loss of what to do. While they were all assembled, the Spirit of the Lord came upon Jahaziel. He spoke prophetically the word that God gave him: *"Do not be afraid. The battle is not yours, but God's. Take up your positions. Go through the motions, but you will not have to fight this battle"* (my paraphrase).

With the word of the Lord proclaimed, instead of being distressed and filled with anxiety, now the people of Judah were encouraged and very relieved. All of Judah bowed low to worship the Lord. That next morning, the army of Judah was led out confidently with praise and singing. The Lord, true to His word, performed a miraculous victory.

Agree with God. It's not your battle to carry. Lay it down and let Him replace your worry with confidence and rejoicing. It's His battle!

God of glory, there are battles that need Your attending. They are bigger than me, but are nothing to You. Replace my fears with Your word. Amen.

July 28

2 Chronicles 21:1–23:21; Romans 11:13–36; Psalm 22:1–18; Proverbs 20:7

A Doxology

Oh, the depth of the riches of the wisdom and knowledge of God! How unsearchable his judgments, and his paths beyond tracing out! Who has known the mind of the Lord? Or who has been his counselor? Who has ever given to God, that God should repay him? For from him and through him and to him are all things. To him be the glory forever! Amen.
—Romans 11:33–36

Paul inserts a doxology of praise, extolling the wisdom of God. Not coincidentally, it comes after he explains the wisdom of God's plan to extend mercy to the Jews after having extended mercy to the Gentiles.

Israel is the source of God's blessing. They are loved on account of the patriarchs. The root is holy, but there have been branches broken off because of unbelief. Because of their transgression, salvation has come to the Gentiles—in hopes to make Israel envious. God's kindness was extended to graft in the Gentiles by faith, even as a wild olive branch. But Israel can recover. If they will put away unbelief, they may be grafted back in, as natural branches. God's wisdom is that His mercy will come to all, but mercy only comes after disobedience.

Doxologies are strewn throughout the Bible intermittently. In the New Testament, as here in Romans, they are short, unique and spontaneous expressions of praise to God for an aspect of His divine nature. It may have been sung as a hymn, as many are sung in worship circles today. Paul draws from Isaiah and Job in an eloquent writing to laud the wisdom and justice of God. Power and wisdom belong to Him. God alone is worthy to be praised.

Father, it is fitting to pause and give You praise for Your wisdom and Your mercy. Thank You for the kindness You have extended to Gentiles throughout the world. Bring Your plan for the Jews, whom You love, to fruition. Amen.

July 29

2 Chronicles 24:1–25:28; Romans 12:1–21; Psalm 22:19–31; Proverbs 20:8–10

Be Transformed

Therefore, I urge you, brothers, in view of God's mercy, to offer your bodies as living sacrifices, holy and pleasing to God—this is your spiritual act of worship. Do not conform any longer to the pattern of this world, but be transformed by the renewing of your mind.
　　—Romans 12:1–2a

I remember well Derek Prince used to say: *"If there is a 'therefore,' you need to see what it's there for!"* Paul takes us to a pinnacle in these verses, and it begins by looking back upon God's mercy, that he had just previously mentioned in chapter eleven. *"Therefore, in view of the fact that God had mercy on us in our disobedience, we ought to offer our bodies to God."* God's mercy gives me another chance. God's mercy means not giving me the judgment I deserved. I would say God's mercy is a good basis to offer anything you have back to God.

Aren't you glad Paul included the word "living" before "sacrifices?" But we already knew that Christ was the fulfillment of the sacrificial system. *Yay!* Paul brings us back to what we saw already in chapter six *(July 20)*—where we *know*, then we *count*, and then we *offer*. It is underscored again, in light of God's mercy, that we can offer the parts of our bodies to God as instruments of righteousness. Here, we see that God considers it a holy act that pleases Him. That's incredible!

Paul shows us in verse two what the two polar opposites produce. Our life used to be given to *conforming* to the whims of the world. These whims are always changing with the wind and rely upon what pop culture dictates. True *transformation*, on the other hand, comes by renewing our minds with the truth of God's Word over and over. This transformation process changes us from the inside out for real.

Father, I pledge my body as a living sacrifice and my mind for truth. Amen.

July 30

2 Chronicles 26:1–28:27; Romans 13:1–14; Psalm 23:1–6; Proverbs 20:11

Love Fulfills the Law

Give everyone what you owe him. Let no debt remain outstanding, except the continuing debt to love one another, for the one who loves his fellowman has fulfilled the law. The commandments are summed up in this one rule: "Love your neighbor as yourself."
—Romans 13:7–9

I have always considered this good advice way before I got to the part about loving my neighbor. I always got caught up on the line, *"Let no debt remain outstanding."* I need that direct approach for my finances! But there is a further point to be made, isn't there.

Paul says: *"Give everyone what you owe him or what is due him."* So if you know someone who is worthy of honor, don't hold back. If someone is due respect, then you be the first to give it. James says: *"Anyone who knows the good he ought to do and doesn't do it, sins" (4:17).* Yet, there is one debt that is constant and remains, and that is to love one another.

Why this obligation? *That's easy.* Think of the magnitude of Christ's love poured out upon you! That's why Paul sums up his point with the greatest commandment Jesus gave us: *"Love your neighbor as yourself."* It's actually the love of God—that changes my heart—that allows me to love another. I can't even love on my own. It's His reservoir of love I draw from that never runs dry. When I love sincerely, as a response to His love toward me, then my love is not selfish in order to get. Love gives, in order to be a blessing. By loving my neighbor, I fulfill the law of God. And when I love, it becomes less and less of an obligation. Christ's love motivates me. God's love compels me to love genuinely.

Father, when I consider the love that You have lavished upon me, I want to love You back. Loving others is the best way I can show You my love. Amen.

July 31

2 Chronicles 29:1–36; Romans 14:1–23; Psalm 24:1–10; Proverbs 20:12

The Kingdom of God

For the kingdom of God is not a matter of eating and drinking, but of righteousness, peace and joy in the Holy Spirit.
—Romans 14:17

This is such a practical passage on how to conduct ourselves with others in the faith, since we are all at different places in our walk with the Lord. It's easy to cast your own convictions onto others as the one correct version. But Paul says, concerning those who may be weaker than you are, if it is a disputable matter, then withhold your judgment of that person. God has accepted him and is not finished with him.

Now concerning your points of view, it is equally important that you be fully convinced in your mind. Know what you believe and why you believe it. The Holy Spirit helps you form those convictions. You will stand before the Lord and give an account for the revelation you received and your manner of obedience. But concerning things that are not critical to points of salvation, be careful to cast judgment on your brother. It may be something you feel strongly about, and that's for your benefit—between you and God. The point of our passage is that you don't want to be a cause for your brother to stumble.

The bottom line is what the kingdom *is* about. The kingdom of God is the rule of God in my life that takes expression in righteous choices. It's about being governed and led by His peace. It's about knowing the joy that comes from a life in the Holy Spirit. There are too many aspects of our faith that we can share together that bring about mutual edification. Don't get stuck on the finer points that may matter more to you. We are not a finished product yet either!

Father, I thank You for what You have taught me by the Holy Spirit. I won't trade those convictions for anything. Help me to encourage others. Amen.

August 1

2 Chronicles 30:1–31:21; Romans 15:1–22; Psalm 25:1–15; Proverbs 20:13–15

Endurance and Encouragement

For everything written in the past was written to teach us, so that through endurance and the encouragement of the Scriptures we might have hope. May the God who gives endurance and encouragement give you a spirit of unity …
—Romans 15:4–5

A theme that has been a thread through several chapters now is to grant mercy to others, not to judge those weaker, extend love to your neighbor, and here, actually to bear with the failings of the weak. Accept one another, just as Christ accepted you. This will promote a spirit of unity among the family of God—that brings praise to God.

Endurance and encouragement are the words that jump out in these verses. Endurance and encouragement is the goal of the Scriptures for us to draw upon. All the stories and testimonies of God's faithfulness throughout the Old Testament give us hope that we, too, can endure the challenges and battles that engage our faith. We can do this! We are encouraged by the saints of old. If God can use Elijah, for example, who was just a man like us, then I am encouraged that God will answer *my* prayers, as well *(James 5:17)*. It is God who encourages us and strengthens us to endure, so that we can encourage others in the faith and bear with their weaknesses.

The end result is hope. Through endurance and the encouragement of the Scriptures we have hope. And again, it is God who is the God of hope. He is the Author. We overflow with hope by the power of the Holy Spirit who dwells within us. The reservoir that we draw from to love is the reservoir we draw from to hope. It overflows to others.

Father of glory, Your Word encourages me to endure this race. I am filled with hope as I see Your faithfulness over and over. Use me to be a blessing. Amen.

August 2

2 Chronicles 32:1–33:13; Romans 15:23–16:7; Psalm 25:16–22; Proverbs 20:16

Too Far Gone?

He (Manasseh) sacrificed his sons in the fire … practiced sorcery, divination and witchcraft. He did much evil in the eyes of the Lord, provoking him to anger. In his distress he sought the favor of the Lord his God and humbled himself. The Lord was moved by his entreaty and listened to his plea …
—2 Chronicles 33:6,12–13

Manasseh was a vile king. His credentials are many. He was not only wicked, but he led all of Judah and the people of Jerusalem astray. He promoted sin and rebellion. He "undid" the good that his father had established. He provoked the Lord to anger. That's like staring God in the face and saying, "I dare you to do something about it!" If there was ever a single person who you could argue that there was absolutely no hope for, you'd be talking about Manasseh. He actually sacrificed his own sons to pagan gods on the altar.

And yet, the Lord spoke to Manasseh and his people, but they paid no attention. He sent prophets with the word of the Lord, and to no avail. God gave Manasseh every opportunity to turn. But with Manasseh, like many of us, we have to receive a measure of God's judgment to know who it is we are dealing with. God justly brought correction to Manasseh when he was taken captive by the Assyrians to Babylon.

It was here, in his darkest hour, that he humbled himself before the Lord. It is heartfelt repentance that gained God's attention. He listened to Manasseh's prayer and was moved by it. Is there ever anyone too far gone that they have moved beyond God's hand of mercy? *Never.* It is how we know what mercy is.

Father, I pray for that one who seems beyond repair. Pursue their heart by Your Spirit as the hound of heaven. In Your kindness, bring them to repentance. Amen.

August 3

2 Chronicles 33:14–34:33, Romans 16:8–27, Psalm 26:1-12, Proverbs 20:17-19

Personal Greetings

Greet Priscilla and Aquila … Greet Andronicus and Junias … They are outstanding among the apostles, and they were in Christ before I was. Everyone has heard about your obedience, so I am full of joy over you; but I want you to be wise about what is good, and innocent about what is evil.
—Romans 16:3,7,19

Paul has finished his teaching points, and now ends his letter with personal greetings to those precious to him. He has not yet been to Rome, but he has worked with many who were from Rome and there are many who have impacted his life and ministry. With varied backgrounds, they are men and women who were tested and approved in the faith and were called out by Paul and commended for their service to the Lord. We'll note just a few.

Paul's list comprises all of chapter sixteen. Eleven of the twenty–nine are women. They were game-changers in the development of the early church. Phoebe led the way, a deaconess from the church in Cenchrea. Priscilla and Aquila were personal friends who ministered as a couple in Rome and Ephesus. Three are mentioned as relatives of Paul's. Another, Rufus' mother, was a mother to Paul, as well. One couple that stands out is Andronicus and Junias. These two were seasoned in the Lord, and had even spent time in prison for the sake of the gospel, with Paul. And it is noted that they, *both,* were outstanding among the apostles. They were acknowledged by their peer as leaders in the establishing and developing of the early church.

Perhaps you have people in your life who have impacted your faith. Right now is a good time to list them. Then personally thank them.

Father God, I cannot thank You enough for putting godly, committed people in my path that have influenced my life and called me to a higher place. Amen.

August 4

2 Chronicles 35:1–36:23; 1 Corinthians 1:1–17; Psalm 27:1–6; Proverbs 20:20–21

One Thing

One thing I ask of the Lord, this is what I seek: that I may dwell in the house of the Lord all the days of my life, to gaze upon the beauty of the Lord and to seek him in his temple.
—Psalm 27:4

In this Psalm, David declares the driving passion of his life.

In the context of being surrounded by enemies and evil men and the day of trouble, David affirms his confidence in the One who is able to conquer the fears and insecurities that ensue. It is often in the vulnerability of our weakness that we most recognize our need for God's intervention. We gain a right perspective.

In his desperate place, David was able to pin down the one thing that superseded all others as the desire of his heart. One affection preoccupied his mind—to dwell in the sweet presence of the Lord. Nothing else compares. Nothing else satisfies the longings of the soul. Once exposed to the richness of His presence, you are ruined for all that would vie for your allegiance. David knew the presence of the Lord. He spent hours and hours before the Lord—many times with guitar in hand. It was the basis for an intimate relationship with God that shaped his life forever. Look at the verbs of David's quest: to *dwell* (in His presence), to *gaze* (upon His beauty) and to *inquire* (of the Lord). You cannot be in a hurry to dwell and gaze and inquire.

To entertain God's presence every waking day is David's motivation. In your life today, what one thing do you desire above all else?

Father God, the longing of David's heart was fulfilled by Your presence. Cause me to accept nothing less. Let me gaze upon Your beauty. Give me a seeking heart. You long to dwell with me and I long to dwell with You. So be it.

217

August 5

Ezra 1:1–2:70; 1 Corinthians 1:18–2:5; Psalm 27:7–14; Proverbs 20:22–23

The Foolishness of God

*For the message of the cross is foolishness to those who are perishing, but to us who
are being saved it is the power of God. Jews demand miraculous signs and Greeks
look for wisdom, but we preach Christ crucified … Christ the power of God and the
wisdom of God …*
—1 Corinthians 1:18,22–24

The message of salvation through Jesus alone sounds foolish to many. That
notion has not changed through the years. Yet to us — we who are the recipients of
this great salvation—we are witness to the delivering power of God to transform.

The Jewish mindset saw the Messiah as a conquering king, but Jesus was
condemned as a criminal. The Greeks entertained mythological ideology
and eloquent speakers and called it wisdom. But again, death was not viewed
as a pathway to victory. For us, the cross is our leg to stand on. What Jesus
accomplished at the cross is why we stand uncondemned and forgiven. Jesus took
the penalty of my sin to the cross. He was the acceptable sacrifice that atoned for
sin once for all. The sin issue has been dealt with entirely. My part is simple faith.

The wisdom of the world cannot wrap their minds around this concept. There
must be more to it than that. *You must be good enough. You must earn your way to
the favor of God.* To a society that craves power and affluence, bowing in humility
to acknowledge Jesus is unthinkable. It sounds foolish to many, but repentance is
the wise plan of God. It is not such a hard thing to grasp—only to do.

*Father, thank You for Your plan of redemption, for Jesus' sinless life of obedience and
the sacrifice He made for my cleansing. Thank You for demonstrating Your power
over death and the grave by raising up Jesus to Your right hand in heaven. I bow my
knee and say "Yes" to Jesus. Amen.*

August 6

Ezra 3:1- 4:24; 1 Corinthians 2:6–3:4; Psalm 28:1–9; Proverbs 20:24–25

Returning from Captivity

Jeshua and his fellow priests and Zerubbabel ... began to build the altar of the God of Israel. When the builders laid the foundation of the temple, the priests with trumpets, and the Levites with cymbals, took their places to praise the Lord ... And all the people gave a great shout of praise to the Lord ...
   —Ezra 3:2,10–11

In fulfilling Jeremiah's prophecy, the Lord moved upon King Cyrus' heart to permit the Jewish people to return to their homeland in order to rebuild the temple in Jerusalem. This followed many years of captivity. Isaiah's prophecy (44:28-45:6) actually names Cyrus, written over a century prior. Once the initial group settled, the altar was built first and then the foundation of the temple was laid.

A celebration of praise followed the completion of the foundation. It was an extremely emotional occasion. For many, they were shouts of joy. Finally the temple was being restored back to it's central place. How could it be anything less? But for many of the older Levites, it was a weeping of sorrow, remembering the past glory of Solomon's temple. This temple would not hold the same grandeur, but it was a monumental step to restore their house of worship.

In the meantime, while progress was being made, jealousy arose among the enemies of Judah. They did not want to see the temple and the Jews become strong again. It's true that the adversary, Satan, hates any progress to advance the kingdom of God. His first line of attack is to accuse and discourage. That is always a sign that you're doing something right—when the enemy tries to hinder the work.

Father, Your word is true. You stirred the hearts of men to rebuild and restore after You brought a strong correction. I pray that you would undergird the people of God. Replace discouragement with courage and boldness. Amen.

August 7

Ezra 5:1–6:22; 1 Corinthians 3:5–23; Psalm 29:1–11; Proverbs 20:26–27

The Prophets Get Results

Now Haggai the prophet and Zechariah the prophet ... prophesied to the Jews in Judah and Jerusalem in the name of the God of Israel, who was over them. Then Zerubbabel and Jeshua set to work to rebuild the house of God in Jerusalem ... and they were not stopped until a report could go to Darius.
—Ezra 5:1–2,5

The work on the house of God had come to a standstill. The enemies of Judah who lived around them had set out to discourage the people of Judah—to cause them to fear, to intimidate them and frustrate their plans to build. For several years now they were held in limbo.

The prophets Haggai and Zechariah knew the mission God had given them—to rebuild and restore. They saw the bigger picture and encouraged them to resume and continue on. They also knew that they needed only to have the original documents revisited.

The prophets spoke the word of the Lord to strengthen, encourage and comfort *(1 Corinthians 14:3)*. But they also joined their fellow-Jews in the trenches to do the work. Most importantly, the eye of God was watching over them *(5:5)* in the midst of their trial. Besides all this, they knew the truth of the original edict. They acted on what was rightfully theirs. It only needed to be brought out into the light.

When the mission appeared impossible, the prophets helped them focus back to what God had called them to. No devil in hell can thwart the plans of God. What is the Lord encouraging you to persevere in?

Father God, You have a great mission for this season in my life. I embrace it and ask that Your Spirit would keep me focused on what's important to complete it. Direct me through the challenges I will face. Give me victory over my adversary. May Your name be praised and receive all the glory. Amen.

August 8

Ezra 7:1–8:20; 1 Corinthians 4:1–21; Psalm 30:1–12; Proverbs 20:28–30

Faithful to a Trust

Now it is required that those who have been given a trust must prove faithful. My conscience is clear, but that does not make me innocent. It is the Lord who judges me. He will bring to the light what is hidden in darkness and expose the motives of men's hearts. At that time each will receive his praise from God.
—1 Corinthians 4:2,4–5

Ultimately, I will answer to God for the trust He has given me. How I am deemed by others is inconsequential in light of the Giver of that trust. The Lord is my Judge. The Lord will also judge the fruit of another man's calling, not I. It's a matter of who we answer to.

Verse five holds a surprise! There will be a day and an hour when we will have an appointment with God—a conversation. He will bring to light what is hidden and expose the motives of my heart. What comes next is the surprise … I am ready to hear the judgment pronounced for the hidden sins I harbored or every wrong thought that whisked through my mind. Perhaps so, but that is what we conjure up when we hear the word *"judgment."* A more appropriate word may be *"accounting."* Because the end result of this encounter will be to receive a report from the accounting God made on the faithfulness of the trust He granted me. *At that time, I will receive praise from my God!*

God knows all the thoughts of our hearts. And He knows how you have desired to serve Him and love Him. He knows the fallenness of mankind. But He knows and delights in the thoughts You have harbored for His glory and honor, how you have longed for His righteousness in your life. Man cannot know these thoughts, but God knows each one, and He is a good accountant. Take heart.

Father God, I will answer to You alone. I consecrate my thoughts, desires and my body as an instrument of righteousness to bring You praise. Amen.

August 9

Ezra 8:21–9:15; 1 Corinthians 5:1–13; Psalm 31:1–8; Proverbs 21:1–2

Keep Your Distance

But now I am writing you that you must not associate with anyone who calls himself a brother but is sexually immoral or greedy, an idolater ... slanderer... drunkard or a swindler. With such a man do not even eat. What business is it of mine to judge those outside the church? Are you not to judge those inside?
—1 Corinthians 5:11–12

Corinth was a seaport city where immorality was rampant. Society's acceptance of sin had influenced many inside the church into compromise. When Paul received a report of sexual sin that had gone uncorrected, his message was clear: *Deal with the sin.* You cannot grow indifferent about something that will pollute the body of Christ.

We're not talking about the unbelievers of the world. You expect impurity from the impure. No, Paul is addressing those who profess to be believers and, yet, continue to indulge in sin that is expressly forbidden in Scripture. They justify their misbehavior and are not remorseful or repentant. In other words, they show no evidence that their confession is authentic. They have trampled underfoot the Son of God by their willful sin. (See also Hebrews 10:26-29.) Paul's exhortation is strong. To summarize, *"Don't ignore the obvious. Have nothing to do with that man. He is deceived and needs correction for there to be purity and unity in the body of Christ. Open sin cannot go unchecked."*

The larger issue is that, here, the Bible instructs us to judge and deal with those inside the church whose sins can dilute the faith of others. Confronting sin within is actually a strong hand of love. Who will love that one enough to yank them out of the fire *(Jude 23)*?

Father God, You said that we are to let our light so shine in a dark world, not to blend in and be like them. I pray that Your deliverance would be complete in my life. Let there be no grey areas of compromise. My delight is in You. Amen.

August 10

Ezra 10:1–44; 1 Corinthians 6:1–20; Psalm 31:9–18; Proverbs 21:3

My Body is a Temple

Flee from sexual immorality … he who sins sexually sins against his own body. Do you not know that your body is a temple of the Holy Spirit, who is in you, whom you have received from God? You are not your own; you were bought at a price. Therefore, honor God with your body.
—1 Corinthians 6:18–20

Some things necessarily need to be spelled out. The promiscuous culture of Corinth was very similar to ours today, and the message has an equal application. Engaging in sexual relations with prostitutes was a prominent aspect of the worship of the love goddess, Aphrodite. But no matter how socially acceptable it becomes, Paul explains that the body is not meant for sexual immorality—but for the Lord.

Paul refers to God's design in marriage, from Genesis 2:24, as when two committed people become one flesh. There is an undeniable bond that occurs when the sex act is consummated. Our culture today promotes the idea of "instant intimacy," but sex outside the covenant of marriage always has far-reaching harmful affects. But the union is real. That is why Paul declares that when we unite with the Lord, we are one in spirit. Our spirit is one with the Spirit of God.

Make no mistake—sexual sins are sins against your own body and the sexually immoral have no place in God's kingdom. Sexual promiscuity may have been a part of your past, but that can be forgiven. When you come to the Lord, you are cleansed and given right standing with God. Now your body is a housing, a temple, for the Spirit of God to dwell and operate in. You are not your own any more. Now, with the Holy Spirit's influence, you can honor God with your body.

Father God, my body is not my own any longer. I have been united with You in spirit, so I commit my members to Your Lordship. Amen.

August 11

Nehemiah 1:1–3:14; 1 Corinthians 7:1–24; Psalm 31:19–24; Proverbs 21:4

Nehemiah Responds

Hanani said … "Those who survived the exile and are back in the province are in great trouble and disgrace. The wall of Jerusalem is broken down, and its gates have been burned with fire." When I heard these things, I sat down and wept … I mourned and fasted and prayed before the God of heaven.
—Nehemiah 1:2–4

This story of the broken down wall and the broken down people of Judah seems so typical of the state of God's people throughout the Scriptures. They have already had two envoys return from exile to Jerusalem in order to reestablish the temple and their culture (in Ezra). And without the wall, they are defenseless. They are stuck.

But also typical throughout the Scriptures, God raises up a leader who will answer the call to bring deliverance and unite the people of God. Nehemiah was that man. Already in a position of leadership, Nehemiah hears the news report concerning Jerusalem and is grieved. His heart is gripped with what was gripping God's heart. He fasts and prays. He inquires of the Lord. *"What can I do?"*

Armed with the favor of the king (of Persia) and the mission of God, Nehemiah made the three month journey and went to work. He didn't make a big political announcement of the grand building plan. Instead, he examined the wall himself by night, to assess and proceed with a plan that took fifty-two days *(6:15)*. Nehemiah was undaunted by opposition that arose. He encouraged the Jews, saying, *"The God of heaven will give us success" (2:20)*. Nehemiah led by example, himself devoted to working on the wall *(5:16)*. And perhaps most notable was the way he organized all of Judah to join in the work. The detailed list of those contributing is incredible—common folk united for a cause.

God of heaven, the greatest ability I have is my availability to You. Amen.

August 12

Nehemiah 3:15–5:13; 1 Corinthians 7:25–40; Psalm 32:1–11; Proverbs 21:5–7

Nehemiah Stands Tall

They (the men of Ashdod) plotted together to come and fight against Jerusalem and stir up trouble ... But we prayed to our God and posted a guard day and night to meet this threat. When our enemies heard that we were aware of their plot and that God had frustrated it, we all returned to the wall ...
—Nehemiah 4:8–9,15

You've heard that the shortest man in the Bible is *Knee-high Miah,* right? Well, none stood higher than this man among leaders.

Nehemiah had the uncanny ability to engage everyone along the wall to repair the area in front of them properly and with pride. They each knew the importance of their role. How impressive it is to note the specific names and details of each contribution made, from Shallum's daughters *(3:12)* to Malkijah, one of the goldsmiths *(4:31).* *"The wall... reached half its height, for the people worked with all their heart" (4:6).*

When the enemies' jealousy was aroused, it was Nehemiah who had his spiritual ears perked to intercept their plans. He had a savvy tenacity to maneuver and stay ahead of the game, and still keep the people of Judah motivated to finish. Nehemiah's first response was always one of prayer. In each case, God would disclose the right response in order to frustrate the attacks.

Some of the attacks were mental and from physical exhaustion. Some of them were from being geographically separated from each other. There was even a significant challenge within their own ranks. But God used Nehemiah, in each scenario, to bring the calm. In each case, God proved to be awesome. Our God will fight for us!

God of glory, we sorely need men of integrity who will lead Your people today. Raise up men and women who will hear Your strategies to overcome. Amen.

August 13

Nehemiah 5:14–7:60; 1 Corinthians 8:1–13; Psalm 33:1–11; Proverbs 21:8–10

The Attacks Get Personal

I realized that God had not sent him (Shemaiah), but that he had prophesied against me because Tobiah and Sanballat had hired him. He had been hired to intimidate me so that I would commit a sin by doing this, and then they would give me a bad name to discredit me.
—Nehemiah 6:12–13

Leaders are always targets for attack. That's the nature of the beast. But when you are called to lead the people of God, it is more so, and you openly pose a threat to the enemies of God. When God has met every challenge made, a last strategy is used to discredit the integrity of God's servant. It gets personal. *Does the adversary never tire?*

Nehemiah had been appointed as the governor in the land of Judah. Out of reverence for God, he devoted his energy on the primary task of rebuilding the wall. Almost complete, now the governor of Samaria is desperate. Sanballat and his side-kick, Geshem, scheme up a plan to harm Nehemiah. Four times they attempt to arrange a meeting. Four times they are spurned. The fifth visit reveals their hand. It's a lie to generate fear. Nehemiah prays, "Now strengthen *my* hands" (6:9).

Some of the greatest discouragement to leaders comes from their own staffers who are not on-board. They have their own self-seeking agenda. Shemaiah was one who became a "Judas" for the other side. The prophetess Noadiah also tried her hand to intimidate. Other nobles sent letters of complaint. But Nehemiah discerned the scrutiny and the deceit. Hearing God and maintaining integrity in every decision was absolutely critical. And so the work was completed.

Father in heaven, grant discernment and favor to those who call upon Your name. Undergird Your leaders. Strengthen our hands. Receive all the glory. Amen.

August 14

Nehemiah 7:61–9:21; 1 Corinthians 9:1–18; Psalm 33:12–22; Proverbs 21:11–12

The Word is Prominent

*He (Ezra) read it (the Law) aloud from daybreak till noon as he faced the square ...
in the presence of the men, women and others who could understand. And all the
people listened attentively ... Then they bowed down and worshipped the Lord with
their faces to the ground.*
  —Nehemiah 8:3,6

It is refreshing to see the attention that is given to the reading of the Word of
God in a public place of worship. Much of what happened in this gathering is
what we design our worship services around today.

Once the Jews had settled in their towns, Nehemiah gathered the people together.
Ezra, the priest and scribe, led the Levite team of teachers to instruct the people
of Judah. The people all stood up when the book was opened. The people listened
attentively to the Book of the Law as it was read. When they heard the word
of the Lord, they were moved and they wept. They spent time in confession of
their sins. They would stand and call out with loud voices to the Lord their God.
They bowed down and worshiped the Lord with their faces to the ground. All
are appropriate responses when we gather together. Does your place of worship
give opportunity for any of these?

The one final activity had to do with obedience. You can make a covenant or
renew a promise, but until you do it, the unfaithfulness of your past overshadows
all good intentions. Here, Ezra gave them an opportunity to obey the word. They
found written in the Law that they were to live in booths during a feast in the
seventh month. When they obeyed the word, it was said that their joy was *very
great*. The response of active faith is answered by the great joy of the Lord.

*Father, restore to the church a holy reverence for Your name and Your Word. Let us
be moved to respond in obedience. Your joy is my strength. Amen.*

August 15

Nehemiah 9:22–10:39; 1 Corinthians 9:19–10:13; Psalm 34:1–10; Proverbs 21:13

Training and Temptation

Everyone who competes in the games goes into strict training. Therefore I do not run like a man running aimlessly;. No temptation has seized you except what is common to man. And God is faithful; he will not let you be tempted beyond what you can bear … he will also provide a way out.
—1 Corinthians 9:25–26; 10:13

I believe that the training we incorporate for preparation is inextricably tied to the temptation we must overcome. I have run in many races, but I've never run just to run. I have always ran with a goal to beat a previous best time. I was not an elite runner and I never won a race, but I was competitive in my age group and achieved satisfying results because of my strict training and work ethic. I was not aimless, but focused. I conditioned my body to produce results.

As believers, we have the Scriptures to show us the state of mankind from the past to the present. They were given us as examples to keep us from setting our hearts on evil things, as they themselves did. We all know what happened when they committed idolatry and sexual sin, and tested the Lord and grumbled. These are all temptations that we are prone to. Be careful. You are not above them.

The good news is that there is no unique temptation. The devil will try to tell you that yours is a special case. God will always provide a way of escape, so that you are not overwhelmed. That is providing that you have trained for the race and have resisted the easy way out. Temptation is going to happen, but temptation itself is not sin. Temptation is an opportunity to prove again the faithfulness of God. But continuing to fall to temptation disqualifies us from being an effective witness and from the prize of finishing well.

Father, I subject my body and mind to Your training and Lordship. Amen.

August 16

Nehemiah 11:1–36; 1 Corinthians 10:14–33; Psalm 34:11–22; Proverbs 21:14-16

Liberated to Love

"Everything is permissible"— but not everything is beneficial. "Everything is permissible"— but not everything is constructive. So whether you eat or drink or whatever you do, do it all for the glory of God. Do not cause anyone to stumble, whether Jews, Greeks or the church of God ...
    —1 Corinthians 10:23,31–32

An exciting truth as believers is that we have freedom in Christ. We no longer have to follow a set of rigid rules to determine our righteousness. Everything originates from God and is given for us to enjoy. I can eat my pulled pork sandwich with a glass of wine with gratitude. The tension comes when my liberty interferes with another brother's weaker conscience.

Matters of conscience are the principles we have been taught relating to right and wrong. Some things are expressly forbidden in Scripture, while others are not so clearly defined. But to an ex-alcoholic, that glass of wine may absolutely be out-of-bounds.

Paul gives us sound wisdom when he says that our overriding motive ought to be—in all things—to glorify God. Will this action I do be honoring to God? *And* ... can this action be misconstrued to cause another to stumble? It's a rule of love that precipitates our actions. I am free, yes, but will it promote the good of others. My guiding principle becomes being sensitive to those around me and graciously deferring if it does. There is nothing wrong with that glass of wine. But why would I put a stumbling block before my brother, whom I love and Christ died? What's interesting is that we can glorify God in all things, even in our eating and drinking.

Gracious Father, You have liberated me to serve You and to serve others. May my actions reflect my love for You while it is a blessing to others. Amen.

August 17

Nehemiah 12:1–13:31; 1 Corinthians 11:1–16; Psalm 35:1–16; Proverbs 21:17-18

Restoring Order

(I, Nehemiah) came back to Jerusalem. Here I learned about the evil thing Eliashib had done in providing Tobiah a room in the courts of the house of God. I was greatly displeased ... I rebuked the officials and asked them, "Why is the house of God neglected?"
—Nehemiah 13:7–8,11

The wall of Jerusalem had been completed, and now was being dedicated. Joyful songs of thanksgiving with musical instruments and two choirs accompanied the great celebration. The sound of rejoicing could be heard far away, because God had given them great joy. But it was a finale following many reforms instituted by Nehemiah.

A key phrase describing the event comes in chapter 13, verse 4: "Before this..." *Before this* day of dedication, Nehemiah describes what happened while he was away. If you recall, when Nehemiah originally requested permission to travel to Jerusalem, he gave a time (twelve years) to finish his business, then return to Babylon. While absent, several details surrounding the temple were abused.

One such issue had to do with Eliashib the priest, who was put in charge of the temple storerooms. It happened that Eliashib married Tobiah's daughter, and gave Tobiah his own room at the temple—*yes,* the same Tobiah who had given Nehemiah so much grief over the building of the wall! Furthermore, Levites and singers had returned back to their own farms because the support designated to them had been cut off. Sabbath laws, also, were being violated. All in all, the temple affairs were being neglected. Likewise, the church today will only be effective when God is honored and purity is maintained.

Father God, let the affairs of Your kingdom be maintained with integrity. May those who lead the church be stewards of Your presence. Amen.

August 18

Esther 1:1–3:15; 1 Corinthians 11:17–34; Psalm 35:17–28; Proverbs 21:19–20

The Lord's Supper

The Lord Jesus, on the night he was betrayed, took bread, and when he had given thanks, he broke it and said, "This is my body, which is for you; do this in remembrance of me." In the same way he took the cup, saying "This cup is the new covenant in my blood; do this, whenever you drink it, in remembrance of me." For whenever you [do], you proclaim the Lord's death until he comes.
—1 Corinthians 11:23–26

Paul elaborates upon the Lord's Supper, recalling Jesus' words at Passover. Today, communion is a sacrament that we are invited to partake in, but it's more than a ritual in a church service. It is a holy engagement to commemorate the broken body of the Lord Jesus and His blood that was shed on the cross. It was this offering of love that purchased our salvation, taking our sins upon His back, once for all. *Whenever* you eat of the bread and drink of the cup, it is a personal declaration of His victory in your life because of the cross. It's a renewal of covenant—and covenant is what this is essentially about.

Jesus said, "This cup is the *new* covenant in my blood…" Covenant is God's promise of deliverance. It's God's guarantee of the agreement that He establishes to make good the salvation He provides. It is the new covenant because Jesus was the fulfillment of everything the old covenant looked forward to. *(See Jeremiah 31:31-34.)*

That is why Paul points out that we ought to examine ourselves before partaking, because it is a holy thing that we do. Every time we partake of the elements that symbolize the body and blood is an opportunity to commemorate the benefits of the cross. We renew our commitment. We show our gratitude for all the cross signifies.

Father God, thank You for giving Your Son to make sacrifice for my sins and for giving me a way to continually respond to the work of the cross. Amen.

August 19

Esther 4:1–7:10; 1 Corinthians 12:1–26; Psalm 36:1–12; Proverbs 21:21–22

A Queen's Faith

Do not think that because you are in the king's house you alone of all the Jews will escape. For if you remain silent at this time, relief and deliverance for the Jews will arise from another place, but you and your family will perish. And who knows but you have come to royal position for such a time as this?
—Esther 4:13–14

Our story is found at the king's palace in Susa, the Persian capital, where Xerxes reigned during the time of the Jewish exile. Mordecai, a prominent Jew, adopted and raised his uncle's daughter, Esther. She won the favor of the king and, following an elaborate beauty contest, was made queen. Even a holiday was proclaimed in Esther's honor.

Things get interesting when the king elevates one of his nobles-—Haman—to a higher position. When Mordecai refuses to bow to the wicked man in reverence, Haman sets out to destroy not only Mordecai, but all of Mordecai's people throughout the kingdom. The edict is granted by the king. Now the Jews face certain annihilation.

When Mordecai learns of the edict, he tears his clothes, putting on sackcloth and ashes, and weeps loudly at the king's gate. His words to Esther challenge her to action. Her favor with God and the king are not for nothing. Following three days of fasting and prayer, Esther approaches the throne to find favor once again. The risk she takes before the king is life and death, but ultimately spares the Jewish nation. Once again, God raises up a deliverer for the people of God.

Esther's faith came with a call to action. It might surprise you to know that God has anointed you and positioned you to give witness to the light and truth of the Lord right where you are at, for such a time.

Father God, use me to boldly influence someone who needs You today. Amen.

August 20

Esther 8:1–10:3; 1 Corinthians 12:27–13:13; Psalm 37:1–11; Proverbs 21:23–24

Eagerly Desire

And in the church God has appointed first of all apostles, second prophets, third teachers, then workers of miracles, also those having gifts of healing, those able to help others, those with gifts of administration, and those speaking in different kinds of tongues. But eagerly desire the greater gifts.
   —1 Corinthians 12:28,31

We are entering into three hallmark chapters that deal with the spiritual gifts and how they operate to edify the church. The famous "love" chapter *(13)* is sandwiched between the instruction *(12 & 14)* so we can know how it is all designed—from the platform of love. When the motive is anything other than love and the benefit of others, then gifts can become self-serving. The need for the gifts in operation is not diminished, but motives matter for them to be fully beneficial.

What caught my attention is how we are to approach this topic of the gifts. After listing several gifts, Paul interjects a summary point: *"But eagerly desire the greater gifts" (v.31)*. I would first ask what the "greater gifts" might be, but then he answers that in just a minute. The larger issue is the "eagerly desire" part. This is a very convicting statement. Just what do I eagerly desire—in all of life—anyways?

It turns out that Paul makes a similar summary point twice more: *"Follow the way of love and eagerly desire spiritual gifts, especially the gift of prophecy" (14:1)*, and, *"Therefore, my brothers, be eager to prophesy" (14:39)*. Paul's exhortation is that the body of Christ be built up by the prophetic now-word the Lord is speaking, words that strengthen, encourage and comfort (14:3). *Eagerly desire* to be the one who hears the Lord's heart and speaks it to one who needs it.

Father, thank You for gifts that encourage the body of Christ. I desire to know Your heart and Your word that I might speak forth blessing. Amen.

August 21

Job 1:1–3:26; 1 Corinthians 14:1–17; Psalm 37:12–29; Proverbs 21:25–26

Job's Heart is Tested

One day the angels came to present themselves before the Lord, and Satan also came with them. The Lord said …, "Have you considered my servant Job? There is no one on the earth like him; he is blameless and upright, a man who fears God and shuns evil." "Does Job fear God for nothing?" Satan replied.
—Job 1:6,8–9

God describes Job as a godly man. His life has had the blessing of the Lord upon it. Job has prospered. He is described as the greatest man among all the people of the East. He prays for his children. Job is even cited in *Ezekiel 14* with Noah and Daniel as recognizably godly men.

Enter Satan. Described similarly by Peter, *"Your enemy the devil prowls around like a roaring lion looking for someone to devour" (1 Peter 5:8).* He comes before God to incite Him to lift the protective hedge and so ruin Job. But it is God who brings up the integrity of Job. He permits the devil to strike his possessions and test the heart of Job. Satan is sure that Job will curse God and abandon his faith.

Job was made to endure heartbreaking grief and agonizing pain. Most of us will face a severe test two or three times in a lifespan. Satan's scheme by them is to ruin the believer. But in our circumstance, God has not turned His head. He is with us. God permits tests to reveal what is in our heart. Remember, the devil is limited by what God will authorize. As long as God is in control, we know that God will achieve a greater purpose in and through it. In the end (that we don't see), our faith is tried and found to be true as pure gold. These momentary light afflictions are a bump in the road in light of eternity.

Father, thank You for the hedge of protection You have over my life and my family. I confess that Your grace is enough for whatever You allow to test my heart. Help me in my trial to be steady. Receive glory in Jesus' name, Amen.

August 22

Job 4:1–7:21; 1 Corinthians 14:18–40; Psalm 37:30–40; Proverbs 21:27

When You Come Together

What then shall we say, brothers? When you come together, everyone has a hymn, or a word of instruction, a revelation, a tongue or an interpretation. All of these must be done for the strengthening of the church.
—1 Corinthians 14:26

Has there been abuse of the gifts in the church? Of course. That's why Paul is addressing the issue. But God has so designed these gifts to build up and edify the church. They are an essential aspect of church life. Why act as though they are invalid? Something that is alive and interdependent upon discerning, yet weak human beings, only means that we need taught and that we need opportunities in a safe environment to practice (and yes, fail). The Holy Spirit still has a word to speak, and He uses humans to deliver them.

The larger issue that strikes my heart today is the way we come together in our gatherings. Paul assumes that when we come together in our worship services that we have something to share! He has already explained in chapter twelve that each part of the body of Christ is necessary and needful. Here, we are each encouraged to come prepared to share something with each other. I would interject that, depending upon the manner of the service structure, it may be on a congregational level or a personal level. Either way would be beneficial to the hearer. *A song? An admonishment? A word from Scripture?* My concern is that far too many of us, if we attend church at all, go with the attitude of, "What will I get out of it today?" rather than, "What do I have to contribute that may strengthen another?" You may issue the grace and kindness someone so desperately needs.

Father, fill me to overflowing with Your presence. Instill in me the word of the Lord for someone today. Put a song in my heart to share. Let me be a giver and not only a taker. Use me to build up the body of Christ today. Amen.

August 23

Job 8:1–11:20; 1 Corinthians 15:1–28; Psalm 38:1–22; Proverbs 21:28–29

An Innocent Job Speaks

How then can I dispute with him? How can I find words to argue with him? Although I am blameless, I have no concern for myself; I loathe my very life; therefore I will give free rein to my complaint and speak out in bitterness of my soul.
   —Job 9:14,21; 10:1

Indeed, only one who knows he is righteous before God can be so confident. What's more, pain has a perspective that forsakes the pleasantries of safe conversation and deals with the gut-honest truth.

There is little doubt that Job's perception of God is affected by his present circumstance. Not that Job is sinning with his mouth, either. He understands the omniscience of His Creator. *"Your hands shaped me and made me. Will you now turn and destroy me?" (10:8).* What Job cries out for is a mediator. *"If only there were someone to arbitrate between us" (9:33).* God is not put off by our honesty.

Interestingly enough, our reading in Psalm 38 shows us that searing pain and anguish of heart can also be attributed to iniquity and sin. There is no question that guilt and shame can have an effect on our health. Thankfully, confession and repentance are remedies for this.

"Friends" who observe from a distance cannot always know the reason why suffering is permitted. God knows. His innocent Son Jesus knew what it was to suffer intensely. But for the child of God, there is an intended outcome for good. What Satan means for harm, God uses to redeem. In the end, faith polishes the witness of God ever brighter.

Father, You alone can know all the reasons for which suffering is permitted. But You do all things well, and there are benefits to all that You allow. May the testimony of Jesus be made evident in the season of suffering. Amen.

August 24

Job 12:1–15:35; 1 Corinthians 15:29–58; Psalm 39:1–13; Proverbs 21:30–31

We Will All Be Changed

So will it be with the resurrection of the dead. The body that is sown is perishable, it is raised imperishable; it is sown a natural body, it is raised a spiritual body. Listen … we will not all sleep, but we will all be changed …
  —1 Corinthians 15:42,44,51

In a church we served in many years ago, appropriately hung on the nursery door was a sign that read: *"We will not all sleep, but we will all be changed!"* I still chuckle when I think of it.

Paul gives us great insight into the process of our natural exit and what we can expect to happen thereafter. What a hope that we have! We all come to know the frailties of our natural bodies over time. They were never designed to go the eternal distance. They are the seeds that must die in order to be raised up. We want them to last forever, but they never do. They were never meant to.

Because Christ has been raised from the dead, He became the firstfruits of those who have died and belong to Him. When Jesus comes again, we (who belong to Him) will all be changed and bear the likeness of the man from heaven. The last enemy to be destroyed is death. It will be swallowed up in victory—a victory we will realize.

We all want the new spiritual body. It's the process we don't particularly look forward to. But it will all be worth it. The hope of a resurrected body is a certain hope. We all know those who are elderly or have disabilities who long for this promise—the sooner the better!

Father, Your plans for me far exceed the seventy or eighty years that I could live out here in this life. When that time comes, I know that Your promise will be proven true. You will resurrect my body to be glorious and imperishable. Best of all, I know that I will be found in Your presence forever. Amen.

August 25

Job 16:1–19:29; 1 Corinthians 16:1–24; Psalm 40:1–10; Proverbs 22:1

The Household of Stephanas

You know that the household of Stephanas were the first converts in Achaia, and they have devoted themselves to the service of the saints. I urge you, brothers, to submit to such as these ... For they refreshed my spirit and yours also. Such men deserve recognition.
   —1 Corinthians 16:15–16,18

When my wife and I were pastoring, we initiated an annual day of celebration called "Stephanas Day." On that day, in utmost secrecy leading up to it, we gave recognition to a person or couple who were notable in service like that of Stephanas. Perhaps you know a few.

First, they were seasoned in the Lord. They were not new on the scene. They had a track record of service. They were devoted to the building up of the local body. They were givers. They freely served. They were people you could follow, because they led by example.

Stephanas, Fortunatus and Achaicus refreshed those they came into contact with. They supplied what was needed for the moment. You know who they are. They have touched you. They have touched me. They have been faithful and diligent, not necessarily the most charismatic or flamboyant. I see that it is loyalty that God so values. They are the stalwarts who can be counted upon. Paul says that such men and women deserve recognition.

Perhaps you could take Paul's tip here and honor someone you know that has been a stabilizer in your spiritual life. Treat them to lunch. They would never ask for it, but they deserve your acknowledgment.

Father, thank You for those whom You have placed in my life as examples. Encourage those faithful who are weary today. Lift their spirit. Cause them to know that their labor in the Lord is not in vain. Crown them with joy. Amen.

August 26

Job 20:1–22:30; 2 Corinthians 1:1–11; Psalm 40:11–17; Proverbs 22:2–4

The God of All Comfort

Praise be to the God and Father of our Lord Jesus Christ, the Father of compassion and the God of all comfort, who comforts us in all our troubles, so that we can comfort those in any trouble with the comfort we ourselves have received. For just as the sufferings … flow, so also … our comfort overflows.
—2 Corinthians 1:3–5

In order to know the comfort and compassion of God, you must first have an acquaintance with suffering and trouble. It's not something you sign up for, as with Job, but you are allowed to experience a side of God's persona that you were not privy to without them.

My wife, Alaine, knows the comfort and compassion of God. She has been diagnosed with cancer—twice. Her faith in the Lord has been unwavering, actually strengthened. She has been flooded with the reality of God's presence. She has experienced the comfort of the Holy Spirit. What's most impressive is how she has been an inspiration to others going through a similar season in their life. She ministers to people I never could, because she's been there. She is able to pass on what she knows to be true, and it resonates with those hurting.

God never wastes an opportunity to bring life and hope to a situation. God meets us where we are at. If it is a fiery trial or a devastating loss, His compassion rushes in. He enables us to understand what is truly important. His eternal perspective prepares us well beyond our dilemma. While we wait to see His deliverance, we always know that He is there with us and beside us. Many times, God's compassion is witnessed through the kindness and prayers of God's people, like you.

Father of compassion and God of all comfort, You have allowed me to know Your presence closely. In my need, I rely not on myself, but look to You, who raises the dead. You do all things well. Thank You for Your favor. Amen.

August 27

Job 23:1–27:23; 2 Corinthians 1:12–2:11; Psalm 41:1–13; Proverbs 22:5–6

Stand Firm in Christ

Now it is God who makes both us and you stand firm in Christ. He anointed us, set his seal of ownership on us, and put his Spirit in our hearts as a deposit, guaranteeing what is to come ... it is by faith you stand firm.
—2 Corinthians 1:21–22,24

Several times we read Paul exhorting us to stand firm in the faith: *"My brothers, stand firm. Let nothing move you." (1 Corinthians 15:58). "Be on your guard; stand firm in the faith..." (1 Corinthians 16:13). "Therefore put on the full armor of God, so that when the day of evil comes, you will be able to stand your ground" (Ephesians 6:13-14).* Today, Paul explains that we cannot stand in our own strength. It is God who enables us to stand firm in our faith. You see, it is difficult to maintain a steady faith in a cultural environment that is ever-shifting and where a deceiving devil prowls around spewing lies round-the-clock.

Paul's confidence for a steady faith is bolstered by three significant facts. *First,* God has anointed us. He has chosen us and placed His hand upon us infused with His life, His purpose and His authority. God empowers us to accomplish His purposes beyond our natural abilities. *Next,* God has placed His seal of ownership on us. He marks us to declare who we belong to. I am wholly His. *Lastly,* God places His Spirit within our hearts. The third person of the Godhead actually dwells within our person, joined with our spirit, and is uniquely positioned to counsel and empower us. That His Spirit is put in our hearts as a deposit means that it is a foretaste of much more to come. Paul told the Ephesians *(1:13-14)* that it was this deposit that guarantees our inheritance. So when I understand that He has given me this great advantage, my faith enables me to stand firm.

Father God, You bolster my faith with Your claim on my life. I stand in You. Amen.

August 28

Job 28:1–30:31; 2 Corinthians 2:12–17; Psalm 42:1–11; Proverbs 22:7

The Aroma of Christ

But thanks be to God, who … through us spreads everywhere the fragrance of the knowledge of him. For we are to God the aroma of Christ among those who are being saved and those who are perishing. To the one we are the smell of death; to the other, the fragrance of life.
  —2 Corinthians 2:14–16

I love the imagery in this. And I believe it is quite fitting. Your life is a testimony before all the world, wherever you venture. Your witness and your message are perceived like a scent that you can smell.

When you walk into a room, you carry with you a sense, an aroma, that is caught by those in the room. To those who are open to the gospel, it is a welcome scent. It is pleasant, like an expensive perfume. It is not overbearing or obnoxious. The message of the gospel is life-giving, so it is meant to be a sweet smelling fragrance.

To others, the good news of the gospel is not received as good news. To the one whose heart is hardened, that same aroma is a foul stench. Your witness reminds them of their choice that shuts out the God of glory. The aroma you carry is repugnant and your message repulsive. Your intentions are pure, but your stout witness causes them to keep you at a distance. You can even feel their rejection of you. It's bothersome, but in reality it is a complement to the Spirit of God at work in you that you don't apologize for.

We spread the knowledge of the Lord. It is our life's mission. We are compelled to share the message, but we want to share it with grace and sincerity. Is your witness changing the complexion of the room?

Father of glory, You desire for me to affect those I come into relation with. Allow the aroma of Christ to permeate the room and draw them to You. Amen.

August 29

Job 31:1–33:33; 2 Corinthians 3:1–18; Psalm 43:1–5; Proverbs 22:8–9

Reflecting Ever-Increasing Glory

And we, who with unveiled faces all reflect the Lord's glory, are being transformed into his likeness with ever-increasing glory, which comes from the Lord, who is the Spirit.
—2 Corinthians 3:18

The awesome conclusion to this passage reveals the glory we reflect as growing believers in the Spirit. Just as we can't suppress the aroma that exudes from a life in the Spirit, God's glory manifests more and more and in greater measure as we are transformed into His likeness.

Paul first makes the comparison, which is no comparison at all, of the former glory of the law to the greater glory of the new covenant. Not that there wasn't glory in the former—Moses' face radiated with glory! The Israelites could not look steadily upon his face even with a veil covering him. But the ministry of the Spirit far supersedes the old covenant. In fact, it is when anyone turns to the Lord, the veil is taken away. Just as the eye is the lamp of the body, so the face radiates the glory of the Lord. With the limitations of a veil removed, the freedom and glory of the Lord is allowed to shine without encumbrance.

Cutting to the core of our verse, you can say … we all reflect the Lord's glory. You may initially want to refute that: *Maybe not me so much!* But I will declare to you that if the Spirit of God dwells within you, then there is a glory that comes forth. It honors the Lord Jesus. Granted, there are degrees of glory. There will always be degrees of glory. Paul explains that we grow from one place of glory to another place of glory, as we are transformed. And transformation is a process that takes place over the course of my life. The glory only increases!

Father, I desire to grow to that next level of glory. Transform my mind and life to reflect the likeness of Your Son. Let Your glory be revealed in me. Amen

August 30

Job 34:1–36:33; 2 Corinthians 4:1–12; Psalm 44:1–8; Proverbs 22:10–12

Jars of Clay

But we have this treasure in jars of clay to show that this all-surpassing power is from God and not from us. For we who are alive are always being given over to death for Jesus' sake, so that his life may be revealed in our mortal body.
—2 Corinthians 4:7,11

Paul describes here a phenomenon so well. What the Lord can do through frail human vessels is such an impressive thing, don't you think? The transforming message of the gospel and the power of the Holy Spirit are priceless treasures that we have been entrusted with. What He does in and through us is truly beyond anything I could ever muster up. And that's the point. It's not about "me" at all. I am only a conduit of His Spirit at work in me.

If there were ever a time that I thought perhaps I had something to do with it, God has gently and kindly shown me what it is I am made of. After all, I can be filled with pride over "my accomplishments" as easily as the next person. But I am a mere human, flawed at best. It is wisdom to come to this conclusion—the sooner the better.

Paul describes the dying process that we all undergo as we discover our new life in the Lord. Our bodies are subject to trials and suffering. We know the squeeze. We tire. We hurt. We age. We inhabit limited frames that house the Spirit of God. But while we are vulnerable and very perishable, His Spirit always finds a way to reveal His life and power through us. Our strength and our ideas are not what God is looking for, but our availability to allow the Spirit to use us—*however.* There is absolutely no limit to what God can do in your life.

Father God, You can do amazing things when I make myself available to You. I feel the limitations of my flesh often. I wonder how You could ever use me, but Your Spirit is the treasure that finds a way to express Your glory. Amen.

August 31

Job 37:1–39:30; 2 Corinthians 4:13–5:10; Psalm 44:9–26; Proverbs 22:13

Inward Renewal

Therefore we do not lose heart. Though outwardly we are wasting away, yet inwardly we are being renewed day by day.
—2 Corinthians 4:16

This verse confirms something I've always known. I know that I am aging with every passing birthday, but I don't *feel* old. My body tells me that I'm not the young whipper-snapper I used to be, but the years have not affected my inner man. In fact, I feel the vigor and zest of a growing relationship with the Lord.

Inwardly I am being renewed day by day by day. When I feed my spirit with the Word of truth, I grow inside. When I allow my spirit to soak in the presence of the Lord, I know that I am being nurtured by His Spirit. My heart is being enlarged. This process doesn't follow the way of my physical aging. It does quite the opposite. I am renewed and made new as I tap into the Source of all livelihood. So, therefore, I do not lose heart. I am encouraged by what the Lord is doing in me.

The context in which Paul makes this statement is in the midst of momentary light afflictions. They are serious enough to cause us to contemplate the life we have after our physical life here is over. Momentary light afflictions are only light and momentary in the light of eternity. They are very weighty when they stare us in the face. But our heavenly dwelling is very much a reality and something we long for when our earthly tent is set to expire.

So I make it my goal to please Him and long for renewal on the inside.

Giver of life, You cause me to come alive on the inside. I come to You for guidance and deliverance through the afflictions that I am to endure. Thank You for hope and for the zeal of the Lord that You renew each day. Amen.

September 1

Job 40:1–42:17; 2 Corinthians 5:11–21; Psalm 45:1–17; Proverbs 22:14

A Final Word on Job

After[wards] … the Lord said to Eliphaz the Temanite, "I am angry with you and your two friends, because you have not spoken of me what is right, as my servant Job has. My servant Job will pray for you, and I will accept his prayer and not deal with you according to your folly."
—Job 42:7–8

For thirty chapters, Job discourses with his so-called friends, Eliphaz, Bildad and Zophar. They spar back and forth on the reasons why Job has incurred the Lord's wrath and judgment. Even a young Elihu weighs in on the argument when all their speeches are exhausted. But in the end, the Lord has the last say. God speaks a resounding word, leaving Job overwhelmed and nearly speechless.

When God addresses Job's accusers, He causes two important things to happen. *First,* God exonerates Job. He declares that the reasoning they used was flawed. Job's sin was not the reason for his misfortune. Twice God declares, *"You have not spoken of me what is right, as my servant Job has."* Job didn't sin with his mouth either. They are corrected and humbled, yet still given the opportunity for restoration. Even that will come from the righteous one they have accused. *Second,* Job is humbled by being the one who prays for his misguided friends. This directive of God sets Job's heart free from offense and unforgiveness. By obeying the Lord and praying his friends, Job becomes a candidate for blessing and prosperity by the Lord. It had to happen in that order. In Job's case, he is doubly-blessed.

If you've wondered why Job did not receive twice the number of children after, remember that he never really lost his first ten kids. The math still works when you consider their place in heaven.

Father, help me to forgive those who are quick to criticize or judge me. Amen.

September 2

Ecclesiastes 1:1–3:22; 2 Corinthians 6:1–13; Psalm 46:1–11; Proverbs 22:15

There is a Season

There is a time for everything, and a season for every activity under heaven: a time to be born and a time to die, a time to plant and a time to uproot, a time to weep and a time to laugh, a time to mourn and a time to dance …
—Ecclesiastes 3:1–2,4

If you will remember, Solomon was the one who asked God for wisdom and discernment to lead Israel. God granted that earnest prayer and gave him so much more. Leaders the world over were awed at Solomon's insight. He became the wisest man in the world, but then did not heed his own advice. His words written in this book appear negative and cynical, but they are indeed true. It's just that his perspective now is looking back as an aged man and seeing all the futility in pursuing things that cannot result in true happiness—things that can only be fulfilled in God alone. He knew of what he wrote.

Among Solomon's conclusions is that God works in seasons. I have found this to be so true. I look back and reminisce on the stages of life that I've experienced, many pleasant, some bitter, but all have been preparation for the next season God was leading me into. I believe that having that God-sense discernment about where He is leading will help you to know whether to embrace the next open door, or to close it and refrain. But there are other things we cannot see coming.

One thing I know. If the season I am in is heartbreaking and difficult, I know that it is just a season—it will not last forever. Conversely, if you're in a season where things are smooth and steady, then also know that a rough patch is ahead that you will need to endure. It's the way of life. *"But He has made everything beautiful in it's time" (3:11).*

Father in heaven, give me grace for the season that I am in, so that much fruit may follow and that You may be glorified. I look to You for wisdom. Amen.

September 3

Ecclesiastes 4:1–6:12; 2 Corinthians 6:14–7:7; Psalm 47:1–9; Proverbs 22:16

Purifying and Perfecting

Since we have these promises, dear friends, let us purify ourselves from everything that contaminates body and spirit, perfecting holiness out of reverence for God.
—2 Corinthians 7:1

Paul's exhortation today is that we would purify ourselves from those things that would contaminate, and to perfect holiness. We do that in light of "these promises" mentioned in the latter verses of chapter six.

Paul reiterates the "promises" that God had declared through the prophets that He would live with them and walk among them and be their God, and they would be His people *(Leviticus 26:12, Ezekiel 37:27)*. Because of this extraordinary relationship with the living God, we have a part to play in maintaining the purity of that union, namely to resist binding relationships with ungodly people who may influence us in an adverse way. We don't avoid relating to unbelievers, but we avoid relationships that may compromise our faith.

Because we are the dwelling place of the living God, we desire to be pure, just as He is pure. We avoid the things that contaminate our body and our spirit. Think of it as filtering out the toxins that would compromise your health. It is true with your spiritual body as well as your physical body. So it is a resisting of harmful sin, but it is also embracing the holiness that comes from reverence for God. We actually see holiness perfected in our lives over time when we learn to fear the Lord. It's a healthy fear that commands total allegiance. It is a respect that learns to love what He loves and to hate what He hates. What are some contaminants that you know you must resist?

Father, thank You for Your promise to live with me and to walk with me. I choose the fear of the Lord and I resist those things that pull me down. Amen.

September 4

Ecclesiastes 7:1–9:18; 2 Corinthians 7:8–16; Psalm 48:1–14; Proverbs 22:17–19

Godly Sorrow

For you became sorrowful as God intended … Godly sorrow brings repentance that leads to salvation and leaves no regret, but worldly sorrow brings death. See what this godly sorrow has produced in you: what earnestness, what eagerness to clear yourselves, what indignation, what alarm, what longing, what concern, what readiness to see justice done.
—2 Corinthians 7:9–11

Today Paul describes a critical step in the process of salvation that brings about real change. *Godly sorrow* is the conviction we feel that makes us uncomfortable with our present condition. It is a deep work of the Holy Spirit that leads us to repent of our sinful ways and to desire God's way. Godly sorrow is more than getting caught in a sin or being sorry for what it may have caused. We were stuck in our sin until the Holy Spirit revealed the chasm that sin created with God.

The conviction of the Holy Spirit is a step that cannot be overlooked or dismissed. Knowledge of God is not enough. Repeating a prayer is not enough, if it is not accompanied by the pull of the Spirit upon your heart that cries out to be delivered. As strange as it may sound, it is the kindness of God that leads us to a desire to repent, because we want to become aligned with God's ways.

The resulting affect is the longing and the concern to follow God in truth. It produces an earnestness and holy zeal to do the right thing. Peter disowned Christ, but his remorse—in response to the prompting of the Spirit—opened the door for his full restoration. Is the Lord dealing with you about a particular sin that keeps you at a distance?

Father, thank You for Your Spirit, who tenaciously works to keep my relationship with You close and free from the entanglements of sin. Shine Your light on anything that would put distance between us. Amen.

September 5

Ecclesiastes 10:1–12:14; 2 Corinthians 8:1–15; Psalm 49:1–20; Proverbs 22:20-21

The Grace of Giving

For I testify that they (the Macedonian churches) gave as much as they were able, and even beyond their ability. Entirely on their own, they pleaded with us for the privilege of sharing in this service to the saints. But just as you excel in everything—in faith, in speech, in knowledge, in complete earnestness and in your love for us—see that you also excel in this grace of giving.
—2 Corinthians 8:3–4,7

Paul was writing this letter to the Corinthian church from the region of Macedonia. During his journey, he was collecting an offering for the severe needs of the Jerusalem believers from the likes of Philippi, Thessalonica and Berea. It wasn't that they had an overabundance of extra money sitting around to give—quite the opposite. They were needy themselves. But they gave sacrificially to help their fellow believers in their time of crisis. It was a natural outflow from a heart dedicated to Christ that produced this response—to love in deed.

Several times this giving is referred to as a grace *(8:1,6,7)*. That means that it is not something you would do on your own. It's something God inspired and enabled you to do. It's the genuine sincerity and eager desire to help another in a practical way, but it's also the completion and follow-through of that kind intention. In their minds, this service to the saints was considered a privilege.

The Corinthians had excelled in many areas. They had made great gains in their faith and love and knowledge of the Lord. Paul says: *"Now add this grace of giving to your repertoire. Know the joy of giving."* The amount of your gift is not as important as your willingness to give so that others may be blessed. Do you know this joy of giving?

Father, You have turned my heart from selfishly clutching to generously giving. May I respond eagerly when You direct me to help another. Amen.

September 6

Song of Songs 1:1–4:16; 2 Corinthians 8:16–24; Psalm 50:1–23; Proverbs 22:22

Poems of Love

Let him kiss me with the kisses of his mouth—for your love is more delightful than wine. Pleasing is the fragrance of your perfumes; your name is like perfume poured out. No wonder the maidens love you! Take me away with you—let us hurry! Let the king bring me into his chambers.
　　—Song of Songs 1:2–4

God is a Bridegroom God. Never more descriptive is the love a bridegroom has for his bride than in these eight chapters penned by a young Solomon. It is a celebration of love and intimacy between a husband and his wife, for sure. It is also a picture of God's devotion and passion for His people, the church.

The Song of Solomon is a dialogue between the *Lover* (King Solomon) and the *Beloved* (the Shulammite maiden). They share their emotions and longings for each other through a series of seven poems. In them, they affirm each other with words of praise. The intimate details, initiated in the mind of God, are sacred within the marriage covenant. It is the closest human example of the overwhelming love of God that touches us on the deepest and innermost level of our person.

Isaiah spoke, *"For as the bridegroom rejoices over the bride, so shall your God rejoice over you"* *(62:5)*. Intimacy with God is the desired goal— pursuing God while He is pursuing you. David's one desire was to gaze and encounter the beauty of the Lord *(Psalm 27:4)*. To know His heart and His emotions for us is to respond with wholehearted love and faithfulness in return. It is the message of the Bridegroom and His beloved bride. *"Your love is more delightful than wine!"*

Father, show me the depths of intimacy that can be reached as I give myself wholly to You. My desire is to know You and be known by You. I'll be Your bride. Come be my Groom. Awaken my heart to love You. Amen.

September 7

Song of Songs 5:1–8:14; 2 Corinthians 9:1–15; Psalm 51:1-19; Proverbs 22:23-25

The Cry of a Repentant Heart

Have mercy on me, O God, according to your unfailing love; according to your great compassion blot out my transgressions. Against you, you only, have I sinned and done what is evil in your sight… Create in me a pure heart, O God, and renew a steadfast spirit within me.
   —Psalm 51:1,4,10

David is confronted by the prophet Nathan concerning his adultery with Bathsheba. David had become desensitized to his own sin. In the wake of his lust is a faithful husband and a newborn child—both now deceased. What's more, the thing David had done displeased the Lord *(2 Samuel 11:27)*. David's heart now pounds out of his chest with conviction. His pleading reveals a sincere repentance.

Look at the verbs: *blot out, wash away, cleanse me, hide your face, do not cast me from.* These are the cries of a repentant heart. Prior to this incident, David may have known mercy in theory. But now he comes face to face with his greatest need for forgiveness.

The best definition of mercy I know is one contrasted with grace: *Grace is getting what you don't deserve. Mercy is not getting what you do deserve.* It's God whom we ultimately sin against, because we've spurned His commands, and it's God alone who is able to forgive us the great debt of that iniquity.

The weight of David's sin was real. The joy he had known was gone. What David needed now was a pure heart, a steadfast spirit and God's abiding presence. All David had to offer God was a broken and contrite heart, but that is an offering that God will gladly accept.

Father, You know me in my weakness, and yet, Your mercy picks me up when I stumble. May I know joy in forgiveness, and then get back up again. Amen.

September 8

Isaiah 1:1–2:22; 2 Corinthians 10:1–18; Psalm 52:1–9; Proverbs 22:26–27

Strongholds Demolished

For though we live in the world, we do not wage war as the world does. The weapons we fight with are not the weapons of the world. On the contrary, they have divine power to demolish strongholds. We demolish arguments and every pretension that sets itself up against the knowledge of God, and we take captive every thought to make it obedient to Christ.
—2 Corinthians 10:3–5

The apostle Paul appeals to the Corinthians that we do not live by the standards of this world. We are as foreigners in a hostile environment where our ideals and faith are not welcome. The tactics of the god of this world are predictable enough—intimidation, lies, deception, manipulation—whatever might bend our will to conform. But we do not answer the lies of the adversary with the weapons he resorts to.

Since Paul doesn't mention what the weapons are, what does he want us to know from this? (He gives us more on the weapons later in his letter to the Ephesians—6:14-18.) What we draw from this is that God has equipped us with tools of divine power that will expose and even demolish strongholds. Strongholds are false belief systems that have embedded themselves into our thought life as acceptable. They are lies that the devil wants you to believe. So it is no wonder that we are to take captive every thought. Every accusation and argument that the world accepts to minimize or displace the truth, we must dismiss.

So the equipment I need to war with is a renewed mind in the Word of God, a keen discernment to know the lie when it presents itself and a bold faith to answer it. We cannot be passive in an aggressive war.

Father God, You have equipped me with all that I need to be an overcomer in my faith. I will give myself to Your Word so that lies and deception are filtered out. Let me stand tall for the truth that sets the captive free. Amen.

September 9

Isaiah 3:1–5:30; 2 Corinthians 11:1–15; Psalm 53:1–6; Proverbs 22:28–29

Simplicity of Devotion

I am jealous for you with a godly jealousy. I promised you to one husband, to Christ, so that I might present you as a pure virgin to him. But I am afraid that just as Eve was deceived by the serpent's cunning, your minds may somehow be led astray from your sincere and pure devotion to Christ.
—2 Corinthians 11:2–3

Paul's earnest desire for all who have received from his ministry is to somehow lead them into a purity of faith. Paul has made quite an investment. Strong feelings of a righteous jealousy naturally follow, since he has poured his life into them. He is the parent who has raised his child with every precaution of truth so that he might succeed and avoid the obvious entrapments. But as every mom or dad knows, there comes a day when that child is going to launch out on his own and he will have to stand up to those challenges by himself.

What Paul was hoping to see maintained was what had already been established—a sincere and pure devotion to Christ. This is the goal for *every* believer. Our faith needs not to be complicated or convoluted. Our devotion needs only to be simple, sincere and uncorrupted.

What grieved Paul was that these precious believers had already put up with self-exalting rival preachers who had presented a different gospel and a different Jesus than what Paul had already proclaimed. They masqueraded as "super-apostles," deceiving those who naively gave place to their logic. No one ever thinks they are capable of being deceived, but the devil is cunning and will stop at nothing to make you question the very foundation of your faith. Remember, it's not a confusing puzzle. Embrace the simplicity of faith in the Savior.

Father, guard my heart and mind from harmful heresy. May I trust You fully and sincerely. Cause me to be that pure bride made ready for Your Son. Amen.

September 10

Isaiah 6:1–7:25; 2 Corinthians 11:16–33; Psalm 54:1–7; Proverbs 23:1–3

A Holy Encounter

I saw the Lord seated on a throne, high and exalted, and the train of his robe filled the temple. And they (seraphs) were calling to one another: "Holy, holy, holy is the Lord Almighty; the whole earth is full of his glory." "Woe to me!" I cried. "For I am a man of unclean lips … and my eyes have seen the King."
—Isaiah 6:1,3,5

Isaiah has a vision of the Lord God Almighty seated on a heavenly throne. Seraphs attend the King, but cover their faces. High and lifted up is the Lord exalted. This encounter changes Isaiah's life forever. The glory and holiness of the Lord fill his senses.

In the presence of glory, only worship is the right response, but from an unclean vessel. God's lofty standard had been missing. In this holy moment, a keen awareness of his own condition is made obvious. Isaiah cries out and is cleansed. The coal of forgiveness touches him.

In this awakening, Isaiah answers the call of the Lord to carry His message to the wayward people of Judah. His encounter forms the constitution of his soul that is necessary to represent Him rightly. It establishes his path and perspective for the rest of his days.

Somewhere along the line—hopefully sooner than later—the Lord will beckon us to engage the nature of His holiness. He wants to reveal His splendor and the fire of His holiness, because He is truly awesome. He bears the standard of a righteousness we can know by knowing Him. While we live among a people of unclean lips, we need the vision and clarity of a holy God who can lift us out of the mire and shine a light of hope and rescue.

Father of glory, cause me to know Your majesty and holiness, so that I may represent You rightly in a world that is in desperate need of cleansing. Amen.

September 11

Isaiah 8:1–9:21; 2 Corinthians 12:1–10; Psalm 55:1–23; Proverbs 23:4–5

A Thorn in the Flesh

To keep me from becoming conceited because of these … great revelations, there was given me a thorn in my flesh, a messenger of Satan, to torment me. Three times I pleaded with the Lord to take it away from me. But He said to me, "My grace is sufficient for you … my power is perfected in weakness."
—2 Corinthians 12:7–9

Paul had received revelations from the Lord that were inexpressible—visions of paradise, third heaven knowledge in the first person—stuff that the most imaginable minds could not dream up.

With such privileged supernatural understanding, it would be easy to exalt yourself above the rest. But God knows how the heart works, and He has remedies for such pride. It's called "a thorn in the flesh." A *thorn* is a physical affliction, a weakness, a recurrent problem or some direct hindrance. Paul does not disclose what his *thorn* is, but he pleaded with the Lord to remove it. That was Paul's prayer.

God's answer was otherwise. God's answer brought humility and an earnest seeking to the very capable Paul. God would enable Paul to do mighty exploits in spite of his obvious human weakness. God's power is not dependent upon energy levels or talent, but is demonstrated in weak humans who rely upon God. When my strength is absent, His strength rests upon me. It takes the "me" out of the equation, so that people aren't confused about who gets the credit.

This gives me a very different take on difficult circumstances. Instead of blaming the devil, I can humbly seek the Lord's strength to overcome in my situation, in spite of my limitations and frailties.

Father in heaven, my strength only gets in the way of Your deliverance. Your grace is always enough. I defer to You. I lean upon Your strength. Amen.

September 12

Isaiah 10:1–11:16; 2 Corinthians 12:11–21; Psalm 56:1–13; Proverbs 23:6–8

The Spirit upon Messiah

A shoot will come up from the stump of Jesse; from his roots a Branch will bear fruit. The Spirit of the Lord will rest on him—the Spirit of wisdom and of understanding, the Spirit of counsel and of power, the Spirit of knowledge and of the fear of the Lord—and he will delight in the fear of the Lord.
—Isaiah 11:1–3

Isaiah speaks prophetically of a day when the Messiah will come and rule in righteousness. The imagery is that of a shoot to arise from the stump of Jesse, a promise that God will raise up a descendent from the line of Jesse's son, David, to rule forever. Jesus is the Messiah. He is referred to as the Root of Jesse, or the Branch who will bear fruit. He will come to enact justice. He will gather His remnant to Himself.

The Spirit of the Lord will rest on Him. He will bring the government of God to the earth. Jesus quoted Isaiah *(61:1-2)*, acknowledging the Spirit's anointing upon Him to release the oppressed and proclaim the Lord's favor *(Luke 4:17-21)*. This time, He will bring with Him the day of vengeance. The Spirit of God is upon Him to execute righteousness and justice. Imagine a government of divine justice!

The Spirit of God quietly saturates the record of the Bible from beginning to end. Here, the Spirit of the Lord rests upon the Messiah. The dimensions of the Spirit that are tangibly at work are of wisdom, understanding, counsel, power, knowledge and the fear (reverence) of the Lord. This anointing upon Jesus will be evident as He ushers in a new day. That is a hope we can look forward to. Our future is bright.

Father God, You have a divine strategy. The work of Your Son is not finished. He will rule and reign over the earth in righteousness to establish Your kingdom forever. I am encouraged, and I long for this day. You have the final word. Amen.

September 13

Isaiah 12:1–14:32; 2 Corinthians 13:1–14; Psalm 57:1–11; Proverbs 23:9–11

Prayer for Perfection

He is not weak in dealing with you, but is powerful among you … we are weak in him, yet by God's power we will live with him to serve you. Examine yourselves to see whether you are in the faith; test yourselves … and our prayer is for your perfection. Aim for perfection.
  —2 Corinthians 13:3,5,9,11

Concluding remarks are intended to bring the letter to a focal point of recollection and response. Paul has announced his upcoming arrival for a third visit, and wants to see that his words are taken to heart.

Paul's prayer and his charge is for their perfection—an attainable perfection. A better expression might be to aim for maturity or completeness. This focus keeps us humbly seeking a more complete obedience. We consciously choose to walk in His strength and in conformity to His will. In a society where faith is an inch deep and a mile wide, we need the bold witness of Christ to be made evident.

One thing we can do, and should do, is to inspect our own faith. Look introspectly. Examine yourself. Ask the questions. Do your convictions and actions stand by the truth? Does the Lord Jesus Christ manifest His life in and through you in service to others?

One thing is certain: Jesus is powerful in His dealings with us. Don't underestimate the strong arm of the Lord. He is jealous over you with strong desire. Jesus intercedes for you at the Father's right hand. His Spirit dwells within you to bring about needed change. Just as the trinity is named in our concluding verse, so they unite to work in you!

Father, I acknowledge that You are dealing mightily in my life to bring about a perfection that reflects Your glory. Speak to me, even now, regarding the areas where I tend to rely upon my own strength. Complete my faith. Amen.

September 14

Isaiah 15:1–18:7; Galatians 1:1–24; Psalm 58:1–11; Proverbs 23:12

A Different Gospel

I am astonished that you are so quickly deserting the one who called you by the grace of Christ and are turning to a different gospel—which is really no gospel at all. Evidently some ... are trying to pervert the gospel.
—Galatians 1:6–7

There is the authentic, and then there is a similar facsimile. There is the original, and then there is a doctored replica. One has power and the other is a weak imitation. Regarding the basic elements of faith, it really does matter that the original recipe is not altered.

What Paul is alarmed about, and devotes his letter to, is that disciples from his first journey were being influenced to desert key tenets of faith that make it faith. It conjured up confusion. Paul calls it a perverted gospel. A watered-down version of the truth destroys the impact. Here, Jewish laws and man-made regulations are imposed as necessary to salvation. In so doing, they deny the power of the cross.

Paul knew firsthand the power of the gospel. He had his life literally turned around on the road to Damascus *(Acts 9)*. He had been as zealous as any man for the cause of Judaism. But His revelation of Jesus changed all that. Now Paul was a preacher of the same gospel he once had persecuted—by the transforming grace of God.

God's plan from the beginning was to save us from our sins by the sacrifice of His Son. The power of this gospel still rescues us today—from sin, and the pull and deception of the evil age in which we live.

Father God, thank You for the sacrifice of Your Son for the remission of my sins. Your deliverance rescues me in this era of lawlessness. Nothing I do can add to your gospel of grace. Display Your power through the saving of souls, in Jesus' name, Amen.

September 15

Isaiah 19:1–21:17; Galatians 2:1–16; Psalm 59:1–17; Proverbs 23:13–14

A Tenacity for Truth

I set before them the gospel that I preach among the Gentiles. I did this privately to those who seemed to be leaders, for fear I was running my race in vain. James, Peter and John, those reputed to be pillars, gave me and Barnabas the right hand of fellowship when they recognized the grace given to me.
—Galatians 2:2,9

We get a really good peak into Paul's life in his early years as a believer—in his own words *(a.k.a. Saul)*. While having been trained in Judaism under the expert leadership of Gamaliel, Paul is now being tutored by the Holy Spirit. He makes it clear that the message he received was not from any man, rather a revelation from Jesus Christ *(1:13)*. Paul had learned to be sensitive to the revealing of truth by the Spirit. It was by a revelation that Paul even traveled to Jerusalem.

Paul appears unimpressed toward "those who seemed to be leaders." But God showed him, again by revelation, that being submitted to church leadership was essential. By being given the right hand of fellowship, they were acknowledging God's anointing upon him. By this, too, Paul could know that he was not running his race in vain.

Listed among the prophets and teachers of Antioch *(Acts 13:1)*, this fiery young man had a zeal for truth and was not afraid to confront an issue head-on. Even when it involved these same leaders, Paul calls them out for their hypocritical stance concerning a critical point of doctrine. Paul calls attention to the fact that all people, including Gentiles, can become believers without having to obey Jewish laws. Now the gospel could truly be global, to Jews and non-Jews alike.

Glorious Father, give me a tenacity for truth, as Paul had. Impart to me the Spirit of wisdom and revelation so that I may know You better. May the eyes of my heart be enlightened to the riches of Your Word. Amen.

September 16

Isaiah 22:1–24:23; Galatians 2:17–3:9; Psalm 60:1–12; Proverbs 23:15–16

Faith is Enough

I would like to learn just one thing from you: Did you receive the Spirit by observing the law, or by believing what you heard?... After beginning with the Spirit, are you now trying to attain your goal by human effort? Does God give you his Spirit and work miracles among you because you observe the law?
—Galatians 3:2–3,5

Paul is making his case against a virus that has infiltrated the ranks. When the gospel was originally spread from the disciples of Jesus, the message was first carried by Jews to their fellow-Jews. But their efforts reached out well beyond their boundaries to become a global movement. Many Jewish believers were deceived into believing that they had to continue living under the law of Moses. With this added expectation, these false brothers insisted that the believing Gentiles, also, must obey the law of Moses, including the rite of circumcision.

The truth that Paul wants to defend is that we are saved by God's grace alone. Believing in the Savior Jesus is the lone requirement for salvation. If righteousness can be gained by keeping the law, then Christ died for nothing *(2:21)!* To think that I can gain favor by my works is to discredit the work of the cross.

Paul shoots to the point: *"Did you receive the Spirit by observing the law?"* Of course not. You received the Spirit by believing and embracing the message you heard preached. What you gain in Christ will always and forever be received by faith in Christ alone. The added yoke of following a rigid set of rules or jumping through hoops is unnecessary and burdensome. Changes made in our behavior will follow as a result of our faith, but are not a prerequisite to our faith.

Father, there is nothing I can do to add to my salvation. The life I now live, I live by faith in the Son of God, who loved me and gave Himself for me. Amen.

September 17

Isaiah 25:1–28:13; Galatians 3:10–22; Psalm 61:1–8; Proverbs 23:17–18

Perfect Peace

You will keep in perfect peace him whose mind is steadfast, because he trusts in you. Trust in the Lord forever, for the Lord … is the Rock eternal. Lord, you establish peace for us; all that we have accomplished you have done for us.
—Isaiah 26:3–4,12

Isaiah 26 is a song that will be sung in the land of Judah *in that day* when the Lord Jesus comes to rule and reign over the earth. In that song is a timeless truth that applies likewise for us today. God will keep the one who trusts in Him in perfect peace.

We can be governed by God's perfect peace when our minds are stayed on the Author of our faith. It should be no surprise that our mind has everything to do with being able to apprehend God's peace. Our minds are the gateway to our inner man. It is in the mind where battles are won and lost against an adversary who plants the seeds of doubt and unbelief. Our thought life—what we choose to dwell upon—influences a response of faith or a reflex of fear. *We've all experienced it* …an alarming circumstance arises and we initially believe the worst. A wave of fear ensues and peace somehow vanishes. When we re-assess the situation with God as our immovable Rock, we can respond with trust. He has been faithful in times past. He will prove faithful again. In the Rock of Ages is everlasting strength. Regardless of the size of the storm, God has established peace for us to walk in.

Of course, there are other choices that can steal away our peace. Sin is the biggest thief. But the principle is the same. We selfishly attempt to satisfy our longings without any consideration of God, and we are robbed of His peace and His presence in the process.

Father, You are my Rock. Banish fear and unbelief from my thought-life. I choose to dwell upon Your truth, Your faithfulness and Your peace. Amen.

September 18

Isaiah 28:14–30:11; Galatians 3:23–4:31; Psalm 62:1–12; Proverbs 23:19–21

Sons of God

You are all sons of God through faith in Christ Jesus, for all of you who were baptized into Christ have clothed yourselves with Christ. There is neither Jew nor Greek, male nor female ... you are all one in Christ. Because you are sons, God sent the Spirit into our hearts ... who calls out, "Abba, Father."
—Galatians 3:26-28; 4:6

We are all sons of God through faith in Christ Jesus. Don't let the gender thing bother you. We are also the bride of Christ! It works both ways. But embrace what is being declared about you.

Paul explains that faith could not be revealed until the promised Seed had come *(3:19)*, namely Christ. When God sent Jesus, faith became the key to draw us into relationship with God—something that the law was unable to do. It is the act of believing and trusting in Jesus that identifies us as belonging to Christ. Baptism, then, is the outward tangible decision we make to lay aside the old raiment of the past and put on the righteous adornment of Christ. It's your new look!

Faith in Christ is also the common denominator amongst all His family members—no matter your heritage or gender. That's because there is no partiality with God. He values the heart response of each one. He views us as one in Christ Jesus; as family.

God's design is that we might receive the full rights of sons. He sent the Spirit of His Son into our hearts so that we might have the closest possible relationship, and call upon Him as "Abba, Father." We are even named as heirs, so all that we are and have comes from Him.

Abba, You have sent Your Son, and I have believed upon Him. My spirit has been made alive. May I walk in my new identity as a son and with others who call on Your Name. You are my Father. You have called me Your son. Amen.

September 19

Isaiah 30:12–33:12; Galatians 5:1–12; Psalm 63:1–11; Proverbs 23:22

Earnestly I Seek You

O God, you are my God, earnestly I seek you; my soul thirsts for you, my body longs for you, in a dry and weary land where there is no water. I have seen you in the sanctuary and beheld your power and your glory. Because your love is better than life, my lips will glorify you.
    —Psalm 63:1–3

Have you ever been hot and thirsty where there was no resource at hand to refresh you? This Psalm exemplifies so well the heart of David at a lonely time of his life, seeking refuge in the barren Desert of Judah. Hiding from his enemies, David cries out to God. He uses his immediate surroundings to describe the longings of his soul to meet with God. Earnestly, and with intentionality, David sought the Lord. The truth be told—all David has is the companionship of his God. There is desperation in his voice. *"My soul clings to you!"(v.8).*

Even through the three watches of the night, David, in his sleeplessness, ponders the goodness of the Lord. Instead of stressing and fretting over the situation, David took that time to reflect and worship. He had time on his hands, and he utilized it to his benefit.

At this juncture of his life, David has a history with God. He has witnessed the power and the glory of the Lord. He has beheld the presence and protection of God. It has been a life made full by the love of God. Acknowledging that he has been so abundantly blessed, David resolves to sing praises, lift up his hands and glorify the Lord.

"Blessed are those who hunger and thirst for righteousness, for they will be filled" *(Matthew 5:6).* How hungry are you for the things of God?

Father, Your love is better than life. You alone have satisfied my soul. I resolve to seek You with all my heart and to praise Your wonderful name. Amen.

September 20

Isaiah 33:13–36:22; Galatians 5:13–26; Psalm 64:1–10; Proverbs 23:23

Live by the Spirit

So I say, live by the Spirit, and you will not gratify the desires of the sinful nature. But the fruit of the Spirit is love, joy, peace, patience, kindness, goodness, faithfulness, gentleness and self-control. Against such things there is no law.
—Galatians 5:16,22–23

Paul brings his argument to some exciting conclusions. What counts is faith expressed by love *(5:6)*. Serving one another in love is the goal *(5:13)*, and loving your neighbor *(5:14)* sums it all up. But the motivation is defined by whether we choose to live by the Spirit or by the flesh. God gave us the Spirit so that we could overcome the pull of the sinful nature. The question is: Do you live under the natural impulses of your flesh, or do you submit to the wisdom and lordship of the Spirit of God within you?

The natural results of this trail are obvious. Live by your sinful inclinations and every sort of selfish impurity will follow. You won't have to work hard at it either. On the opposite spectrum—if you live by the Spirit, you will repel those sinful desires, because the Spirit and the sinful nature are contrary to each other, like oil and water. The natural outflow of a Spirit-led life is the fruit of love and joy, peace, patience, kindness, goodness, faithfulness, gentleness and self-control. You cannot manufacture these attributes in your flesh. No law can produce what is birthed by the Spirit. But live by the direction of the Spirit and each of these will develop and manifest in your life.

We can live the crucified life over sinful passions only by the power of the Holy Spirit. We overcome when we live and love by the Spirit.

Father God, I pray that spiritual fruit will grow exponentially as I give myself to the leading of Your Spirit. Empower me to walk this out every day. Amen.

September 21

Isaiah 37:1–38:22; Galatians 6:1–18; Psalm 65:1–13; Proverbs 23:24–25

Sowing and Reaping

Do not be deceived: God cannot be mocked. A man reaps what he sows. The one who sows to please his sinful nature will reap destruction; the one who sows to please the Spirit … will reap eternal life. Let us not become weary in doing good, for at the proper time we will reap a harvest if we do not give up.
   —Galatians 6:7–9

The principle of reaping and sowing is like the law of gravity. It's just as certain as that. Like it or not, you cannot beat the system. You may perhaps pull one over on some, but you will not fool God. And over time, it becomes increasingly evident what seeds you have sown.

If you plant cucumber seeds in the spring, you're going to get cucumbers in late summer. If you sow seeds of anger, you can blame the other guy, but it will progress to bitterness and worse, in your own heart. By giving place to it and rehearsing it over and over in your thoughts, it grows and is sure to manifest. It's the same with lust, or any other vice that feeds off the sinful nature. Destruction in some form is sure to follow. You only deceive yourself if you think you can sow to the flesh and not reap a very corrupt consequence.

But the equalizer is that the law of sowing and reaping works the same when you sow to the Spirit. When you give yourself to the reading of God's Word and to prayer, to times of worship and serving others, you will also reap a harvest of rich fellowship with the Spirit of God. You will be refreshed in your spirit. You will hear what is on the heart of God. Wisdom will be accelerated in your life. You will love people sincerely. You will creatively and thoughtfully imagine ways to bless those in your path. What seeds are you sowing in this season?

Almighty God, today, in this season, I commit to You my time and energy in order to please the Spirit. May an abundant harvest follow. Amen.

September 22

Isaiah 39:1–41:16; Ephesians 1:1–23; Psalm 66:1–20; Proverbs 23:26–28

Prayer for Revelation

I keep asking that the God of our Lord Jesus Christ, the glorious Father, may give you the Spirit of wisdom and revelation, so that you may know him better. I pray also that the eyes of your heart may be enlightened in order that you may know the hope that he has called you, the riches of his glorious inheritance in the saints, and his incomparably great power for us who believe.
—*Ephesians 1:17–19*

Paul has spent considerable time with the Ephesian believers, and so pens this letter of encouragement to them while imprisoned in Rome. He details the truth about the church in such extravagant language, but it's his personal prayer for them that resounds today.

Paul prays for his friends. He has invested in them. He thanks God for them often. He asks, and he keeps asking, that God would meet with them and disclose new layers of revelation of Himself. The Spirit of God is the Spirit of wisdom and the Spirit of revelation. Simply put, prayer is talking to God, and revelation is God talking back to us. When we ask, we can anticipate that God will impart His perspective. We can expect that God will download into our spirit truth from His Word. He is a speaking God. We only need the eyes of our heart to be enlightened. The goal is to engage with the Spirit, so that we may come to know our glorious Father better and more intimately.

God wants us to know Him in truth. He desires that we would be able to grasp and discern what He has for us. There is a great wealth of hope and riches and power for those who believe and apprehend what God has provided. Ignorance is not bliss. It is the inheritance of every believer to hear the voice of the Spirit and draw near.

Father, open the eyes of my understanding that I may perceive the promptings of the Spirit. Cause me to internalize what You have declared to be so. Amen

September 23

Isaiah 41:17–43:13; Ephesians 2:1–22; Psalm 67:1–7; Proverbs 23:29–35

You Are Mine

But now, this is what the Lord says— "Fear not, for I have redeemed you; I have summoned you by name; you are mine. Since you are precious and honored in my sight, and because I love you … whom I created for my glory, whom I formed and made."
—Isaiah 43:1,4,7

Isaiah articulates the strong emotions of a loving Father in spite of continued resistance of His own people. Their propensity to stray does not change His heart of mercy and the plans He has purposed for their future benefit. Most of us, as parents, have understood this crisis. When our child approaches adulthood, we want them to know that they are loved for who they are. We have lofty dreams for their success. They can make grievous decisions, but we do not stop loving.

Isaiah specifies that it is Israel who God has formed and created. But the passage has a dual application. It is meant for you and I, as well. It is God's heart for *you*. Hear His desire for you. He has called you by name. You are precious to God. You are honored in His sight. He has created you for glory. Why? *…because He loves you.*

When life happens, you are never alone. When the fire of adversity strikes, the Lord, your God, is with you. The Holy One of Israel is your Savior. You can walk in confidence and without fear, because He is with you. You are never alone. He takes you by the hand *(42:6)*.

This is the heart of the Father for everyone who has ever strayed. He does not wring His hands in disgust. He is patient towards the wayward and longs to grant redemption. He declares, *"you are mine!"*

Father, You have made this personal. Your emotions for me are very real. You declare over me that I am yours. I am grateful and long to reflect Your glory.

September 24

Isaiah 43:14–45:10; Ephesians 3:1–21; Psalm 68:1–18; Proverbs 24:1–2

The Girth of God's Love

And I pray that you, being rooted and established in love, may have power, together with all the saints, to grasp how wide and long and high and deep is the love of Christ, and to know this love that surpasses knowledge—that you may be filled to the measure of all the fullness of God.
—Ephesians 3:17–19

When I last mailed a parcel to my daughter in the UK, the friendly postal clerk computed the cost by figuring the width and length and the girth—or the circumference—of the package. It represents the greatest measurement around the middle. So when I consider how massive and inexhaustible the love of Christ is, I am reminded of the "girth dimension." It is God's love in bulk proportions.

In our verses, Paul is praying again for believers—this time for *power*. First, we need to be strengthened with *power* in our inner man by His Spirit so that Christ may dwell in our hearts. His power enables us to have faith and believe. Next, Paul prays that we would have *power* to grasp the magnitude of Christ's love. Our unrenewed mind cannot fathom such things! We need to be empowered on the inside in order to somehow comprehend this love even a little bit. God's love supersedes knowledge. It's revelation. It is to be known and experienced on a personal level—to be rooted and grounded in love— so that we may be filled with all the fullness that God has for us.

We will spend a lifetime swimming in the depths of God's great sea of love. We will discover more and more as we go, and yet, never see the end of the reaches of His lovingkindness.

Father, You have strengthened me in my inner man to know You and Your inexhaustible love. Your power is at work in me beyond what I can imagine. Establish me in love. Cause me to know the girth of Your love. Amen.

September 25

Isaiah 45:11–48:11; Ephesians 4:1–16; Psalm 68:19–35; Proverbs 24:3–4

Office Gifts

It was he (Christ) who gave some to be apostles, some to be prophets, some to be evangelists, and some to be pastors and teachers, to prepare God's people for works of service, so that the body of Christ may be built up until we all reach unity in the faith and in the knowledge of the Son of God and become mature.
—Ephesians 4:11–13

Paul gives us insight into God-ordained church leadership, in order for the body of Christ to be built up, prepared for service and become mature. Mentioned are five distinct offices that God has instituted to bring about the attaining of the full measure of Christ *(v.13)*.

Pastors are the personable nurturers who can build, oversee and coach a group of people, and lead by example. Apostles establish, oversee and care for the nurturing of many congregations. Teachers explain the gospel in a most apprehendable manner. Prophets are black and white in their perspective. They hear the word of the Lord for the moment. The thrust of the evangelist is primarily soul-winning.

In the western church, we are accustomed to having "pastors" who fill the pulpits. While, in fact, many times the person filling the position is called a pastor, he may have the calling and anointing for the office of the evangelist. So we shouldn't be surprised when a local "pastor" preaches salvation each week to his congregation, because God has gifted him to be an evangelist. These callings are equally important to bring about the full counsel of God, but are also reliant upon the other offices to bring about the balance. One leader cannot wear the hats of all five offices. The body of Christ needs the impartation that each office presents. Can you tell which office your "pastor" is gifted?

Father, You have placed godly leaders in the body of Christ with a variety of gifts so that I might grow in Your truth. I honor your servants. Amen.

September 26

Isaiah 48:12–50:11; Ephesians 4:17–32; Psalm 69:1–18; Proverbs 24:5–6

The Great Put On

You were taught, with regard to your former way of life, to put off your old self… and to put on the new self, created to be like God in true righteousness and holiness … And do not grieve the Holy Spirit of God …
—Ephesians 4:22,24,30

Paul now exhorts the new believer to live out of a new identity. We are no longer among the ignorant and darkened of understanding. Paul has carefully laid out our identity as believers. Now it is time for us to shake off the former way of life in regard to everyday choices.

We now consciously and intentionally put off the old man of corruption and put on the new self. We can do this because our minds are being renewed in the truth of God. We don't just put on the façade of a happy face. We act out of a new nature that reflects the righteous and holy nature of God. The Spirit of God dwells within to empower us to make that break with old patterns and habits.

The pull of the old corrupt desires can be strong, especially if habits have formed a lifestyle. That's why Paul warns us not to give place to the devil. You don't want the foothold to become a stronghold. Then a more complete deliverance is needed. When we cave in to the old desires, it actually grieves the Spirit of God within us.

Listen. New attitudes only arise when we bathe our mind in the truth of God's Word. Give yourself to it. Become a student of the Word. You will find yourself loving the things that He loves and hating the things that He hates. You will be amazed, as the transformation will become very apparent. You are being fashioned to reflect the glory of Jesus.

Father, You have given me a new identity to walk in. Today, I lay aside my old manner of life and put on the new self You have created me to be. Amen.

September 27

Isaiah 51:1–53:12; Ephesians 5:1–33; Psalm 69:19–36; Proverbs 24:7

A Man of Sorrows

He had no beauty or majesty to attract us to him, nothing in his appearance that we should desire him ... He was despised and rejected by men, a man of sorrows, and familiar with suffering ... But he was pierced for our transgressions, he was crushed for our iniquities; the punishment that brought us peace was upon him, and by his wounds we are healed.
—Isaiah 53:2–3,5

What an incredible foretelling Isaiah describes 700 years before the Lord's servant bursts onto the scene. The Messiah who will bring salvation is described no doubt differently than they would imagine.

The Messiah-to-come is described as a man who is very ordinary in appearance—nothing stands out in particular. But he is no ordinary man. He will bear the iniquity of a sin-laden people. He will carry our rebellion to the cross. The Lord's righteous servant is despised by men. He is also rejected by men. He would come to know extreme sorrow and emotional grief. He would suffer excruciating pain. In the midst of his affliction, he is speechless and will not retaliate. The suffering he endures cannot be overstated. *But why must it be?*

It was the Lord's will to crush him and cause him to suffer in order to make his spotless life an offering for sin. In this manner, he justified the many. He bore the punishment we deserved. By his sacrifice, we are introduced to forgiveness and peace and healing. By this supreme act of love, we are made acceptable before a holy God. Isaiah saw it all. He could also report that this same Jesus would be lifted up and highly exalted. He will rule and reign triumphantly!

Father, You designed a plan to deal with my brokenness and sin once and for all. You brought it to fruition because of Your great love. Thank You for Jesus, who humbly accepted Your assignment to bring salvation and healing. Amen.

September 28

Isaiah 54:1–57:13; Ephesians 6:1–24; Psalm 70:1–5; Proverbs 24:8

The Armor of God

Finally, be strong in the Lord and in his mighty power. Put on the full armor of God so that you can take your stand against the devil's schemes. For our struggle is not against flesh and blood, but ... against the spiritual forces of evil ...
—Ephesians 6:10–12

The wily devil is relentless in his attempts to assault the believer, to lie and deceive and uproot faith. There is most definitely a struggle involved, but Paul wants us to know how we can win the skirmish.

First, remember that it is not people with skin who are the real problem here. Yes, it may involve people, but it is the unseen demonic forces behind the people that bring the fight. This helps us to deal with the real culprit, not the mindless pawns who are being used. The goal, then—that Paul states four times—is to stand your ground. To be unmovable in your faith is Paul's point. So how do we take our stand?

We confront the enemy with the armament that God provides. Truth is central. We deal in truth. We speak the truth. We protect our heart with right choices. We ready our feet to spread about peace. Even our faith is a shield in the midst of fiery onslaughts. We guard our minds by reminding ourselves over and over the truth of the gospel. Verbally speaking the Word of God over the situation is our offensive weapon to secure victory. Spirit-directed prayers are mighty because we release God to war on our behalf. It is His mighty power we stand in.

Isaiah adds this word of the Lord: *"no weapon forged against you will prevail, and you will refute every tongue that accuses you" (54:17).*

Father, I appeal to You when the enemy strikes. I do not shrink back, since You have provided for my deliverance. Help me to stand to the end. Amen.

September 29

Isaiah 57:14–59:21; Philippians 1:1–26; Psalm 71:1–24; Proverbs 24:9–10

Where God Dwells

For this is what the high and lofty One says—he who lives forever, whose name is holy: "I live in a high and holy place, but also with him who is contrite and lowly in spirit, to revive the spirit of the lowly and… the heart of the contrite."
—Isaiah 57:15

To appreciate this verse, consider the greatness of our God. He is the high and lofty One. He lives forever. Holy is His name. He is the Maker of heaven and earth. He is the God of Israel. He is the God over all the kingdoms of the earth. He is enthroned between the cherubim and He is seated above the circle of the earth. He stretches out the heavens like a tent to live in *(Isaiah 37:16; 40:22)*. What majesty and honor surround Him.

Now, imagine the God of glory coming down to dwell with man. This is what King Solomon was grappling with as he prayed at the temple dedication: *"But will God really dwell on earth with men? The heavens, even the highest heavens, cannot contain you … how much less this temple I have built!" (2 Chronicles 6:18)*.

But here is the stroke of genius: God is attracted to humility. He is drawn to the humble, the contrite and the repentant heart. A lowly spirit is a magnet for the God of Awesome to come and dwell, because he knows his true condition. He knows that all he is and has comes from God. David prayed… *"a broken and contrite heart, O God, you will not despise" (Psalm 51:17)*. Think of it … God moves in to revive the heart that bows low to welcome Him. The very thought is humbling.

High and lofty Father, You are greatly to be praised. There is none like You in all the earth. Cause me to know my barren condition without You, so that I will each day acknowledge my need for You. May I walk in humility so that I will always be squarely in Your gaze. In Jesus' name, Amen.

September 30

Isaiah 60:1–62:5; Philippians 1:27–2:18; Psalm 72:1–20; Proverbs 24:11–12

Humility Personified

Your attitude should be the same as that of Christ Jesus: Who, being in very nature God, did not consider equality with God something to be grasped, but made himself nothing, taking the very nature of a servant ... made in human likeness... he humbled himself and became obedient to death—even on a cross!
—Philippians 2:5–8

Oddly enough, we have the message of humility extended by the very example of Jesus. Paul explains that Jesus was Himself God, but He voluntarily clothed Himself in human flesh and subjected Himself to human limitations in time and space. Jesus was wholly God, and yet, wholly man. He set aside the right to His glory and power so that he could identify with our sins and the human condition.

Jesus humbled himself by becoming obedient to the Father's plan, a plan that would include dying on the cross for the sins of all humanity. By this, Paul admonishes us: *"Your attitude should be the same as that of Christ Jesus."* Humility is first expressed by an attitude of willing obedience to the Father. He has a plan, and it is God who works in you to bring about the good purposes of His plan.

Humility is further expressed in our selfless attitude towards others. That's exactly what Jesus did. He laid aside his own agenda to consider the overarching interest of others. He resisted self-interest and self-preservation in order to bring salvation to us all.

Obey God and serve people. It's the way of humility and the way we mature. *"In humility, consider others better than yourselves"* (2:3).

Father God, I thank You for Your plan of salvation and the willing obedience of Your Son to carry it out. May I express my love to You with the same attitude that serves others and brings honor to Your name. Amen.

October 1

Isaiah 62:6–65:25; Philippians 2:19–3:4a; Psalm 73:1–28; Proverbs 24:13–14

Give Him No Rest

I have posted watchmen on your walls, O Jerusalem; they will never be silent day or night. You who call on the Lord, give yourselves no rest and give him no rest till he establishes Jerusalem and makes her the praise of the earth.
—Isaiah 62:6–7

Isaiah gives us compelling reason for night and day prayer to be offered on behalf of Israel. Clearly his desire for the salvation of his people is cause for intercession. Our passage today continues from yesterday: *"For Zion's sake I will not keep silent, for Jerusalem's sake I will not remain quiet, till her righteousness shines out like the dawn, her salvation like a blazing torch" (62:1).*

The prophet gives us a glimpse into the future plans the Lord has for His own. His zeal for Zion is unquestioned. They will be called "the Redeemed of the Lord," and "the City No Longer Deserted," because God will take delight in them. The salvation of Israel will blaze like a torch to show forth the glory of the Lord. All the nations will witness their turnabout. They will be a crown of splendor in His hand.

Paul explains that … *"Israel has experienced a hardening in part … "*but *"all Israel will be saved. Just as you who were at one time disobedient to God have now received mercy as a result of their disobedience, so they too have now become disobedient in order that they too may now receive mercy as a result of God's mercy to you" (Romans 11:25–26,30–31).* The beauty of mercy is that it is revealed to the disobedient. God's claim is upon them by covenant. God is jealous for Jerusalem. So we persist in prayer for the promises of God to come to fruition.

Father, I bring before You the nation of Israel. Reveal Your mercy. Cause their eyes to be opened to the one true Messiah. May they receive Your kind gift of salvation and show forth Your splendor in all the earth. Amen.

October 2

Isaiah 66:1–24; Philippians 3:4b–21; Psalm 74:1–23; Proverbs 24:15–16

Press in for the Prize

Brothers, I do not consider myself yet to have taken hold of it. But one thing I do: Forgetting what is behind and straining toward what is ahead, I press on toward the goal to win the prize for which God has called me heavenward in Christ Jesus.
—Philippians 3:13–14

There is a goal—a prize—and I have not yet obtained it. But I'm in good company, because Paul hadn't yet either. I press on, because there is more to embrace. We are not talking about our righteous standing before the Lord. Our legal position before God is assured through the cross of Christ by simple faith. But there is more to press in for. I have not attained to all that Christ died for. There is more for me, but it is not granted without the reach. It must be sought after.

Christ took a hold of me for grand purposes. I don't want to live a life of regrets, or look back and wonder what could have been. There is more to apprehend. Paul said, *"I want to know Christ and the power of his resurrection,"* and yes, even *"the fellowship of sharing in his sufferings" (3:10)*. There is a deep intimacy of knowing Christ in this way—in demonstrations of His power *and* suffering in the face of persecution. Trusting God through every possible challenge in this life will carry us to the final goal of attaining resurrected bodies at Jesus' coming.

My contribution is to not dwell on what I cannot change, but to let go of the past and focus on the prize that is before me. I pursue and strain to finish my race strong. I am not passive. I press in to win. I live up to what I have already attained, but I also cannot afford to drift in neutral. I seek Him for more, because there is more to seize.

Father, I want to embrace all that You have intended for me. I want to know You and be known by You. I press in to the upward call. Amen

October 3

Jeremiah 1:1–2:30; Philippians 4:1–23; Psalm 75:1–10; Proverbs 24:17–20

Rejoice and Pray

Rejoice in the Lord always. I will say it again: Rejoice! Do not be anxious about anything, but in everything, by prayer and petition, with thanksgiving, present your requests to God. And the peace of God, which transcends all understanding, will guard your hearts and minds in Christ Jesus.
—Philippians 4:4,6–7

As Paul addresses his friends at Philippi, he writes from a unique perspective—he is imprisoned in Rome. It's in this context, ironically, that Paul encourages them to live in the reality of joy. The joy of the Lord is cultivated by walking in the Spirit and is not dependent upon our circumstances. Sixteen times in this short epistle Paul refers to *joy*, or the verb, *rejoice*. We rejoice because He has made our hearts glad.

It's a natural reaction to become anxious when challenging circumstances arise. But Paul has a right strategy when adversity comes knocking: rejoice and pray. The Lord says: *"Talk to Me. Give it to Me. There is nothing too small or great. Do not entertain fear. I am near you. I know your situation. I will meet you where you are at."*

You see, God knows that what we need in the moment is His peace. The peace of God is a monitor upon our heart that affirms that He is near. We can trust Him. His peace protects our minds from imagining the worst. Even when we don't understand or have an answer or an ability to control it, God will guide us through with an uncanny peace.

The exhortation is to present your request with every sort of prayer. Pray, and in the midst of your circumstance, give thanks, because the Lord has your back. Affirm your trust and acknowledge His presence.

Father, I don't give in to fear, because You are near. I can proceed confidently because Your peace guides me. I rejoice in You and give thanks. Hallelujah!

October 4

Jeremiah 2:31–4:18; Colossians 1:1–20; Psalm 76:1–12; Proverbs 24:21–22

An Adulterous Heart

This is what the Lord says to the men of Judah and to Jerusalem: "Break up your unplowed ground and do not sow among thorns. Circumcise yourselves to the Lord, circumcise your hearts ... because of the evil you have done."
—Jeremiah 4:3–4

However agonizing and alarming, the prophet Jeremiah proclaims the message of the Lord to a faithless people. The truth of their heart-state has to be spoken in order for Judah to repent and turn from their waywardness. But Judah is not listening. Jeremiah describes the condition of their heart in dramatic terms.

"Does a maiden forget her jewelry, a bride her wedding ornaments? Yet my people have forgotten me, days without number. How skilled you are at pursuing love!" (2:32-33). *"Yet you have the brazen look of a prostitute; you refuse to blush with shame"* (3:3). *"Return, faithless people; I will cure you of backsliding"* (3:22).

It is the endless pursuit of other loves that drew away the heart of Judah. Searching for fulfillment outside the perimeters of God's love and provision became an adultery of the heart. Their infatuation over lesser gods defiled them. Judah was deceived about their sin and their hearts became hardened and desensitized to God's ways.

It is a wake-up call for us all. While there are many alluring options to captivate the heart, they are all idols. God says: *"Plow up the ground of your heart. Do not waste your life where no fruit is able to grow."* As circumcision is a cutting away of the outer flesh, God says: *"Cut away the fleshly desires that surround your heart. I am jealous for you."*

Father, You know my heart well. Forgive me for pursuing other loves. Purify my desires that I may be wholly yours, for You are a faithful Husband. Amen.

October 5

Jeremiah 4:19–6:14; Colossians 1:21–2:7; Psalm 77:1–20; Proverbs 24:23–25

The Process to Perfection

Once you were alienated from God ... now he has reconciled you by Christ's physical body through death to present you holy in his sight, without blemish and free from accusation. We proclaim him, admonishing and teaching everyone with all wisdom, so that we may present everyone perfect in Christ.
—Colossians 1:21–22,28

When is the last time you have reflected back on your life to see where God has brought you from? What a mess we were. Paul reminds us that we were alienated from God and were enemies by our behavior. But through the cross of Jesus, our relationship was restored. By his atoning sacrifice, we were made holy in His sight. Where we were once only to blame, now we are declared blame*less*. This is the way the holy God of heaven sees us now—through Christ.

Yet Paul labored in the power of the Holy Spirit so to be able to present every man and woman perfect in Christ. *Wasn't I already declared perfect? Isn't that enough?* The gap lies in the "legal position" that Christ affords us through faith and our "living condition" in real time. Thank the Lord for our perfected status before the Father. He accepts us just the way we are, but He loves us too much to leave us that way! The life we live ought to reflect what is true of our righteous standing. It is a process that will continue throughout our lifetime.

This process to full maturity comes as we daily submit to the Lord, continuing in the faith, not moved from the hope that we have and obeying the Lord completely as we know to do. The Holy Spirit is the best teacher and divine enabler to coach us to this desired end.

Father, thank You for reconciling me back into fellowship through Jesus. You see me now as perfect, and I want my life to reflect that holy position. Empower me by the Spirit to live righteously before You in this world. Amen.

October 6

Jeremiah 6:15–8:7; Colossians 2:8–23; Psalm 78:1–31; Proverbs 24:26

Stand at the Crossroads

This is what the Lord says: "Stand at the crossroads and look; ask for the ancient paths, ask where the good way is, and walk in it, and you will find rest for your souls. But you said, "We will not walk in it."
—Jeremiah 6:16

Jeremiah is imploring the hardened rebels of Judah to turn back from their sin. They do not listen or pay attention to the word of the Lord. They only continue their impulses bent upon evil *(7:24)*. Truth has vanished from their lips. Their sin deceives them. They think they can prance into the house of God while continuing their same detestable practices *(7:10)*. They don't realize that they will be thrust from God's presence. Judgment is inevitable. Yet God beckons.

The Lord says to the rebellious heart: *"Stand at the crossroads."* We may not even recognize it at first. But the crossroads is a place of decision. The Lord is good at positioning us like that. He places us at a fork in the road that forces our hand to decide what direction we are going to commit to. The Lord says: *"Look."* Stop to pause and assess what you are doing and where this is going. It's not too late. But don't be fooled. It's late enough. Consequences will follow, either way. The Lord says: *"Ask."* Inquire of the Lord. Seek godly counsel. Ask for the ancient paths. The wisdom that has worked for generations is still pertinent today. Why can't we learn from our fathers before us? The precepts and principals of God do not change. Lastly, the Lord says: *"Walk in it."* Walk in the good way provided. A decision leads to action.

The impact of obedience is rest for your souls. Instead of angst and torment, you can know peace that can actually be felt.

Ancient of Days, thank You for the fork in the road that causes me to pause and inquire of You. I turn from my selfish inclinations to follow You. Amen.

October 7

Jeremiah 8:8–9:26; Colossians 3:1–17; Psalm 78:32–55; Proverbs 24:27

Word Dwell Richly

Let the word of Christ dwell in you richly as you teach and admonish one another with all wisdom, and as you sing psalms, hymns and spiritual songs with gratitude in your hearts to God.
—Colossians 3:16

In this passage, Paul speaks of our newfound identity as believers and gives practical ways for us to walk it out. For example, you have died and your life is now hidden with Christ, therefore, put to death all that belongs to your earthly nature. Again, you have been raised with Christ, therefore, set your hearts and minds on things above. Put on the new self. Clothe yourselves with kindness. Forgive. Put on love.

The most proactive thing I can do to walk out this new identity is to saturate my mind with the Word of God. The Spirit of God breathes life into my spirit when I dwell upon His truth. It changes me from the inside out. When I am full of His Word, I am ready to overflow with a helpful insight or encouragement. It's on my tongue. I am looking for an opportunity to bless someone. This treasure was given me, not to hoard, but to give away. I don't have to be a teacher or a preacher to share what God is imparting. Life-giving wisdom will spill out of my mouth to bless whoever God has in front of me in that moment.

Singing songs unto the Lord is another avenue to affirm the truth of God's Word and release gratitude that wells up inside. Proclaiming His Word with melody and song is powerful three ways: to the hearer, even more so to the proclaimer, and ultimately to the One Whom we are proclaiming to and about. God loves to hear it from your lips.

Father, You know that just as my body craves food, my spirit craves Your Word. You designed me to be refilled and refreshed each new day. Your well is endless. Let Your Word dwell richly in me that I may be a giver. Amen.

October 8

Jeremiah 10:1–11:23; Colossians 3:18–4:18; Psalm 78:56–72; Proverbs 24:28–29

Wrestling in Prayer

Devote yourselves to prayer, being watchful and thankful. And pray for us, too, that God may open a door for our message, so that we may proclaim the mystery of Christ, for which I am in chains. Pray that I may proclaim it clearly, as I should. Epaphras … is always wrestling in prayer for you, that you may stand firm in all the will of God, mature and fully assured.
　—*Colossians 4:2–4,12*

Just as you or I would write a letter to a friend, Paul concludes his letter to the Colossian believers with personal updates on those relationships they had in common. Some of those he mentions are even being sent to them from Paul. With Paul, relationships are paramount, and prayer is the most effective way we nurture those relationships, because we keep them before us and before God.

One who sent greetings was Epaphras. He was the one who actually founded the Colossian church. It was said of Epaphras that *"he always wrestles in prayer for you."* That sounds impressive, but what does it mean? In high school, I wrestled my sophomore year. I was the junior-varsity wrestler in the 105 lb. class. I concluded that no other sport was more exhausting. It taught me life skills and discipline I will never forget. Translating my experience, I would claim that wrestling in prayer is to labor fervently on behalf of another. It is not being vague in my appeals to the Father. It is pressing in and not letting go. It is confronting the spiritual adversary that would hold you back.

Epaphras was resolute and determined to bring about all the will of God in those of his circle. He travailed for those precious to him. *Think about it:* since it is God alone who can bring about change, the most thoughtful thing I can do is lift those before the Father of glory.

Father, I call forth prayer warriors to contend for the body of Christ. Amen.

October 9

Jeremiah 12:1–14:10; 1 Thessalonians 1:1–2:9; Psalm 79:1–13; Proverbs 24:30-34

A Steady Witness

Our gospel came to you not simply with words, but also with power, with the Holy Spirit and deep conviction. You know how we lived among you for your sake. Your faith in God has become known everywhere.
    —1 Thessalonians 1:5,8

On Paul's second missionary journey, he and Silas traveled through Macedonia, running into jealous Jews in Philippi and Thessalonica *(Acts 17:5)*. But the gospel was proclaimed nonetheless. In this adversarial situation, the message was received even more effectively, because it endured the scrutiny of it's enemies. *This gospel was real!*

What conviction poured from their lips and their lives. Paul and Silas were not in the business of impressing their audience with eloquent sermons. Either this message worked in the trenches or it didn't work at all. In spite of severe opposition, the Holy Spirit impacted the Thessalonians to turn from their idols and serve the true and living God. They witnessed the gospel at work in the lives of those who were sharing it. They saw with their eyes the power of the Holy Spirit. From that testimony, now they were welcoming their message with open arms. Faith welled up. The joy of the Spirit enveloped them.

In these rigid circumstances, the gospel rang true and loud. Thank God for the compassion and tenacity of these apostles. Their love was evident and their testimony true. From this, the young faith of these Macedonians was on display and became known everywhere. When the opportunity presents itself, does your light shine in season and out? Is your witness steady in the good times *and* the bad?

Father, I only ask that my words pour forth with conviction by the Holy Spirit and that my life will affirm the message I proclaim. Draw all men unto You. Amen.

October 10

Jeremiah 14:11-16:15; 1 Thessalonians 2:10-3:13; Psalm 80:1-19; Proverbs 25:1-5

My Response to the Word

And we also thank God continually because, when you received the word of God, which you heard from us, you accepted it not as the word of men, but as it actually is, the word of God, which is at work in you who believe.
—1 Thessalonians 2:13

When your words came, I ate them; they were my joy and my heart's delight.
—Jeremiah 15:16

It is quite intriguing when a similar theme is echoed throughout the day's verses. Today, three instances surface concerning the response of the writer to the word of the Lord.

Paul was exhilarated to find the Thessalonians so accepting of the spoken word that was proclaimed. Even amidst persecution, they received it as God's words. The word of God, inspired by the Holy Spirit and received by faith, is an agent of change to conform us to the image of Jesus. The word continues to work within yielded hearts.

Jeremiah heard the word of the Lord usually as a conversation *(i.e. "Then the Lord said to me …").* Whether it was audible or not is not important. Jeremiah discerned God's voice distinctly. When His words came, Jeremiah consumed them. He delighted to hear what was on the Lord's heart. Delivering the word as God spoke it was Jeremiah's primary occupation, whether the people of Judah received it or not.

Proverbs 25:2: "It is the glory of God to conceal a matter; to search out a matter is the glory of kings." God has hidden treasure in His Word, not to keep you from it, but for you to seek it out and discover it.

Father, I welcome your Word into my heart. I position myself before Your printed Word to search out matters of wisdom and to know You. It is my joy to hear Your Spirit speak. What is on Your heart for me today? Amen.

October 11

Jeremiah 16:16–18:23; 1 Thessalonians 4:1–5:3; Psalm 81:1–16; Proverbs 25:6–7

Called to Purity

It is God's will that you should be sanctified: that you should avoid sexual immorality; that each of you should learn to control his own body in such a way that is holy and honorable, not in passionate lust like the heathen … For God did not call us to be impure, but to live a holy life.
—1 Thessalonians 4:3–5,7

You want to know what God's will looks like? Here it is … in part. God has called us to be sanctified. Sanctification is that process of cleansing that starts when we accept Jesus into our lives. We are declared righteous before God, but the process of cleansing my thoughts and behavior has to be worked out. It's not automatic.

The Holy Spirit of God now dwells within us to convict us and coach us along. So we are not left to ourselves. We first notice the change when it bothers our conscience that we even thought that thought, because it didn't use to. Now, we want to do right, even if our flesh wants it kicking and screaming. I used to give in so easily. But now I sense the battle that rages within me.

Enter again the Holy Spirit. Temptations may send up the high alerts, but I have also been renewing my mind in the truth of God's Word. Now I have help I didn't use to have. The Spirit enables me to say a resounding "No." It's called self-control. It's a fruit of a life lived in the Spirit. It's our responsibility in this relationship with a holy God. He provides the supernatural strength to run from anything that even remotely smells of a compromising situation. Do what Joseph did. He didn't hang around or entertain the idea. He ran. *What a man!*

Father, in an age where immorality floods the streets, raise up a remnant of men and women who will pledge their bodies to purity with the help of the Holy Spirit. Cleanse my mind and my motives. In Jesus' name, Amen.

October 12

Jeremiah 19:1–21:14; 1 Thessalonians 5:4–28; Psalm 82:1–8; Proverbs 25:8–10

More of God's Will

Be joyful always; pray continually; give thanks in all circumstances, for this is God's will for you in Christ Jesus. Do not put out the Spirit's fire; do not treat prophecies with contempt. Test everything. Hold on to the good. Avoid every kind of evil.
—*1 Thessalonians 5:16–22*

We just read yesterday that it was God's will that we should be sanctified. Ready for some more of God's will for your life?

You have to love this passage. They are like rapid-fire power verses. No fluff here. Compact, but mighty, and we need to be reminded.

Denny's version: **16.** You are allowed to be joyful. I don't believe God wears a frown, so why should we? Joy is a natural outcome of walking in the Spirit, and is not dependent upon your circumstances. **17.** You can formulate short, effective prayers all through the day. Give people and situations to God as they pop up in your mind. **18.** Give thanks in every situation, knowing that God is right there with you. By it, you acknowledge that He knows what He is doing and has your best interest in mind. He has not turned His head. It has not taken Him by surprise. **19.** The Spirit, He is God, and He is active in His people. Do not stifle what He is doing just because you cannot rationalize it all. **20.** Do not minimize or dismiss the prophetic voice. **21.** Don't be passive or gullible. Evaluate all things according to the Word of God. Embrace what is beneficial and faith-building. **22.** Be discerning and wise, so that you are not associated with any expression of evil.

To live out God's will is to walk in the Spirit every conscious moment.

Father, I covet Your will for every aspect of my life. I embrace Your counsel. Let Your joy overflow upon my countenance as I trust in You. Amen.

October 13

Jeremiah 22:1–23:20; 2 Thessalonians 1:1–12; Psalm 83:1–18; Proverbs 25:11–14

God is Just

We boast about your perseverance and faith in all the persecutions and trials you are enduring. God is just: He will pay back trouble to those who trouble you and give relief to you who are troubled ... This will happen when the Lord Jesus is revealed from heaven in blazing fire with his powerful angels.
—2 Thessalonians 1:4,6–7

Paul's greeting to the Thessalonians in his second letter commends them for enduring persecutions and trials from both Jews and their fellow Gentiles. Not only did they endure it, but they were actually growing in their faith and their love for each other was increasing.

These believers knew the truth—that opposition is an element of believing. Not everyone approves. Persecution is very real. Suffering is painful. People are martyred for their faith. Christianity is not a club that protects you from mean-spirited people. The only way to avoid much of the direct hit is to allow your testimony to blend into the woodwork. Become a chameleon. Let your level of commitment fade.

The good news is that God is perfectly just. We don't get all the vindication up front. But when the Lord Jesus returns in glory to establish His kingdom upon the earth, everything will be dealt with. No details will go missing. He keeps really good records. King Jesus will come in blazing fire to judge the earth with His mighty angels.

For those who have known and served Him, we will marvel at the majesty of His power. And while we wait for the great equalizer, we remain faithful to His call to affect our world with a bold witness.

Father in heaven, My hope rests in Your divine justice. It is an honor to carry Your Name to this needy generation. Empower me on the inside to represent You forthrightly. May I be found worthy of Your call. Amen.

October 14

Jeremiah 23:21–25:38; 2 Thessalonians 2:1–17; Psalm 84:1–12; Proverbs 25:15

Like a Hammer

"Let the prophet who has a dream tell his dream, but let the one who has my word speak it faithfully. For what has straw to do with grain?" declares the Lord. "Is not my word like fire," declares the Lord, "and like a hammer that breaks a rock in pieces?"
—Jeremiah 23:28–29

The ministry of the prophet is to speak the word of the Lord—whatever that word is. To an obstinate people, these people of Judah did not listen or receive God's plea to turn from their wickedness. They would have none of it. But they went even beyond that. To justify their sinful lifestyle choices, so-called prophets would arise and speak forth lies *"from their own minds" (23:16)*. They would say in the name of the Lord: *"You will have peace. No harm will come to you" (23:17)*.

Jeremiah calls out these lying prophets: *"I did not speak to them, yet they have prophesied. But if they had stood in my council, they would have proclaimed my words ... and would have turned them from their evil ways..." (23:21-22)*. By pacifying the rebellious with words they wanted to hear, they were sanctioning their sin and leading them away from God. But in the end, lies only keep you from the truth.

The one who proclaims the word of the Lord is held accountable for his words. Jeremiah compares the true and false prophets to straw and grain. One is without substance; the other is nourishing food. The prophetic word is given by God for impact and looks for a corresponding response. That's why His word is like a hammer. It is able to shatter the lies and deceptions that lead hearts away from the truth. We do well to shine the light of truth to expose a deception.

Father, let my words and my life proclaim Your truth, to turn back the one who has been deceived by the lies of sin. Shatter darkness with light. Amen.

October 15

Jeremiah 26:1–27:22; 2 Thessalonians 3:1–18; Psalm 85:1–13; Proverbs 25:16

The Thessalonian Prayer Request

Finally, brothers, pray for us that the message of the Lord may spread rapidly and be honored, just as it was with you. And pray that we may be delivered from wicked and evil men, for not everyone has faith.
—*2 Thessalonians 3:1–2*

"Finally" indicates that we are nearing the end of Paul's letter. Kind of like when the preacher says, "In conclusion …" That just means there is another point yet to be made:)

Paul is committed to praying for his new disciples. *"Night and day we pray most earnestly that we may see you again and supply what is lacking in your faith" (1 Thessalonians 3:10).* Again, *"we constantly pray for you, that our God may count you worthy of his calling…" (2 Thessalonians 1:11).* Prayer was his commitment of love for his friends while away. Paul knows how prayer binds the heart together, so he wants to enlist the Thessalonians to share the spiritual burden with him.

Paul is requesting prayer for three things: **(1)** that the word of the Lord may run swiftly, **(2)** that the word of the Lord may be honored, and **(3)** that Paul's missionary team may minister without the interruptions and the struggle from the ungodly. There is an urgency that Paul senses to get this gospel out. There are hungry souls who need to hear this message. For these upcoming efforts, if they will respond as these Thessalonians had, then the word of the Lord is honored and received. To pray for deliverance is quite an honest request. There is work to be done, and the less entanglements to that end, the better. But even in that request, Paul affirms God's faithfulness to strengthen and protect. While doing so, Paul is building up *their* faith for those same situations. Who are you praying for and who is praying for you?

Father, put an urgency in my heart to evangelize. Go before me today. Amen.

October 16

Jeremiah 28:1–29:32; 1 Timothy 1:1–20; Psalm 86:1–17; Proverbs 25:17

Fight the Good Fight

Timothy, my son, I give you this instruction in keeping with the prophecies once made about you, so that by following them you may fight the good fight, holding on to faith and a good conscience. Some have rejected these and so have shipwrecked their faith.
—1 Timothy 1:18–19

Paul writes this very personal letter to his true son in the faith. Timothy is a young minister over the church in Ephesus, and Paul takes him under his wing to counsel and encourage. The spiritual landscape there brings many challenges and conflicts to grapple with. False teachers stir up controversy by focusing on non-essentials to faith. Meaningless chatter rivals the sound doctrine they need.

What a mentor Paul is—having wisdom to offer through the turbulence has to be a great comfort and confidence-builder to a new pastor. What Timothy is in for is a fight. No question. But it is a fight worth fighting. It is the fight for the souls of men. It is the struggle for the truth to be employed in order for fruitful lives to flourish with God's blessing. It is a war that we engage in order to turn a culture from the wicked entrapments they promote. It is the constant daily battle of shining light on the dark areas we live among.

We know the fight is before us. What may surprise us is how the struggle can dishearten so many. Those who are not fully committed can be easily swayed. If their anchor isn't rooted deep, their faith can become shipwrecked. So we embrace faith and maintain a clear conscience. God, in turn, strengthens us on the inside by His Spirit.

Father, I need Your steady guidance to navigate past the potholes that would trip me up. I look to Your Word, so I may discern what to embrace and what to discard. I accept Your call to fight the good fight, in Your strength. Amen.

October 17

Jeremiah 30:1–31:26; 1 Timothy 2:1–15; Psalm 87:1–7; Proverbs 25:18–19

Pray for Everyone

I urge, then, first of all, that requests, prayers, intercession and thanksgiving be made for everyon— for kings and all those in authority, that we may live peaceful and quiet lives in all godliness and holiness. (God our Savior) wants all men to be saved and come to a knowledge of the truth.
—1 Timothy 2:1–2,4

This title comes from the first verse and seems rather simplistic. That's the way small children make sweeping prayers—for the whole world—in a one-line utterance. Upon consideration, perhaps it would be better to say that every person alive can be affected by prayer.

Certainly pray for everyone you know individually and by name. Thank God for them. Intercede on their behalf. It is God's design that every person whom He created come to know the saving knowledge of Jesus Christ. The sacrifice that Jesus made wasn't just for some—but for all who would call upon His name. So pray for that neighbor or cousin. Lift up your co-worker before the Lord. Ask God to come in power, to reveal His kindness and remove the scales from their eyes. Earnest prayer moves the heart of God. Does every man accept God on His terms? Obviously not. But the provision for every man is there, and I know that God can save the hardest heart. *Why wouldn't I pray?*

Paul urges us to pray for governmental leaders. The emperor at this time, Nero, was particularly cruel. Still yet, rulers play a significant role in the spiritual climate of a country. They can bring peace or upheaval to a society of people. There can be fundamental differences in our perspectives on how to govern, but we still need a peaceable environment where we can live to serve and worship our God.

Father, I pray for our president. Put godly counsel around him. Bring him to an encounter with Jesus. Raise up leaders who will seek Your face. Amen

October 18

Jeremiah 31:27–32:44; 1 Timothy 3:1–16; Psalm 88:1–18; Proverbs 25:20–22

Covenant Love

I will make an everlasting covenant with them: I will never stop doing good to them, and I will inspire them to fear me, so that they will never turn away from me. I will rejoice in doing them good and will assuredly plant them in this land with all my heart and soul.
—Jeremiah 32:40–41

Jeremiah's mission is a difficult one. How do you convince a people of the reality of their rebellion? How do you penetrate that kind of defiance? Imagine the pain in God's heart to be refused again and again. *"They turned their backs to me and not their faces; though I taught them … they would not listen or respond to discipline" (v.33).*

In context, the army of Babylon is at the door, besieging Jerusalem. Indeed, God is going to judge Judah for all their evil. They are expecting the worst, but God gives them hope in His overview of the situation to Jeremiah. *"I will bring them back to this place and let them live in safety" (v.38).* Jeremiah even purchases a field from his cousin to demonstrate that properties will again be bought in this very land. With all His heart, and in spite of total rejection, God is committed to building them up again. His covenant is His irrevocable word.

God gives an extraordinary promise to his covenant people. *"I will put my law in their minds and write it on their hearts" (31:33). "I will forgive their wickedness and remember their sins no more" (31:34).* The new covenant Jeremiah refers to will find it's fulfillment in Christ *(see also Hebrews 8:6-13)*, and will be extended to include Gentiles, as well. God has given us a conscience with His Spirit so that we may discern His ways and come to a personal knowing through relationship.

Father, You are a covenant-keeping God. In all Your ways, You are utterly faithful. Instill in me a singleness of heart so that I will honor You. Amen.

October 19

Jeremiah 33:1–34:22; 1 Timothy 4:1–16; Psalm 89:1–13; Proverbs 25:23–24

Godliness Training

Have nothing to do with godless myths ... rather train yourself to be godly. For physical training is of some value, but godliness has value for all things, holding promise for both the present life and the life to come.
—1 Timothy 4:7–8

The verses in this chapter garner my attention for several reasons. I am an advocate of a healthy lifestyle, including physical exercise, so my attention is peaked. But I am also struck by the proactive verbs Paul uses throughout: *train yourself, devote yourself, do not neglect, be diligent in, give yourself wholly to ...* There is nothing half-hearted about shepherding the flock of God. The example lived is paramount.

Training the body involves discipline and focus. You work the muscles with a steady, daily effort. There is value in that. Paul was not discounting physical training. However, it is only one dimensional. Paul used what we know is true about physical training to emphasize something that is true about our spiritual development. Godliness requires the same fierce devotion and works the spiritual muscles that build our faith. Spiritual health doesn't just happen once a week in a church service. We develop those muscles by the Word of God and prayer, by serving and forgiving, by loving and seeking. It's the Sermon on the Mount lifestyle *(Matthew 5-7)*. Our discipline and obedience molds us for the present and shapes our future forever.

For Timothy to be truly effective, to combat the false teachers that were prevalent, he needed to be on his fittest level spiritually. Nothing less than wholehearted commitment would do. *How about you?*

Father in heaven, I commit my body, soul and spirit to the process of spiritual health. I embrace discipline in order to become a true disciple. Let my life be an example for other believers in speech, in love, in faith and in purity. Amen.

October 20

Jeremiah 35:1–36:32; 1 Timothy 5:1–25; Psalm 89:14–37; Proverbs 25:25–27

Family Values

Do not rebuke an older man harshly, but exhort him as if he were your father. Treat younger men as brothers, older women as mothers, and younger women as sisters, with absolute purity. [Children] should put their religion into practice by caring for their own family ... for this is pleasing to God.
—1 Timothy 5:1–2,4

There are two separate thoughts here, both relating to family values.

Our relationships with people on every level ought to be held in high esteem and purity, just as you would an immediate family member. You would treat your mom or dad with dignity and respect, so treat your elders with the same care. There would be no questionable behavior in relating to your sister, so regard other young ladies with the same courtesy. Integrity protects and values every relationship.

When it comes to caring for family members, remember the sacrifices your mom and dad made for you. They provided for your needs gladly while you were under their roof. When they reach the season where they can no longer work as they once did, who should come to their aid but their children? Your faith in God should reflect a compassion for your aging parents. It pleases God. Paul is more frank in his words to the one who does nothing—*"he is worse than an unbeliever" (v.9)*.

Family values have taken a hit in recent years. But Christianity is and always will be about family. It is the core of kingdom life. It's where we live out the details of our faith. We honor the Lord when we honor our parents. We value others when we respect them as family.

Father, You have given me a family to love and a family to love me. Forge purity and honor in the precious relationships you have given me. Amen.

October 21

Jeremiah 37:1–38:28; 1 Timothy 6:1–21; Psalm 89:38–52; Proverbs 25:28

Walls That Protect

Like a city whose walls are broken down is a man who lacks self-control.
—Proverbs 25:28

Timothy, guard what has been entrusted to your care.
—1 Timothy 6:20

City walls were designed to guard and protect its inhabitants from enemy attack. It was a natural defense against passing bands of thieves and villains. Without walls, those in the city were vulnerable. Solomon used this analogy to demonstrate the wisdom there is in setting perimeters around your life so as to protect you from the wiles of the enemy. It's called self-control. These are not just a rigid set of rules, but self-established walls to keep the enemy at bay. It may be abstaining from areas where we are susceptible to temptation. It may include accountability. But it's more than will power. God enables us to establish boundaries and maintain them by the power of the Spirit.

Think of the many blessings God has given you—your faith, integrity, spiritual gifts, family, and so many other meaningful relationships. Then consider that the devil is always looking for an avenue of compromise to steal away or devalue what God has bestowed. That's reason enough to guard and protect that which is precious to you.

While Timothy was the pastor in Ephesus, he was given a charge to guard the purity of the gospel so that opposing ideas and false teachers would not infect the precious saints he was ministering to.

What walls have you built to guard what God has entrusted to you?

Father, by the enabling of the Holy Spirit, help me to establish and maintain walls of self-control in my life to guard the precious gifts You have given me. Amen.

October 22

Jeremiah 39:1–41:18; 2 Timothy 1:1–18; Psalm 90:1–91:16; Proverbs 26:1–2

Fan into Flame

I have been reminded of your sincere faith … For this reason I remind you to fan into flame the gift of God. For God did not give us a spirit of timidity, but a spirit of power, of love and of self-discipline.
—2 Timothy 2:3,5–7

Paul writes his final letter, directed to his true son in the faith, one whom he has invested in and mentored. Paul's words reveal his heart for Timothy. There is a bond between them. You get a sense of urgency as Paul passes the mantle to this next generation of believers.

Paul is constantly praying for Timothy. He is emotionally engaged in Timothy's welfare and ministry. He is drawn to Timothy's sensitive heart and sincere faith. They have wept together. They have shared the joys of ministry. Paul knew his family well. The faith of his mother Eunice and grandmother Lois had impacted Timothy greatly in his formidable years. He has a solid foundation under him to build upon.

Paul's admonishment is for Timothy to *"fan into flame the gift of God."* Paul recognizes the gifts that God has blessed him with. With God's anointing, these gifts become powerful tools to build up the body of Christ, His church. They need to be fanned and developed and utilized. Our own natural fears, coupled with outside intimidation, may attempt to restrain us to remain passive. But by assertively responding to God's call, we are able to witness the power of God at work, motivated by a heart of love. These gifts are not reckless, but are guided by our own Scriptural convictions. It's a boldness we don't have in ourselves—it is an outflow of the Holy Spirit working within.

Father God, You have given me particular gifts that are effective and useful when I rely upon Your Spirit. May they honor You and further the kingdom! Amen.

October 23

Jeremiah 42:1–44:23; 2 Timothy 2:1–21; Psalm 92:1–93:5; Proverbs 26:3–5

The Lord Gives Insight

Endure hardship with us like a good soldier of Christ Jesus. Similarly, if anyone competes as an athlete, he … competes according to the rules. The hardworking farmer should be the first to receive a share of the crops. Reflect on what I am saying, for the Lord will give you insight into all this.
—2 Timothy 2:3,5–7

Paul is encouraging Timothy to be strong in God's enablement and to persevere through hardship. Then Paul gives Timothy three examples to consider that will help him to understand the nature of hardship and suffering. The catch here is that Paul gives him the thought—the visual—but he does not expound upon it. He wants Timothy to think upon it, to reflect and allow God to make a greater application.

If you were to spend a day in the military, you would be able to get a better sense of the dedication and training that is required to become a focused soldier. Spend a day in the life of an athlete and find out the discipline and strategic effort it takes to be among the best. There are tenants of training you cannot skimp on in order to win. Farming, likewise, is laborious work. It's non-stop year-round. Many ground preparations are needed for seed to grow. There is obvious financial risk. The farmer must rely upon God for the proper amounts of water and sunshine. Spend a day in the life of a farmer and take notes. Perseverance and fierce dedication is required in each. But they know that going in. They have counted the cost in order to succeed.

By dwelling and reflecting upon these verses, and any other passage of Scripture, God is able to illuminate, amplify and make personal application to our lives by the Holy Spirit. He is a speaking God!

Father, You have painted a vivid picture of strict discipline and endurance in order to win the prize. Enable me by your grace to go the distance. Amen.

October 24

Jeremiah 44:24–47:7; 2 Timothy 2:22–3:17; Psalm 94:1–23; Proverbs 26:6–8

Last Days Lovers

But mark this: There will be terrible times in the last days. People will be lovers of themselves, lovers of money ... lovers of pleasure rather than lovers of God—having a form of godliness but denying its power. Have nothing to do with them.
—2 Timothy 3:1–2,4–5

While I was a student in Bible college, I remember addressing the youth group of our church with this topic. I thought the title might capture their attention. But it's not a very encouraging passage if you think about it. It's actually rather depressing. As the years have gone by, the truth of these verses has become more and more apparent.

The list here is what we know and can expect from people who do not love God. They have not encountered a heart change from their Creator, so they know nothing else except to fend for themselves. Their baseline for behavior is all about and only what will benefit "me, myself and I!" They are lovers of themselves. They are also lovers of money. We all are pretty sure we need more of the green stuff, but to love money is to make it your primary pursuit. *"The love of money is a root of all sorts of evil,"* and it can lead you away from the faith *(1 Timothy 6:10)*. There is nothing wrong with pleasure. It is a gift of God. But it is exclusive seeking after pleasure that gets us out-of-balance.

A deceptive feature of these last days lovers is that they can wear a cloak of decency. They may go to church, do good deeds and speak the Christian verbiage, but what is truly in their heart becomes very apparent. Paul's warning is frank: *"Have nothing to do with them."*

Father in heaven, as we near the coming of Your Son, may I be found to be a lover of You, of the good, and have a true godliness that trusts Your power. Amen.

October 25

Jeremiah 48:1–49:22; 2 Timothy 4:1–22; Psalm 95:1–96:13; Proverbs 26:9–12

Seasons of Ministry

Be prepared in season and out … discharge all the duties of your ministry. Do your best to come to me quickly, for Demas, because he loved this world, has deserted me. Only Luke is with me. Get Mark and bring him with you, because he is helpful to me in my ministry. I left Trophimus sick in Miletus.
—2 Timothy 4:2,5,9–11,20

As I read today's passage, it reminded me of just what ministry looks like in the real world. As structured as we may intend it to be, life situations aren't that cut and dry. The fact is, people move in and out of your life at a rapid pace.

People leave, for whatever reason. People get sick and their plans are altered. Some get sidetracked from their faith commitment. Others sense the call of God to go to another venue. By nature, the pastor must train up others to carry on the message and work. They are to entrust the Word to faithful men who will in turn teach others *(2:2)*. Jeanie Kay, a dear pastor's wife, reminds me, *"Blessed are the flexible, for they will not be bent out of shape."* Such is the life of a pastor.

Ministry can also be very lonely. *"Only Luke is with me. Get Mark and bring him with you…"* You would think that being among so many friendly faces that this would not be an issue. But think about it. The pastor is the one there for the needs of those he serves. It is difficult to carry on reciprocal relationships within a congregation. But who cares for the pastor? Having Mark come would be a welcome sight. He was another minister who could understand and assist.

In Paul's final farewell, he is aware of the relationships that have meant so much. Indeed, that is what ministry is about—loving people.

Father, thank You for the many friendships You have placed in my life. Amen.

October 26

Jeremiah 49:23–50:46; Titus 1:1–16; Psalm 97:1–98:9; Proverbs 26:13–16

Confronting Untruth

[An overseer] must hold firmly to the trustworthy message as it has been taught, so that he can encourage others by sound doctrine and refute those who oppose it. For there are many rebellious people... They must be silenced, because they are ruining whole households. Therefore, rebuke them sharply, so that they will be sound in the faith ...
—Titus 1:9–11,13

Titus was a traveling companion and close friend of Paul's. After having visited the island of Crete, Paul appoints Titus to oversee the churches there. So Paul gives instruction on how to administrate churches and appoint elders in a similar style as he did with Timothy.

The criteria for elders/pastors/overseers is a high standard, for he is carrying on the work of God *(1:7)*. His life must be above reproach, giving witness to the truth of his message. The man of God must be able to encourage his followers with sound doctrine *and* refute those who oppose it *(1:9)*. In other words, it is imperative to know what you believe and why you believe it, so that you may be able to give an account at a moment's notice, in season and out of season.

The scenario in Crete is not unlike churches elsewhere. There are strong personalities who lead, however misguided they might be. Some are prompted by their own agenda for personal gain. But sound teaching cannot be compromised or corrupted. It is the foundation of faith for generations to come. That is why Paul is so adamant about correcting the false teachers who babble on and deceive. It is not a popular proposition to confront people, but maintaining and restoring truth is the core of our faith. Households are at stake.

Father, deceptions are rampant today. Give me a holy boldness to declare Your truth when the need arises so that even they may be sound in the faith. Amen.

October 27

Jeremiah 51:1–53; Titus 2:1–15; Psalm 99:1–9; Proverbs 26:17

Grace Teaches Us

For the grace of God that brings salvation has appeared to all men. It teaches us to say "No" to ungodliness and worldly passions, and to live self-controlled, upright and godly lives in this present age …
—Titus 2:11–12

Paul continues his emphasis for Titus to teach sound doctrine—to the various ages of both men and women, and how appropriate. Titus gets help, because implied in the very salvation message is that grace is also a teacher.

We know grace to be the favor of God bestowed upon us that we did nothing to deserve. This is the good news that we heard and believed. This grace teaches us that we have been redeemed from the world for a reason. Grace gives us an escape to the wicked ways we were stuck in. The reason Jesus gave his life was to rescue us with finality, setting us free from sin's control, and then to purify us. It would have been an incomplete rescue if we were not given a way to live above the pull of fleshly desires. It is the Holy Spirit who now empowers us to be able to refuse the selfish passions of our flesh and to choose to live upright lives even amongst a godless culture.

Receiving God's favor makes me want to somehow thank Him with my life. He lifted off a great burden. I'm now free to live without that encumbrance. Grace shows me that I can live free. I now see purity as desirable. I am His. I am set apart as His very own. *I'm peculiar!*

Father, thank You for grace and the power You bestow by Your Spirit. I long for and anticipate the glorious appearing of Your Son and my Savior, Jesus. Until He returns, continue the process that will purify me so that I will be wholly Yours. Amen.

October 28

Jeremiah 51:54–52:34; Titus 3:1–15; Psalm 100:1–5; Proverbs 26:18–19

Affecting a Culture

Remind the people to be subject to rulers and authorities, to be obedient, to be ready to do whatever is good ... stress these things, so that those who have trusted in God may be careful to devote themselves to doing what is good. Our people must learn to devote themselves to doing what is good, in order that they may provide for daily necessities and not live unproductive lives.
—*Titus 3:1,8,14*

OK. OK. I get the hint. When a phrase is repeated three times in one chapter, then it must be an emphasis I would do good not to miss.

Paul eludes to the fact that before the kindness and love of God appeared, we all lived in malice and envy and were unfit for doing anything good. Paul even quotes one of their own poets, Epimenides, from 600 years prior, that categorized their behavior as to be *"liars, brutes and lazy gluttons" (1:12)*. This was what they were prone to in their societal landscape, and it affected their livelihood. Sadly, some get locked into an identity that is hard to shake.

But the kindness and love of God did appear. Jesus, by His mercy and grace, saved us so that we might become partakers of hope for eternal life. The work of salvation is a total deliverance. At rebirth, we are washed and cleansed and made new by the Holy Spirit that is poured out upon us. We are granted a new identity that allows us to overcome those predisposed behaviors. We are heirs of hope. We can live productive, fruitful lives that affect our culture in a truly excellent way. True societal change comes from revival, one heart at a time. How has rebirth affected your livelihood in the real world?

Father God, where I thought I was stuck as a sinner with no hope of change, You came and gave me a new lease on life. Your generosity was not withheld. Now I can operate from a new identity by the help of the Holy Spirit. Amen!

October 29

Lamentations 1:1–2:19; Philemon 1:1–25; Psalm 101:1–8; Proverbs 26:20

The Pledge of Integrity

I will be careful to lead a blameless life—when will you come to me? I will walk in my house with blameless heart. I will set before my eyes no vile thing. The deeds of faithless men I hate; they will not cling to me. My eyes will be on the faithful in the land … he whose walk is blameless will minister to me.
—Psalm 101:2–3,6

Early on in his reign, David establishes perimeters in his life so that integrity may be the mark of his leadership. This is precisely what walls of self-control are (referring to Proverbs 25:28 on October 21).

Integrity is not just something you can put on before the public like some garment. Integrity is who you are in the every day when no one else is looking. The inner chamber of your house is where you let your hair down. If there is an area of lax or indiscretion, chances are that it began inside the walls of your own private sanctuary. *No one else could know, right?* Yet David understood that nothing is withheld from God's view, and every thought and detail matters. That's why David pledges his eyes to look upon no vile thing—no object that God calls sin. Integrity begins and ends inside the walls of your own home.

Moreover, David knew the effect that peer pressure and bad company can produce. It was in his heart to position himself around honorable and godly people. The wicked and perverse would not be afforded the opportunity to influence the society in a denigrating way. David's choices led to a kingdom that honored God for generations.

It's about integrity, and it all begins with the personal pledge before a holy God who sees it all. It's about living honestly before His gaze.

Father, I pledge my eyes and thoughts to purity. I choose to walk beside those who are faithful and blameless. With Your help, I will fulfill this vow. Amen.

October 30

Lamentations 2:20–3:66; Hebrews 1:1–14; Psalm 102:1–28; Proverbs 26:21–22

Mercies are New

I remember my affliction and my wandering, the bitterness and the gall ....Yet this I call to mind and therefore I have hope: Because of the Lord's great love we are not consumed, for his compassions never fail. They are new every morning; great is your faithfulness.
—Lamentations 3:19,21–23

It is easy to look at our verses today and recall the catch phrase of God's faithfulness, and then miss the weight of it all. Truth be known, the funeral dirge that Jeremiah pens expresses a heart that is broken over Judah's sins and resulting judgment. Jerusalem is destroyed. Babylon has taken captive its inhabitants. Many are tortured and killed. Jeremiah grieves deeply. He is referred to as the "weeping prophet" for good reason. He mourns over the people he loves because they have rejected God. While he prophesied these events to occur, he took no pleasure in witnessing their fulfillment.

Yet, smack in the middle of the five poems (chapters), Jeremiah shines a light of hope that gives perspective on the character of God and their situation. In the midst of the darkest night, when his soul was at its lowest point, he could call to remembrance from times past the faithfulness of God. Never was there a more sober moment, and yet God is committed now as ever to His people. It is because of mercy that it was not worse. The consequences of their sin brought great pain, but God did not reject them. His compassion was realized. Discipline is never pleasant. But it's meant to bring us to a place where we seek Him again. God promises to turn it around for good.

Father, I know that You are just and You cannot allow sin to flourish in my life. If I happen to stray off the path, put Your finger on my sin, so that I may repent quickly. Give me a heart that grieves over sin. When the sun rises in the morning tomorrow, I will know that Your mercies are new again. Amen.

October 31

Lamentations 4:1–5:22; Hebrews 2:1–18; Psalm 103:1–22; Proverbs 26:23

Remember the Benefits

Praise the Lord, O my soul, and forget not all his benefits—who forgives all your sins and heals all your diseases, who redeems your life from the pit and crowns you with love and compassion, who satisfies your desires with good things so that your youth is renewed like the eagle's.
—Psalm 103:2–5

I will praise the Lord and forget not all His benefits: for providing salvation for me through His Son; for the forgiveness of sins; for making my spirit come alive by the Holy Spirit; for healing all my diseases; for making my life something when it was nothing; for crowning me with love and compassion; for satisfying my desires with good things; for the awesome presence of His Spirit that never leaves me; and for the glories revealed of our Lord Jesus Christ.

I give thanks to my Creator for the sunrise that brings in the new day; for the close friends that have been sent to walk beside me; for the multitudes of stars and the Big Dipper; for the gift of knowing the Father's love, who would never give up on me; for the tender beauty of a rose petal; for righteousness, peace and joy in the Holy Ghost; for providing a job that pays the bills; for an eternal inheritance that cannot be stolen; and for giving me a family to love and that loves me.

I give praise to God for giving me physical and mental strength for the tasks at hand each day; for granting wisdom and revelation into the knowledge of Jesus; for unconditional love; for a clear conscience and restful sleep; for conforming me into the image of Jesus more each day; and for pressing me to continue forward in my faith walk ...

I will forget not all His benefits, but I will run out of room to list them.

Father, I am mindful of Your blessings and am thankful for each one. Amen.

November 1

Ezekiel 1:1–3:15; Hebrews 3:1–19; Psalm 104:1–23; Proverbs 26:24–26

Eat the Scroll

Then he said to me, "Son of man, eat this scroll I am giving you and fill your stomach with it." So I ate it, and it tasted as sweet as honey ... And he said to me, "Son of man, listen carefully and take to heart all the words I speak to you. Go now to your countrymen in exile and speak to them. Say to them, 'This is what the Sovereign Lord says,' whether they listen or fail to listen."
—Ezekiel 3:2,10–11

Ezekiel is called by God to prophesy to Israel as Jeremiah was to Judah. The biggest difference is that the younger Ezekiel is ministering to a nation that is already defeated and captive in Babylon.

It is a difficult task. The Israelites got where they were by being obstinate and stubborn. Yet the Word of the Lord must be delivered. The response of the people was not the responsibility of the prophet. The duty of the prophet is to deliver all that was declared by the Lord. On this scroll were lamentations and warnings overflowing to both front and back sides. No wonder Ezekiel is overwhelmed.

For the one who would take the Word of the Lord seriously, eating the scroll entirely is essential. The Word must be internalized. We consume the whole of it. We must know the passions of God's heart. The Lord says: *"Listen carefully. Take to heart all My words."* We cannot pick and choose only what will gain acceptance and tickle the ears. No, we must have the full counsel of God— the warnings alongside the blessings. There is judgment, and there is also restoration. The one who eats the scroll enjoys the taste of the scroll, that it is *"sweeter than honey, than honey from the comb" (Psalm 19:10).*

Father in heaven, You have given me Your precious Word that I may know You and Your ways. May Your word be on my tongue to declare Your truth. Amen.

November 2

Ezekiel 3:16–6:14; Hebrews 4:1–16; Psalm 104:24–35; Proverbs 26:27

Mixed with Faith

We also have had the gospel preached to us, just as they did; but the message they heard was of no value because those who heard did not combine it with faith. Therefore ... let us hold firmly to the faith we profess. Let us... approach the throne of grace with confidence [to] receive mercy and find grace ...
    —Hebrews 4:2,14,16

Judaism was God's avenue for true worship and prophesied of a day when the Messiah would come and establish a new kingdom. When the Messiah did enter human history in the person of Jesus, many Jews believed. This writing to the Hebrews reveals Jesus as God's complete answer for salvation and superior to the old in every way. It was the ultimate defense so that believers everywhere would not retreat back into what was familiar. Rituals and laws were replaced by simple faith in the Son of God. No add-ons were needed, only faith.

The element of faith is our response of affirmation to God's offer of salvation. It is the "Yes" in our spirit that releases the life and activity of God into our person. To hear the gospel without a response renders no value. Our faith is activated when we listen *and* believe in our heart that Jesus is the Son of the living God and by the confession of that pledge *(Romans 10:9-10)*. Our faith is not baseless. It is rooted in the sinless life of Jesus who, as our high priest, removed any barrier to God's throne. Total access has been granted for every believer.

Everything we receive from God is received by faith. When we need grace and mercy, and we all do, we approach by faith. Because Christ gained this access for us, we can come before God with confidence.

Father, You have provided salvation. My only proper response is to say "Yes," and "Thank You." I come before You, not of my own, but solely on the merits of Jesus' life and sacrifice. From Your throne I receive mercy and grace. Amen.

November 3

Ezekiel 7:1–9:11; Hebrews 5:1–14; Psalm 105:1–15; Proverbs 26:28

Prayers Are Heard

During the days of Jesus' life on earth, he offered up prayers and petitions with loud cries and tears to the one who could save him from death, and he was heard because of his reverent submission.
—Hebrews 5:7

If you have ever wondered just how integral prayer was in Jesus' life while he was physically here on earth, here is your answer. We know He taught us to pray *(Matthew 6:5-13)*, but He also lived it and relied upon it. Jesus was in constant communion with His Father. Yes, Jesus was the divine Son of God, but He was also fully human with all the limitations of time and space and, well, humanity. He demonstrated to us that prayer is the lifeline for a relationship with God.

We know from the gospels that Jesus tucked away often to pray in secret *(Matthew 14:23)*. He spoke only what the Father taught Him *(John 8:28)*. He prayed through the night to receive instruction concerning the choosing of apostles *(Luke 6:12-13)*. Jesus also wept over Jerusalem *(Luke 19:41)*. He showed great emotion, so it is no surprise that His prayers were earnest and heartfelt, even vehement and with tears.

The key to Jesus' prayer life is the same for us—*reverent submission*. Even in His darkest hour, Jesus was able to pour out His heart to the Father, and yet was willing to submit to the Father's sovereign plan. He said, *"yet not my will, but yours be done" (Luke 22:42)*. When we sincerely submit our lives and circumstances to the Father, we can know that our prayers have moved the heart of God.

Father, You love a willing heart that is consecrated to You. I confess that I am in need of Your counsel and strength. I submit my agenda to You, because You always know what is best. Thank You for hearing my prayers. Amen.

November 4

Ezekiel 10:1–11:25; Hebrews 6:1–20; Psalm 105:16–36; Proverbs 27:1–2

A Stern Warning

It is impossible for those who have once been enlightened, who have tasted the heavenly gift, who have shared in the Holy Spirit, who have tasted the goodness of the word of God and the powers of the coming age, if they fall away, to be brought back to repentance … dear friends, we are confident of better things in your case—things that accompany salvation.
—Hebrews 6:4–6,9

A strong word was what the Hebrew believers needed to hear. It's what we needn't avoid today. It's a theme that has surfaced several times already *(2:1-3; 3:12-15; 4:6,11):* a sinful, unbelieving heart turns away from the living God. I am of the opinion that it is just as loving to know both sides of the truth. Yes, give me the positive feel-good encouragement, but I also need to understand the ramifications of a heart that ignores or neglects such a great salvation *(2:3).*

What we are talking about is a continual and deliberate rejection of Christ as God's sole avenue for salvation. Faith is not something you can be casual about. An apostate condition is a hardened heart that continues to refuse God on His terms. This warning heightens my awareness of the tremendous sacrifice Jesus made on my behalf.

Let's not overlook the upside. We who have called on the name of the Lord are described as having been enlightened. We have tasted the heavenly gift, the goodness of the word of God and the powers of the coming age. We have shared in the Holy Spirit. These life-giving deposits all work to tenderize my heart and set me up for a lifetime of fruitful labor. As the Lord said to Ezekiel, *"I will remove from them their heart of stone and give them a heart of flesh" (11:19).*

Father, I desire a heart that responds quickly to Your voice and Your word. I resist apathy and sin that would harden my heart. Guide me by Your truth.

November 5

Ezekiel 12:1–14:11; Hebrews 7:1–17; Psalm 105:37–45; Proverbs 27:3

The King of Salem

Melchizedek was king of Salem and priest of God Most High. He met Abraham returning from the defeat of the kings and blessed him, and Abraham gave him a tenth of everything. Without father or mother, without genealogy, without beginning of days or end of life, like the Son of God he remains a priest forever.
—Hebrews 7:1–3

Enter Melchizedek. We've had a couple of teasers already concerning this man *(5:6,10; 6:20)*. But who is he? *(Let's call him 'Mel' for short.)*

His name means "king of righteousness," and "king of peace." Mel's story is found in Genesis 14. Abraham (when his name was still Abram) met this king of Salem following a victory over four allied kings and having recovered a large group of captives, including his nephew Lot. It is King Mel who reminds Abram that it was *"God Most High who delivered your enemies into your hand" (14:20)*. This king is not of Hebrew origin. As a matter of fact, this king has no ancestry to trace. Yet he is the king of Salem, the city that will later become known as Jerusalem. He is also a priest of God Most High and he proceeds to pronounce a blessing over Abram. In this remarkable exchange, the patriarch Abram gives this man of God a tenth of all his plunder.

The headline today is that Jesus is our high priest forever, as in likeness to Melchizedek. Was Melchizedek a pre-incarnate visitation of Jesus? *Perhaps.* Who can know, but he illustrates Jesus' unique role as Messiah. It is that of a higher priestly order that supersedes human regulations, having offered the perfect atonement for sins once for all.

God Most High, I acknowledge that Jesus was sent to be my high priest forever by his indestructible life in order to provide forgiveness of my sins— and for the sins of all humanity. Thank You for a love so deep. Amen.

November 6

Ezekiel 14:12–16:42; Hebrews 7:18–28; Psalm 106:1–12; Proverbs 27:4–6

The Perfected Version

The former regulation is set aside because it was weak and useless, and a better hope is introduced, by which we draw near to God. Because Jesus lives forever, he has a permanent priesthood. Therefore, he is able to save completely those who come to God ... because he always lives to intercede for them.
  —Hebrews 7:18–19, 24–25

The accolades of Christ continue. For the Jews who were evaluating this new faith, the advantages are growing insurmountable. A better hope is introduced. Jesus is the guarantor of a better covenant.

To this point, the priests of Levi and their laws could not save anyone. Animal sacrifices served as temporary forgiveness and had to be repeated day after day. Priests were relied upon to mediate, yet they, too, were weak men who needed their sins atoned for first. The duties of their office were good as long as they were alive, but death is inevitable. The former system is thus set aside for a perfected version.

Unlike men who were appointed as high priests, Jesus lives forever as a permanent priest, first because he truly does live forever. He is also the permanent high priest because His Father declared it so. Three times now we have seen referenced Psalm 110:4 that declares an oath God spoke: *"You (the Messiah) are a priest forever."* What we needed in a high priest, we have in Jesus. He is holy, spotless and above reproach because He led a sinless life *(v.26)*. He offered Himself as an acceptable sacrifice for sins once for all time *(v.27)*. Finally, He lives now to intercede for us always and forever. He is there right now at the Father's right hand to plead our case. You are never alone in the fight.

Father, You are able to save me wholly and completely through the finished work of the cross, by the intercession of Jesus and the power of the Holy Spirit. Amen.

November 7

Ezekiel 16:43–17:24; Hebrews 8:1–13; Psalm 106:13–31; Proverbs 27:7–9

A New Covenant

For if there had been nothing wrong with that first covenant, no place would have been sought for another. But God found fault with the people and said: "This is the covenant I will make with the house of Israel … I will put my laws in their minds and write them on their hearts."
—Hebrews 8:7–8,10

This is interesting. In between the lines I see a God who is reaching out to the people He cherishes, but they have resisted Him adamantly to this point. He finds fault with the first covenant because, while God is faithful, the people have not remained true to God. So He initiates a new covenant that is made so accessible that they cannot avoid it.

God promises a new covenant. But how does this new covenant improve upon the old? We get a fresh review from Jeremiah 31:31-34. The old was a written code between God and Israel. The better hope by which we draw near to God is a covenant of grace whereby Christ's sacrificial death provides forgiveness and acceptance. His sacrifice is one time for all *(10:10)*, so the access gained is extended now to even the Gentiles. But the most unique feature is that now God's law is fixed upon our hearts and our upon minds. We will know what is required by a conscience that has been quickened to discern right and wrong. The Holy Spirit convicts us of sin and woos us and draws us in our need for a Savior. Now we respond to that inner witness by an affirmation of faith, not by the animal sacrifices of the past. Paul reminds us that *"the word is near you; it is in your mouth and in your heart"* to confess and believe *(Romans 10:8).*

God has made salvation accessible to us all through Jesus. Will you respond to His invitation with a "Yes" from your heart and your lips?

Father, Your covenant of love draws me into fellowship with You. Amen.

November 8

Ezekiel 18:1–19:14; Hebrews 9:1–10; Psalm 106:32–48; Proverbs 27:10

Personal Accountability

The righteousness of the righteous man will be credited to him, the wickedness of the wicked will be charged against him. Rid yourselves of all the offenses you have committed, and get a new heart and a new spirit. For I take no pleasure in the death of anyone, declares the Sovereign Lord. Repent and live!
—Ezekiel 18:20,31–32

Ezekiel gives extensive time to illustrate personal accountability for sins. He wants to correct false notions about being held responsible for the sins of your parents and/or your children. This topic has been broached before: Deuteronomy 24:16 responds to the second commandment that seems to punish the sons to the third and fourth generation for the sins of their fathers (Deuteronomy 20:5). So Ezekiel sets the record straight.

The proverb that is being quoted about Israel is this: *"The fathers eat sour grapes, and the children's teeth are set on edge?" (18:2).* While it is true that we may suffer from the effects of the sins of our parents, God does not judge us for what they did. Neither can we use them as an excuse to continue in their sin. The examples we have in our parents provides us with a choice to follow in their footsteps or to resist the way they have chosen. But the responsibility for our choices will be ours to own. Because my father failed in particular areas doesn't mean I am bound to fail in those same areas. We can resist the propensity of generational sins by the power of the Holy Spirit.

If we inherit a spiritual decay in the culture that was created by the generation before us, then we have the opportunity to reverse that trend. God is just and imparts new life through the gift of repentance.

Father, You have given me an avenue to be forgiven for the sins I have committed. I repent and turn to receive a new heart and a fresh start. Amen.

November 9

Ezekiel 20:1–49; Hebrews 9:11–28; Psalm 107:1–43; Proverbs 27:11

Certainties In Life

Just as man is destined to die once, and after that to face judgment, so Christ was sacrificed once to take away the sins of man; and he will appear a second time, not to bear sin, but to bring salvation to those who are waiting for him.
—Hebrews 9:27–28

This is the passage where we understand the first two certainties in life, the obvious ones: we will all pass from this present existence and then we will face our Maker. We will be accountable for our choices. The timing of when we pass is anybody's guess, but it is unavoidable, and we ought to always live in a readiness. To know God's Son as His source for salvation is the first step of preparedness. These first two certainties are not intimidating when we understand the next one.

The third certainty is that sin has been dealt with by the sacrifice of Jesus on the cross. No other religion has an answer for sin. Simply stated, *(v. 22) "without the shedding of blood there is no forgiveness,"* no remission of sins. But Jesus did, in fact, lay his life down as the perfect sacrifice for sins—once for all and for all time. The blood of Jesus cleanses us on the inside so that we may serve the living God!

The last certainty is that Jesus Christ will appear a second time to bring our salvation to completion. Just as man is destined to die once, and just as Christ was sacrificed to remove the sins of all who would believe, so Jesus will return to those who are living in anticipation of their salvation to be fully realized. It is the blessed hope *(Titus 2:13)*. It is the appearing we long for of the righteous Judge *(2 Timothy 4:8)*. Embrace these realities as the "awards ceremony" of your life.

Father, You have redeemed my past, empowered my present and sealed my future forever. I live in expectation for the coming of Your Son in glory. Thank You for the blood of Jesus that cleanses my conscience to serve You. Amen.

November 10

Ezekiel 21:1–22:31; Hebrews 10:1–17; Psalm 108:1–13; Proverbs 27:12

The Already and the Not Yet

But when this priest had offered for all time one sacrifice for sins, he sat down at the right hand of God … because by one sacrifice he has made perfect forever those who are being made holy.
—Hebrews 10:12,14

Did you catch the verb tenses in the statement about the causal effect of the one sacrifice? He *has made* perfect (past tense) those who are *being made* holy (present tense, active and continuous). The first is an accomplished fact. The second is an ongoing work. They are both true at the same time, and both are to be embraced.

Jesus' sacrifice *has perfected* us. This is my legal position before God. He sees me through the grid of what Jesus did on the cross. Because of a sinless life, the blood of Jesus was the one perfect sacrifice that could atone for sins for all time. Our faith activates a status of total acceptance and justification before a holy God.

The ongoing work of *being made* holy is called sanctification. It is a process whereby I reflect in real life what is already true of me. I have been declared pure and holy, and now it becomes more and more evident in my behavior. I now desire holiness, and the Holy Spirit reveals to me areas in my life that can be purified. It's like looking at my thoughts and intentions under a microscope at 10X power and seeing the impurities that need attention. Just when I think I've got things under control, He shows me again those motivations at 20X power, and another whole set of issues are exposed. I have made progress in my holiness, but there will always be room for further purification. Thank God that I am *being* conformed to His image!

Father, I am a work in progress, and yet, you are pleased. Sanctify me wholly. Instill righteous desires. Continue the good work You have started. Amen.

November 11

Ezekiel 23:1–49; Hebrews 10:18–39; Psalm 109:1–31; Proverbs 27:13

The Need to Persevere

Remember those earlier days after you had received the light, when you stood your ground in a great contest in the face of suffering. So do not throw away your confidence; it will be richly rewarded. You need to persevere so that when you have done the will of God, you will receive what he has promised.
—Hebrews 10:32,35–36

This is an encouragement for me that I must finish well. It is evident from our passage that these Jewish believers have a history with God. They have had some moments of standing strong in the faith to overcome adversity. But somewhere along the way, they have become indifferent. They have lost some of the confidence they once had.

I have discovered that, even as you age, you enter into new seasons that must be met with faith. You never outgrow the need to trust and rely upon the Lord for that next challenge or assignment. Your scope of influence and testimony still requires that you walk circumspectly, giving attention to your steps. Your faith doesn't have to have sunk so low to where you are deliberately sinning. It may be in more subtle ways, where you have just given up on meeting together on Sundays, as some are in the habit of doing. Either way, it reminds me, in every season of life, that I need the encouragement to keep keeping on—to persevere. I need spurned on toward love and good deeds. I need the edification that comes from true fellowship of those of like-precious faith. After all, the prize is given to those who finish the race.

"Let us draw near to God with a sincere heart in full assurance of faith ... Let us hold unswervingly to the hope we profess, for he who promised is faithful" (v.22-23).

Father God, there are many opportunities to put my faith in neutral and coast, but that passivity only promotes unbelief. Empower me to finish well. Amen.

November 12

Ezekiel 24:1–26:21; Hebrews 11:1–16; Psalm 110:1–7; Proverbs 27:14

Elements of Faith

Now faith is being sure of what we hope for and certain of what we do not see. And without faith it is impossible to please God, because anyone who comes to him must believe that he exists and that he rewards those who earnestly seek him.
—Hebrews 11:1,6

We have come to the "Hall of Faith" chapter where the ancients were commended for their lives and exploits of faith. We have these who have gone before us who chose to believe God for the promise or persevered in adversity because they knew the One who was faithful. Some of them received the promise *(v.33)*, while others did not *(v.13)*. In each case, how they maintained a steady faith was what mattered.

Faith is not just hoping for the best or thinking positive thoughts. It is not ambiguous. It is embracing what God has promised. It is seeing what is more real than what is visible. It is a certainty and a knowing directed at a Person, not just a bolstered emotional confidence.

We cannot please God without faith. The converse of that is likewise true. Faith pleases God. Enoch's faith did *(v.5)*. The requirements for faith are that **1)** we believe He exists, and **2)** we believe that He is a rewarder of those who earnestly seek Him. The first part seems easy enough. But do we believe that God rewards the diligent? The truth is that the reward does not come fully (or at all) in this present life. We must believe that God will be faithful to His word and His promise.

Every act of your faith places an approving smile on the face of God.

Father in heaven, You invite me to believe for the naturally impossible. You reward me for seeking You with all diligence. I choose to trust You. In Christ's name I pray, Amen.

November 13

Ezekiel 27:1–28:26; Hebrews 11:17–31; Psalm 111:1–10; Proverbs 27:15–16

The Works and the Wonders

Great are the works of the Lord; they are pondered by all who delight in them. Glorious and majestic are his deeds, and his righteousness endures forever. He has caused his wonders to be remembered.
—Psalm 111:2–4

The works and the deeds of the Lord are things that the Lord has brought to pass that tell of His glory. God has wrought wonders by His mighty strength. They are breakthroughs that we could not bring about on our own. They are benchmark events in our life that we will never forget. They are arranged incidents that show us that we are special in His eyes. We ponder them, because they left an impact.

On a broad scale, you will find the works of the Lord throughout the pages of Scripture. Creation is the most magnificent display of the works of the Lord. The plagues in Egypt and the deliverance of the Hebrews were wonders never to forget. Circling Jericho seven days for the city walls to fall was a work of God. David's one stone to fell a giant; well … you get the idea. Israel's history is full of works and wonders.

On a more personal level, we see that the Lord has proven Himself over and over to us, as well. The events that drew us to salvation. The people who were there for us. The tug of the Holy Spirit. The financial miracle at the twelfth hour. The near miss that kept us from disaster. The healing you received in your body. The circumstances that "just happened" for you to meet your spouse. The doors that opened to launch your career. This list should start your mind to recounting the many, many wonders He has brought about. Then you will say, *"Indeed, the Lord is gracious and compassionate. Great is the Lord!"*

Father, Your works have attested Your love to me over and over. Thank You!

November 14

Ezekiel 29:1–30:26; Hebrews 11:32–12:13; Psalm 112:1–10; Proverbs 27:17

Loving Discipline

Endure hardship as discipline; God is treating you as sons. If you are not disciplined, then you are illegitimate children and not true sons. Our fathers disciplined us for a little while as they thought best; but God disciplines us for our good, that we may share in his holiness.
—Hebrews 12:7–8,10

I don't know anyone who volunteers to be disciplined, but most of us realize that Father knows best. As a parent, I know that I am the one responsible to train up my child in the way he should go. When he fails or cowers, then I am the one to bring clarity or correction or even punishment. Why? Because I know what's best for his development. I know what kind of person he will need to be to succeed in this life. Who better, then, than the Father of our spirits to keep our lives on the straight path. For these Jewish believers, they needed to know that God would use every difficulty to hone their faith.

We live in an era now where corporal punishment (spanking) is viewed as child abuse. This did not use to be the case. Allowing a child to do whatever he wants is no display of love. A child needs limits and perimeters placed upon him. He needs to grow up with a healthy respect for authority. No one signs up for the wood shed experience. No discipline is pleasant at the time. Yet, *"the Lord disciplines those he loves" (v.6). "Better is open rebuke than hidden love" (Proverbs 27:5).*

The upside to being trained by discipline is that it produces a harvest of righteousness and peace. We are permitted to share in His holiness. We exercise the fruit of self-control. We are legitimate sons. When times of hardship come, remember the Lord wastes no opportunity.

Father, Give me perspective so that I will embrace Your discipline. You know what I need to grow in holiness. I submit my soul and spirit to You. Amen.

November 15

Ezekiel 31:1–32:32; Hebrews 12:14–29; Psalm 113:1–114:8; Proverbs 27:18–20

The Throne We Approach

But you have come to Mount Zion, to the heavenly Jerusalem, the city of the living God. You have come to thousands and thousands of angels in joyful assembly, to the church of the firstborn ... You have come to God, the judge of all men ... to Jesus the mediator of a new covenant, and to the sprinkled blood.
—Hebrews 12:22–24

Throughout Hebrews, we have been invited to draw near to God, because now we have access to the throne of grace by the sacrifice of Jesus on the cross *(4:16; 10:19–22).* Because of His shed blood, we are enabled to approach God with all confidence.

In the days when Moses approached the mountain of God's presence, it was an extremely frightful experience on a physical mountain (Sinai). After all, God is a holy God, and we are to worship Him acceptably with reverence and awe. That part hasn't changed. But how fascinating it is to get a peek into the landscape of the heavenly Jerusalem, the place of God's habitation, now, as we approach God.

Mount Zion is not a physical mountain, as Sinai, but the dwelling place of God in the spirit realm. Populated there are multitudes of thousands of angels, the spirits of righteous men made perfect *(no physical bodies needed here),* God the judge, Jesus the mediator and the sprinkled blood that authorizes our access. The atmosphere is the rich presence of God amidst unspeakable joy. How desirable is that ... the gathering place for the community of God's own? What a difference Jesus has made to welcome us into God's very presence.

"Who is like the Lord... who sits enthroned on high?" (Psalm 113:5).

Father God, You have given me a glimpse of Your glorious habitation and an invitation that allows me to draw near to worship You for all eternity. Amen.

November 16

Present-Day Sacrifices

Through Jesus, therefore, let us continually offer to God a sacrifice of praise— the fruit of lips that confess his name. And do not forget to do good and to share with others, for with such sacrifices God is pleased.
—Hebrews 13:15–16

Because Jesus was the sacrifice to end all sacrifices, these Jewish believers now no longer needed to go through the rituals as historically prescribed. The Messiah had fulfilled all the requirements of the law. Access to the Father has been granted. Is there any sacrifice left to give that has relevance? As a matter of fact … yes, there is.

How truly significant, after all that has been said in this letter, that its' writer would suggest to us acceptable sacrifices that we could make that would please God. Sacrifices, after all, were efforts of obedience, but the heart state in which it was processed was the larger factor in whether it was pleasing to God. Here, the sacrifice reflects the heart, because it is a concerted articulation of praise from a thankful heart; and that does truly please Him. The fruit of our lips is what proceeds from our heart *(Matthew 12:34)*. Praise that flows from gratitude is a sacrifice the Father receives as worship. Continuous praise before Him is a fragrant aroma. Speaking forth what is already true about the Lord is wisdom. Thanking Him specifically brings honor to the One from whom all blessings flow. And in the process of lifting up praises to God, there is a profound effect upon us, as well. Our spirit is liberated and made to overflow. Withholding praise, then, is only shortsighted.

But the passage is not finished. Doing good and sharing with others is also a giving of ourselves that blesses the Lord, as it does to others.

Father God, as the one leper returned to Jesus, I give You thanks from a grateful heart. Your touch on my life is everything. Amen.

November 17

Ezekiel 35:1–36:38; James 1:1–18; Psalm 116:1–19; Proverbs 27:23–27

Smiles in Miles of Trials

Consider it pure joy, my brothers, whenever you face trials of many kinds, because you know that the testing of your faith develops perseverance. Perseverance must finish its work so that you may be perfect and complete, not lacking anything. If any of you lacks wisdom, he should ask God …
—James 1:2–5

I'll be honest. When I think about what brings me pure joy, I don't automatically think of "various trials." But that is because I see the discomfort and the inconvenience of the test. I'm not looking at the benefits beyond the trial, like the Lord sees. The fact is that we will endure many trials and testings in life. We don't get an exemption from what God says will make us mature and complete. We just need God's perspective, since God's aim for us is to pass these tests.

Peter elaborates upon his view. Sure, there is grief to suffer in a trial, but our faith is proven to be genuine when it is refined as gold in the fire *(1 Peter 1:6-7)*. Paul adds further that our afflictions are temporary in comparison to the eternal glory that they bring *(2 Corinthians 4:17)*.

I guess the key to making these trials work for us is to face them head on, embracing faith. To persevere in trials is to do more than simply endure them. There is a higher purpose in mind. I have found trials are most often designed to produce humility and a sincere witness. Our core beliefs are challenged. Our convictions rise to the surface and are honed. The substance of our faith is expressed or exposed in our response to the tests. And since we are going to need His grace and insight to benefit from them, God says, *"Ask,"* and He will lavish wisdom on us from above. But pure joy? I need to work on that!

Father, I need You in every dilemma I face. May my faith be proven as gold. Amen.

November 18

Ezekiel 37:1–38:23; James 1:19–2:17; Psalm 117:1–2; Proverbs 28:1

Faultless Religion

Religion that God our Father accepts as pure and faultless is this: to look after orphans and widows in their distress and to keep oneself from being polluted by the world.
—*James 1:27*

James, the brother of Jesus, defines for us what God the Father accepts as an authentic expression of religion. What an astounding call it is—to exhibit a life of purity while serving those in need.

We have seen throughout the Scriptures this year certain groups of people that are close to God's heart. It is those who are needy and in distress, like orphans and widows, that require compassion and kindness. Just two days ago, the writer of Hebrews exhorted us to remember those in prison and those who are mistreated *(13:3)*. Asaph writes in Psalm 82:3, *"Defend the cause of the weak and fatherless; maintain the rights of the poor and oppressed."* We touched upon having regard for the weak *(February 25)*. When we begin to understand what matters to God, we will see needs pop up all around us. We put our Christianity into practice when we do something tangible to help others.

But James takes it a step further. Service rendered to others is an incomplete expression if not accompanied by an uncompromised life. What we offer hurting people is more than a Band-Aid to the physical needs they possess. The whole person—spirit, soul and body—needs the touch of God. We present the gospel in its purest form when we model a life that is uncorrupted by the world's value system. Our lives match up with the message we proclaim and we validate God's love by addressing people at their point of need.

Father, allow my testimony to reflect what is true of You. Show me what I can do today that would show forth Your compassion to the needy. Amen.

November 19

Ezekiel 39:1–40:27; James 2:18–3:18; Psalm 118:1–18; Proverbs 28:2

The Power of Our Words

We all stumble in many ways. If anyone is never at fault in what he says, he is a perfect man, able to keep his whole body in check ... but no man can tame the tongue. It is a restless evil, full of deadly poison. Out of the same mouth come praise and cursing. My brothers, this should not be.
—James 3:2,8,10

The power of our words ... they cannot be underestimated. Death and life are in the power of the tongue. That means that my conversation with you could impart healing or it could stir up a fit of rage. My words could be a fragrance or a stench. They could be a medicine or a hand grenade. The potential for good and bad is equal.

I have witnessed the tragic effects of gossip, spreading an evil report, complaining and slander. So have you. When you are the subject of such ridicule, it hurts to the core. Once words are spoken and the cat is out of the bag, the damage is done. The effects can be lifelong. No wonder James says to *"be quick to listen"* and *"slow to speak" (1:19)*.

What is so bewildering is that we bless and praise with the same instrument that we brag and curse with. It is perplexing really. The truth is that the thought was there in our unrenewed mind to begin with. We only speak what is already residing in the heart.

I believe that the Lord would have us grow towards becoming a perfect or complete man. That implies that we have the members of our body under the harness of the Holy Spirit. I believe that self-control exercised over our tongue is among the final struggles in that fight to perfection. What is your tongue saying that is in your heart?

Father God, I submit my tongue and the members of my body to You. May my words be directed by the Holy Spirit to speak truth and bring healing. Amen.

November 20

Ezekiel 40:28–41:26; James 4:1–17; Psalm 118:19–29; Proverbs 28:3–5

Opposing Worldviews

You adulterous people, don't you know that friendship with the world is hatred toward God? Or do you think Scripture says without reason that the spirit he caused to live in us envies intensely? But he gives us more grace. That is why ... "God opposes the proud but gives grace to the humble."
  —James 4:4–6

James is a leader in the Jerusalem church and he is quite concerned for the Jewish Christians outside Palestine. Their values were being compromised and their double-lives were found in hypocrisy. If you didn't know better, you would not have known they were believers by their actions. James confronts their empty faith head on.

The simple truth is that the values espoused by the world and by the gospel are night and day opposites. God resists pride and cannot bless selfishness. The urge of the flesh to conform to the pattern of the world around us is strong and seductive, but Jesus died so that we might be delivered entirely from that bondage. The great advantage we have is the Holy Spirit who was deposited within us when we believed. The Spirit of God doesn't sit around lamely. His desire is intense that we would walk submitted to God's way of holiness. The conviction of the Spirit makes us feel uncomfortable when we choose to sin. It is God saying, *"I've called you to a higher place than this!"*

The people of God today are faced with the same temptation to cave in as they were in James' day. The steps to humility are likewise the same. Submit yourselves to God. Resist the devil and his ploys. Come near to God. Wash your hands of the past. Grieve over the sins that grieve God. Separate yourself from the association you had with sin, and consecrate anew your mind and heart to serve God alone.

Father, I desire Your way of holiness and humility. Extend your grace. Amen.

November 21

Ezekiel 42:1–43:27; James 5:1–20; Psalm 119:1–16; Proverbs 28:6–7

Pray like Elijah

Is any one of you sick? He should call the elders of the church to pray over him and anoint him with oil in the name of the Lord. And the prayer offered in faith will make the sick person well. The prayer of a righteous man is powerful and effective. Elijah was a man just like us. He prayed earnestly …
—James 5:14–17

We know Elijah to be a prophet of God who did some amazing things in 1 Kings. He brought a dead child back to life in Zeraphath. He had a showdown with the prophets of Baal on Mount Carmel. But it wasn't always so dramatic. Following a windstorm, an earthquake and fire, God spoke to Elijah through a gentle whisper. For Elijah, prayer was birthed out of relationship. God would speak and Elijah would obey. Elijah would pray and God would move. It's what made Elijah famous. But James reminds us that Elijah was a man just like us, with many of the same fears, yet he prayed earnestly to God.

We know what prayer is … it's the way we communicate with God. It's not rocket science. It's not even difficult. So why is prayer too often our last resort? It's because only needy people are desperate enough to pray. We pray when we are in trouble. We pray when we need to be forgiven. We pray when our bodies are in need of healing. It takes faith to trust God for things you cannot do yourself. It takes faith to call upon the elders of your church to ask for prayer. But God says if we will ask and believe, He will make the sick person well.

God loves the fervent prayer of a righteous man. He loves the reach you exhibit in asking and the faith to believe Him for it.

Father, You know my needs better than I, yet You ask me to ask You. So I present my requests before You. You are my Savior, my Healer and my Deliverer. I trust You with the details of my life. In Jesus' name I pray, Amen.

November 22

Ezekiel 44:1–45:12; 1 Peter 1:1–12; Psalm 119:17–32; Proverbs 28:8–10

A Living Hope

In his great mercy he has given us new birth into a living hope through the resurrection of Jesus Christ ... and into an inheritance that can never perish, spoil or fade- kept in heaven for you, who through faith are shielded by God's power until the coming of the salvation ... to be revealed in the last time.
  —1 Peter 1:3–5

While none of us are exempt from hardship, pain, misunderstanding and ridicule, most of us have not had to endure persecution for our faith as Peter's audience did. These Jewish believers were scattered throughout the Mediterranean world in order to survive. Peter's message to encourage his brothers was one of hope— real hope.

When you are on the brink of severe trials and tribulations, you want to know what works and what is real. A sure hope would sustain their faith and build a foundation of confidence. New birth provides us a living hope because Jesus Christ is the basis for our hope, and He is alive right now at the Father's right hand making intercession for the saints. My hope is as certain as Christ is alive. In addition to a living hope, God has promised us an inheritance that cannot be defiled or tampered with. It is reserved in heaven with our name upon it. And while we are here, we may expect to face various trials, but we are shielded by God's power throughout. We are God's chosen, after all.

We can rejoice. Our hope is sure. All members of the Trinity work to make our salvation complete *(v.2)*. We are filled with inexpressible joy in believing. Even in the sufferings, our faith can result in praise, glory and honor when Jesus is revealed. He is proven faithful once again.

Father of glory, You have given me a hope that is sure and a faith that is greater than gold. It will carry me through the trials and the momentary light afflictions that I will face. I lean upon Your power and Your Spirit. Amen.

November 23

Ezekiel 45:13–46:24; 1 Peter 1:13–2:10; Psalm 119:33–48; Proverbs 28:11

Crave Spiritual Milk

Therefore, rid yourselves of all malice ... deceit, hypocrisy, envy, and slander. Like newborn babies, crave pure spiritual milk, so that by it you may grow up in your salvation, now that you have tasted that the Lord is good.
—1 Peter 2:1–3

We all have to start somewhere in our journey with God. We have the living word of God spoken to us by the Holy Spirit sent from heaven *(1:12,23)*, and we are born again. The Father chose us, then we chose Him. He called us out of darkness and into His wonderful light. We have tasted of the goodness of the Lord and we believe. Now what?

The most natural instinct for a newborn is to crave milk. It is a healthy sign to indicate that all systems are go for growth. Craving spiritual milk is to desire the nourishment from the Word of God that we need to grow. Once we get started, our appetite for more increases, and the growth spurts begin. If you have tasted that the Lord is good and you don't crave more, then something is off. This truth cannot be skirted or understated: if your spiritual diet does not include healthy doses of God's Word, you will not grow up as the Lord intends. The sad truth is that many believers never mature. Perhaps you have been leaning upon someone else to feed you. Take the initiative to begin feeding yourself. Get alone and allow the Spirit of God to be your teacher.

The milk of the Word provides the basic foundation on which to grow. Let me say that we will never outgrow the need for milk. Yes, we will advance to a wider selection of solid food, but the basics never change. You will only build upon the truths of salvation and your identity in Christ. The greatest gift is to hunger and thirst for more.

Father, I have tasted of Your goodness and You have given me an appetite for more. Tutor me by Your Spirit so that I grow in the knowledge of You. Amen.

November 24

Ezekiel 47:1–48:35; 1 Peter 2:11–3:7; Psalm 119:49–64; Proverbs 28:12–13

True Beauty

Wives ... be submissive to your husbands so that they may be won over by the purity and reverence of your lives. Your beauty should not come from outward adornment ... Instead it should be that of the inner self, the unfading beauty of a gentle and quiet spirit, which is of great worth in God's sight.
—1 Peter 3:1–4

Beauty is a most sought after identification. We are simply *obsessed* with beauty. It captivates the aspirations and pocketbooks of the vast majority of our society. The fashion industry comes alongside to define and perpetuate this craving. The truth is that beauty is a God-inspired desire. It is right that every woman would desire to enhance what God has bestowed. But outer beauty is only the first layer.

The apostle Peter, of all people, is the chief fashion consultant of the New Testament. His advice is priceless ... Beauty in the eyes of God goes much further than external adornment. The truly attractive traits are those that emanate from your inner person—gentleness, purity, humility and devotion to God. These characteristics are evidence of a life that is led by the Spirit and nurtured by communion with God. Solomon adds: *"Charm is deceptive. And beauty is fleeting; but a woman who fears the Lord is to be praised"* (Proverbs 31:30).

Marriage is an incubator that intensifies the reality of what true love is. God's love is sacrificial and selfless. It shows us how to give and give, and then give some more. Yes, God uses your mate to help you work out the details of your salvation within the school of marriage.

My wife, Alaine, is the most beautiful woman I know. It was that inner purity complimenting her natural beauty that so attracted me to her.

Father, You are the Author of beauty. May we find our true worth in You.

November 25

Daniel 1:1–2:23; 1 Peter 3:8–4:6; Psalm 119:65–80; Proverbs 28:14

A Life Resolve

But Daniel resolved not to defile himself with the royal food and wine, and he asked the chief official for permission not to defile himself this way. Now God had caused the official to show favor and sympathy to Daniel ...
—Daniel 1:8–9

The national tragedy that was Judah's conquer to the Babylonians changed the life and landscape of a young Daniel and his countrymen. But it also afforded him an opportunity. Daniel was among a select few to enter training for the service of the king. While he was chosen for his aptitude, nobility and physique, Daniel quickly became set apart for the fear and favor of God.

The circumstances that surrounded Daniel were sending red flags of caution and compromise. The royal food and wine was a form of defilement to Daniel's keen sense of consecration to God. The favor of God permitted him and his three Israelite friends to prove a better course of nourishment than the lavish rich foods of their hosts. In the end, these four young men entered their service to the king with no equal in every matter of wisdom and understanding. God's blessing was evident, as He positioned them for key roles in the kingdom.

Likewise, God will place us in circumstances where we can make a difference to shine the light of our testimony, but there will always be that opportunity to compromise. If we cave and go with the flow, it diminishes the power of that light. Our consecration will be tested. Our convictions to serve God without defilement will be an issue. Determine now, in the secret place, that you are His and His alone.

Father, You place us in positions to show forth Your honor and Your glory. I consecrate my heart and my mind to serve You primary, and to be unstained by the world. May your favor rest upon me for a witness of Your grace. Amen.

November 26

Daniel 2:24–3:30; 1 Peter 4:7–5:14; Psalm 119:81–96; Proverbs 28:15–16

No Other God

Shadrach, Meshach and Abednego replied to the king, "O Nebuchadnezzar ... if we are thrown into the blazing furnace, the God we serve is able to save us from it, and he will rescue us from your hand, O king. But even if he does not, we want you to know, O king, that we will not serve your gods ..."
—Daniel 3:16–18

Nebuchadnezzar must have heard the portion of the dream that Daniel interpreted that stroked his ego the most—that he was the "head of gold"—because this Babylonian king made an image of gold ninety feet wide and nine feet tall for all to bow and worship. A blazing furnace awaited anyone who dared defy the king's order.

But the three friends of Daniel who administrated over the province were not moved by the edict. It was not a debatable topic. Allegiance to God governed their life choices. Bowing before a rival god was not going to happen. Threats of death could not shake the faith of these three. Deliverance from the circumstance was in God's hands. Certainly He is capable. But they resolved that even if He did not, they would be rescued from the king's hand by death.

They would be martyrs for the Lord's honor. But this time, the Lord gained greater glory through their deliverance. In the midst of their fiery trial, one likened to the Son of God appeared beside them.

As we near the end of the age, more believers in Christ will be required to take a stand before the opponents of the one true God. It has already escalated in regions abroad. What is your position now? *"If you are insulted because of the name of Christ, you are blessed, for the Spirit of glory and of God rests on you"* (1 Peter 4:14).

Most High God, I exalt You. You are worthy of my life's devotion. Amen.

November 27

Daniel 4:1–37; 2 Peter 1:1–21; Psalm 119:97–112; Proverbs 28:17–28

Add to Your Faith

For this very reason, make every effort to add to your faith goodness; and to goodness, knowledge; and to knowledge, self-control; and to self-control, perseverance; and to perseverance, godliness; and to godliness, brotherly kindness; and to brotherly kindness, love.
—2 Peter 1:5–7

The foundation of our faith is and always will be Christ. That does not change. Faith is active believing and trusting. We do not earn that or work for it. It is based upon the finished work of the cross. It is the foundation of our faith in Christ that we build upon. With that in mind, Peter exhorts us to *"make every effort to add to your faith."* In other words, build upon your foundation of faith. Let it take expression.

People are always watching us. What we want them to see is evidence of our faith in Christ. We want them to take notice of a faith that has feet. We display our faith in tangible ways. We demonstrate it with *goodness*. We are not ashamed to share the saving *knowledge* of it. We are enabled to resist temptation and sin through *self-control* and participation in the divine nature. We *persevere* by staying steady and remaining true to the Lord in every circumstance. By the power of the Holy Spirit we emanate *godly character* that resembles the Lord Jesus. Active faith finds ways to show *kindness* to our brothers and sisters in the household of faith. Finally, the ultimate goal of our faith is that we would continue to grow in our *love* for people.

Peter says that if we possess these qualities in increasing measure, we will be effective and productive. Our faith will be growing and it will show. Is your faith evident? Are you making every effort to grow?

Holy Spirit, I need Your divine power to reflect an accurate testimony of Jesus. I have room to grow. Cultivate Your character in me. Amen.

November 28

Daniel 5:1–31; 2 Peter 2:1–22; Psalm 119:113–128; Proverbs 28:19–20

Lot's Righteous Soul

If he rescued Lot, a righteous man, who was distressed by the filthy lives of lawless men (for that righteous man, living among them day after day, was tormented in his righteous soul by the lawless deeds he saw and heard)—if this is so, then the Lord knows how to rescue godly men from trials and hold the unrighteous for the day of judgment, while continuing their punishment.
—2 Peter 2:7–9

Now here lies an enigma. If you make a quick review of some of the choices Lot made in his life, you realize that he was the one who chose to live in Sodom. By all appearances, Lot grew comfortable living amidst brazen sin. He was the one who offered his daughters to the men of the town to save visiting angels. Once delivered from the burning sulfur of judgment, both of his daughters got dad drunk and committed incest to continue the family line. But that would not be the whole story. And we would all draw incomplete conclusions.

2000 years later, we unearth more necessary details about the nephew of Abram. What Peter reveals is quite astonishing. We know that God had mercy on Lot and rescued him from the wicked city of Sodom. What we didn't know was that Lot was tormented by the wickedness around him. His soul was distressed over the lewdness of lawless men. Lot was grieved over the city he chose to reside in. But to draw this out, there must be people who feel compelled to live in such places in order to be a light amongst the darkness. The tricky part is to remain pure and untainted by the very people you mean to reach.

While there might be as many questions as answers, Lot clearly was a righteous man who had a conscience for purity and lost souls.

Father in heaven, I myself am grieved that I am not more grieved for the lost in my city. Give me Your heart for the lost. Time is of the essence. Amen.

November 29

Daniel 6:1–28; 2 Peter 3:1–18; Psalm 119:129–152; Proverbs 28:21–22

Daniel and The Kitty Cats

When Daniel learned that the decree had been published, he went ... to his upstairs room where the windows opened. Three times a day he got down on his knees and prayed, giving thanks to his God, just as he had done before.
—Daniel 6:10

Daniel is over eighty years old now. He has served under three kings and is currently the top of three administrators in Darius' Medo-Persian empire. And, oh by the way, there is a reason why he had so much influence among kings. He is capable, obviously, but he is also a man of integrity and a man of God. And then the plot thickens ...

Daniel is also a man of prayer. There was nothing in his character that could be found to convict him of wrongdoing. But jealousy is a terrible thing. The government workers who were envious of his position plotted a scheme for Daniel's downfall. They appealed to the king's pride for a decree that sentenced any man to the lion's den if they prayed to anyone other than the king himself. The king was fooled, and once authorized, the edict could not be repealed.

Did the threat of death keep Daniel from his prayer closet? That thought never crossed Daniel's mind. He has served God continuously since his youth, and he wasn't about to stop now. Whatever happens happens. I believe this whole incident bothered King Darius more than it did Daniel. He made every attempt to rescue Daniel—even fasting—but to no avail. It was God who sent His angel to stay the execution. God had not yet written the final chapter of Daniel's life.

Father God, may my life demonstrate consistency and faithful devotion to You that would lead to integrity and favor before men. Establish godly people in areas of government and greatest influence. Amen.

November 30

Daniel 7:1–28; 1 John 1:1–10; Psalm 119:153–176; Proverbs 28:23–24

Walk in the Light

This is the message we have heard from him and declare to you: God is light; in him there is no darkness at all. If we claim to have fellowship with him yet walk in the darkness, we lie and do not live by the truth. But if we walk in the light, as he is in the light, we have fellowship with one another, and the blood of Jesus, his Son, purifies us from all sin.
—1 John 1:5–7

As an eyewitness to the life and ministry of Jesus, John testifies to a new generation of believers so they would not be swayed by heretical teachers who denied the incarnation of Christ. As an elder statesman, John wants to validate their faith with the truth that he himself witnessed. He combats false teaching that extends even to this day.

His message is simple and forthright: God is light. He is perfectly holy. In Him, there is no shade of gray. Light exposes all things for what they are, whether good or evil. It is by the light that we are led out of darkness. Darkness cannot survive the presence of light just as sin cannot reside in the presence of God. So when we claim to have fellowship with God, then it must follow that we also live in the light. We welcome the light and refuse any association with darkness. Walking in light invites the Spirit of God to inspect our heart and shine His light on any shadow. This transparency before the Lord allows us to walk in purity and in true fellowship with others.

If we claim to have fellowship with God and still walk in darkness, then we deceive ourselves. Many teachers still claim that if you accept Jesus, then it doesn't matter how you live; *God forgives either way.* But the Lord knows our heart. If we choose the light, then we will choose His way—to confess our sins as the Spirit exposes them.

Father, I choose to walk transparent before You. I invite Your light. Amen.

December 1

Daniel 8:1–27; 1 John 2:1–17; Psalm 120:1–7; Proverbs 28:25–26

We Have an Advocate

My dear children, I write this to you so that you will not sin. But if anybody does sin, we have one who speaks to the Father in our defense—Jesus Christ, the Righteous One. He is the atoning sacrifice for our sins, and not only for ours but also for the sins of the whole world.
—1 John 2:1–2

Here, John affectionately instructs us that Plan A is that we avoid sin. We can live in the light and walk as Jesus walked. We make this our reality by the Word of God and the Spirit of God empowering us within. It sure keeps life less complicated. But since none of us have been perfected in this skin yet, we are grateful for an amended plan.

Sin has a way of disrupting our fellowship with God and with people. It creates a sense of distance and separation. It brings an unsettling disturbance in our spirit. And if we didn't feel bad enough already by missing the mark, the devil jumps in to heap on the guilt. He is rightly called *"the accuser of the brethren" (Revelation 12:10).* That is why we need a good defense attorney to argue our case before the Judge. Jesus Christ is our advocate. He made the necessary sacrifice to atone for our sins, and by it, He has won our case. We have been declared *"not guilty."* So when accusations fly, we remind Satan that the shed blood of Jesus is the legal basis for our righteous standing. Jesus remains at the Father's right hand as our defender, supporter and intercessor.

Owning up to our sin and confessing it for what it is allows us to feel the flow of forgiveness and the joy of restored fellowship. It is God's way to purify us from unrighteous gobbledegoop *(1:9).*

Gracious God, You have called me out of the muck and mire of sin. What's more, You have provided a way for me to enjoy uninterrupted fellowship with You. With Jesus, I am never left to fend for myself. I am never alone. Amen.

December 2

Daniel 9:1–11:1; 1 John 2:18–3:6; Psalm 121:1–8; Proverbs 28:27–28

A Model for Prayer

While I was praying, confessing my sins and the sin of my people ... Gabriel instructed me and said to me ... "As soon as you began to pray, an answer was given, which I have come to tell you, for you are highly esteemed."
—Daniel 9:20,22–23

Do you want a Biblical model of prayer from one acquainted with prayer? The same Daniel who sought the Lord unashamedly three times a day gives us an effective approach to praying for our nation.

First of all, Daniel was extremely committed to this nation that God had ordained and blessed. He was interested in seeing the promises of God fulfilled in regards to Judah, Jerusalem and all Israel. He was also familiar with the existing Scriptures that the prophet Jeremiah had penned concerning the timeline for their captivity *(25:11-12)*. But Daniel was also well aware of the shame and waywardness of his people. It was for this reason that God righteously brought wrath. But rather than pointing a finger of blame upon others, Daniel shoulders the responsibility of Judah's sin. This esteemed man of God confesses the sins of the nation as if they were his own. He took the position of humility and sought the Lord with fervency and urgency. He fasted. He pleaded earnestly. Daniel knew that God was merciful. Daniel made his requests for the sake of His honor and His great name.

In each of the two examples given, God was said to have responded *immediately*. In the second prayer, there was a delay of twenty–one days because of the warfare going on in the spiritual realm, but the answer came nonetheless. In each case, God sent answers. In each case, God was attuned to the heartfelt cry of a humbly-seeking heart.

Father in heaven, I seek you for our nation. We have sinned grievously, O God. I appeal to You. Extend mercy. Forgive us. Bring revival. Amen.

December 3

Daniel 11:2–35; 1 John 3:7–24; Psalm 122:1–9; Proverbs 29:1

For This Purpose Jesus Came

The reason the Son of God appeared was to destroy the devil's work. This is how we know who the children of God are and who the children of the devil are: Anyone who does not do what is right is not a child of God; nor is anyone who does not love his brother. And this is his command: to believe in the name of his Son, Jesus Christ, and to love one another as he commanded us.
  —*1 John 3:8,10,23*

John has a simple and straightforward approach, because it really is that obvious. Made plain, the command John gives is to believe in God's Son for salvation and then to love one another.

When we believe, we are born of God and God's seed is deposited within us. Like any seed that bears the properties of the parent seed, that seed will grow and produce like kind. That seed will develop to resemble the nature and characteristics of the God who loves. There is no mystery to it. For the one who has not believed, then that one is considered a son of the devil, because he does not have the seed of Jesus, but the seed of the first Adam. That spells out what takes place when we are born again: the Son of God destroys what the devil had previously established in that person and creates a new heart that loves, from the new seed. It all starts at the point of believing, or not.

The result that follows is love that is evident and active. Acts of selfless giving bear out the work that God has done in our heart. We are now motivated to love and to serve others. We see people in a new light because we have been born of God's Spirit. We see with His eyes and from His perspective. What deeds are evident in your life?

Gracious God, You sent Your Son to seek and save the lost and to bring about a complete deliverance in me. Destroy the works of the devil. Plant your seed in me. May it bear the fruit of authentic love from a changed heart. Amen.

December 4

Daniel 11:36–12:13; 1 John 4:1–21; Psalm 123:1–4; Proverbs 29:2–4

Confidence on That Day

But at that time your people—everyone whose name is found written in the book— will be delivered. Multitudes who sleep in the dust of the earth will awake: some to everlasting life, others to shame and everlasting contempt. Those who are wise will shine like the brightness of the heavens …
—Daniel 12:1–3

In this way, love is made complete among us so that we will have confidence on the day of judgment, because in this world we are like him.
—1 John 4:17

Daniel received a vision that concerned a great war at the end of the ages. Details are specific and ambiguous at the same time. Kings will emerge and evolve from the north and the south, but the end will arise with the angel Michael. After a time of great persecution and suffering for believers, deliverance will finally be realized. The people of God, whether alive or dead —whose names are written in the book— will awaken to everlasting life. Likewise, the unbelieving will also arise, receiving the sentence of shame and everlasting contempt. It's the final outcome and destiny of our lives for all eternity.

The words Daniel received were closed and sealed until the time of the end, but the promise of an inheritance was given. Those who are wise and believe will shine with the brightness of the heavens. It is the reward we receive when our life here is completed. All of history is racing toward this day when we will stand before the Lord and receive what is due. The day of judgment can be a scary thought for those who don't believe or are uninformed. But for the believer, this is the culmination of all we hope for and believe. With God's life and love within us, we actually look forward to that day with confidence.

I lift up my eyes to Your throne in heaven. I long for the day when my journey leads me to Your presence. Until then, let me love with Your love. Amen.

December 5

Hosea 1:1–3:5; 1 John 5:1–21; Psalm 124:1–8; Proverbs 29:5–8

An Unrelenting Love

I am going to allure her; I will lead her into the desert and speak tenderly to her. There I will give back her vineyards, and will make the Valley of Achor a door of hope. There she will sing as in her youth.."In that day," declares the Lord, "you will call me 'my husband;' you will no longer call me 'my master.'"
—Hosea 2:14–16

Hosea was a prophet to Israel as they were heading towards their fall to Assyria, just as Jeremiah was a prophet to Judah leading into theirs against Babylon. Both were in serious moral decline. While their collapses did not coincide on the same timetable, both prophets depicted their nation in a similar light. Both were acting as an adulterous bride, unfaithful to the One who loved her steadfastly.

As we have seen throughout the Scriptures, marriage illustrates the closest bond a relationship can celebrate. The total disregard of their covenant vows is how Israel is described in resisting God's love. God, in fact, told Hosea to take an unfaithful wife (Gomer) to magnify the point, that the nation of Israel was guilty of spiritual adultery.

What Hosea highlights to us, despite Israel's stubborn refusal, is that not only is God's commitment in tact, but His plans and promises for her were undiminished. Punishment was unavoidable. Her lewdness would be exposed; but He would position her to reconsider His kindness. He would block her path with thornbushes to bring about disillusionment with their idols. A new day of restoration was what God had in mind. Her troubles (the Valley of Achor) would give way to hope. In that day, God will no longer be considered a master to them, but a husband, and He will restore the joy they once knew.

Father, anything that takes prominence over You is an idol. Realign my priorities and take Your rightful place on the throne of my heart. Amen.

December 6

Hosea 4:1–5:15; 2 John 1:1–13; Psalm 125:1–5; Proverbs 29:9–11

Do Not Lose That

It has given me great joy to find some of your children walking in the truth, just as the Father commanded us. Watch out that you do not lose what you have worked for, but that you may be rewarded fully.
—2 John 1:4,8

In this short letter to a dear friend and her children, the elder apostle John writes to encourage her to know the truth and live by the truth. John knew the Savior's life and message firsthand. He was full of grace and truth *(John 1:14,17)*. Jesus was the truth *(John 14:6)*.

One of the greatest compliments that you can receive in life is when someone takes note of your children's wise choices. We remember them as youngsters; now they are making a life of their own. And this chosen lady had modeled a life of following after the truth, and they were following in her footsteps. Their witness made an impression.

It is this life of truth that she lived out that John was giving caution about. *"Watch out that you do not lose what you have worked for."* As you know, it takes a lifetime to build a credible reputation and a name of integrity. It takes only a moment of senseless retaliation or a lapse in judgment for it all to come crashing down.

Another way we can lose what we've worked for is simply becoming negligent of a discipline. We put that gift on the shelf or we get distracted. "Use it or lose it" may apply. Devotion to God through prayer and the Word are critical in maintaining all that the Lord has accomplished in you. Being a good steward of what He has given will bring great reward in the end and will open the door for more. Think about what God has given you. What needs your attention right now?

Father, guard my heart from the thief. Guide me by wisdom and truth. Amen.

December 7

Hosea 6:1–9:17; 3 John 1:1–14; Psalm 126:1–6; Proverbs 29:12–14

Enjoy Good Health

Dear friend (Gaius), I pray that you may enjoy good health and that all may go well with you, even as your soul is getting along well.
—3 John 1:2

Once again, the elder apostle John addresses a dear friend, this time thanking Gaius for the generous hospitality he had shown to traveling preachers. His ministry was a blessing to the recipients, but also the local church. Now John wanted to pray a blessing over Gaius.

God is very interested in your health. He created your amazing body to operate at an optimum level. After all, you need to be running on all cylinders in order to fulfill all the will of God. Your physical well-being is critical in fulfilling what God intends. If you're bogged down with sickness and disease, even your good intentions won't get you out of that bed. You are limited by what your health will allow.

It is God's will that you be whole—physically, spiritually, emotionally, mentally, and in every way. Paul ends 1 Thessalonians with a similar declaration: *"May your whole spirit, soul and body be kept blameless at the coming of our Lord Jesus Christ"* (5:23).

So, be a good steward of your body. Get enough restorative sleep. Eat your vegetables. Exercise regularly and get that heart rate up. Stay away from those colas and candy bars. It's the only body you'll have for a few years. Treat it well. And, by all means, pray for healing. God is still in the healing business. Jesus has made provision for our wholeness on the cross. It is by His stripes that we are made whole *(Isaiah 53:5).*

Jehovah Rophe, You are the God who heals me. I offer my body as an instrument of righteousness for Your sake. Amen.

December 8

Hosea 10:1–14:9; Jude 1:1–25; Psalm 127:1–5; Proverbs 29:15–17

Pray in the Spirit

I felt I had to write and urge you to contend for the faith that was once for all entrusted to the saints. But you, dear friends, build yourselves up in your most holy faith and pray in the Holy Spirit.
   —Jude 1:3,20

Jude is the brother of James and the half-brother of Jesus. But here, Jude refers to himself as the servant of Jesus Christ. He wants to write about the salvation they share, but is compelled to warn them about the false teachers who are attacking the basic tenets of their faith. It's nothing new. Godless men slip in to water down the message. They bring division. They follow their natural reasoning. They do not speak by the Spirit of God because the Spirit does not reside in them.

So what is the most beneficial thing I can do to build up my faith? The answer is to "pray in the Spirit." That means to pray by the direction and unction of the Spirit. But to build yourself up in your most holy faith is to pray in the Spirit as Paul directed in his letter to the Corinthians. Paul is encouraging the use of the gifts of the Spirit to benefit the congregation, but brings about the truth as they are used personally, as well. Listen to Paul: *"He who speaks in a tongue edifies himself…"(14:4).* *"For anyone who speaks in a tongue does not speak to men, but to God" (14:2).* *"For if I pray in a tongue, my spirit prays, but my mind is unfruitful. So what shall I do? I will pray with my spirit, but I will also pray with my mind" (14:14–15).* *"I would like every one of you to speak in tongues …" (14:5).* As believers, we have the option to pray with understanding or to pray in the Spirit, knowing that when we do, we build up our faith in the process. If this is a missing element in your prayer life, ask God who gives freely and generously of His Spirit.

Father, You gave me a way to build myself up in my most holy faith. Thank You for the gift of praying in tongues. I welcome what You make available.

December 9

Joel 1:1–3:21; Revelation 1:1–20; Psalm 128:1–6; Proverbs 29:18

Gracious and Compassionate

"Even now," declares the Lord, "return to me with all your heart, with fasting and weeping and mourning." Rend your heart and not your garments. Return to the Lord your God, for he is gracious and compassionate, slow to anger and abounding in love, and he relents from sending calamity.
—Joel 2:12–13

Joel prophesies as a prophet does. He speaks of the calamities to come if Judah is not willing to repent of their sins. He pleads with his people to turn back to God. Joel warns of the great and dreadful "day of the Lord" that will come for ultimate judgment of sin. But Joel also relates the merciful side of a holy God who desires to bless His people. In those latter days, God will pour out His Spirit upon all people.

The phrase that describes the nature of God's dealings with His people is one that has popped up several times this year: *"… for he is gracious and compassionate, slow to anger and abounding in love."* This phrase first appeared as God's response to Moses when he asked to see His glory *(Exodus 34:6-7). Do you remember that?* I was waiting for a light show, but God chose to give this self-disclosure instead. It was how He wanted Moses to understand His true nature—He deals with us from a heart of love. Moses reiterates it in a prayer following the twelve spies' evil report *(Numbers 14:18)*, adding that God will forgive rebellion. The phrase was passed on, because Nehemiah quotes it in a united prayer to God *(Nehemiah 9:17)*. Three times David quotes the phrase *(Psalm 86:15; 103:8; 145:8)*. Jonah, a contemporary of Joel's, complained to God after Nineveh repented because He knew this was true of God *(Jonah 4:2)*. Let this become a settled issue in your heart—God loves you with an everlasting love. He abounds with mercy.

Gracious God, You know what I am made of, yet You love me. You would rather refrain from sending calamity, but You are just, as You are forgiving.

December 10

Amos 1:1–3:15; Revelation 2:1–17; Psalm 129:1–8; Proverbs 29:19–20

What Happened to Your Passion?

To the angel of the church in Ephesus write: I know your deeds, your hard work and your perseverance. I know that you cannot tolerate wicked men, that you have tested those who claim to be apostles but are not, and have found them false. But I have this against you: You have forsaken your first love.
—Revelation 2:1–2,4

The apostle John writes the first of seven letters to the churches of Asia Minor, but they are not his words. They are instructions he received from Jesus. While they are specific to the church he addresses, they could represent so many church situations today.

What is interesting with Ephesus, is that we are able to see the state of the church in what was about AD 95 and contrast it to what Paul wrote in his letter to the same church around AD 60. He had spent three years there making disciples on his third journey, from about AD 54 *(Acts 19)*. When he met with the elders at his final departure *(Acts 20:29-31)*, he warned them that false teachers would arise to distort the truth and draw people away from the faith. How true these words would be. It was over this very issue that the church of Ephesus was commended. They worked hard, persevered, weeded out the false prophets and endured hardships without growing weary. This was impressive. Could that be said of the church today?

What was not acceptable was that this second generation of believers was losing their zeal and passion for the Lord Jesus. What once was a trademark *(Ephesians 1:15)* was now their downfall. They had allowed their first love to deteriorate to a mechanical duty, and Jesus noticed. Jesus knows our heart state and calls us to keep love alive.

Lord Jesus, You call me to a vibrant personal relationship that will in turn motivate me to serve You wholeheartedly in every other area. I repent. Amen.

December 11

Amos 4:1–6:14; Revelation 2:18–3:6; Psalm 130:1–8; Proverbs 29:21–22

You Have a Reputation

To the angel of the church in Sardis write: I know your deeds; you have a reputation of being alive, but you are dead. Wake up! Strengthen what remains and is about to die, for I have not found your deeds complete ... Remember, therefore, what you have received and heard; obey it and repent.
—Revelation 3:1–3

God's perspective is always the one that counts. He cuts through the veneer of what people see on the outside to unmask the truth about what's really going on. The church in Sardis, by outward appearances, is the hip place to be. They have the cool worship band. They identify with the culture in a non-threatening way. But not is all what it seems behind the scenes. They have the reputation without the substance.

Jesus exposes what is really about to die. Their obedience is an incomplete obedience. They have heard the Lord, but have not followed through. They did things to win the approval of the masses whether God was in it or not. Most of those in the church have soiled their clothes. They have allowed sin to tarnish their witness. The leaders did not call them to holiness or to live above the standards of their society. They were not taught to take responsibility for their actions, nor led to repent of their sins. It was loosey-goosey in Sardis, and that is a dangerous place to be.

The threat was that if they did not wake up from their apathy, they would have no perception as to when the Lord would come again. How tragic. But there are a few who have resisted the trend and have kept their selves pure. They are the ones who see through the hype. There is still time to repent and overcome, but no time to waste.

Jesus, No matter the front I put on to please, Your acceptance is all I really need. You want my total obedience so I can walk without compromise. Amen.

December 12

Amos 7:1–9:15; Revelation 3:7–22; Psalm 131:1–3; Proverbs 29:23

Lukewarm Faith Anyone?

To the angel of the church in Laodicea write: I know your deeds, that you are neither
cold nor hot. I wish you were one or the other! So, because you are lukewarm—neither
hot nor cold—I am about to spit you out of my mouth.
*   —Revelation 3:14–16*

I have to tell you … I am a fan of coffee. I love two or three cups of my favorite
Guatemalan blend every morning, fresh and steamy hot. If it sits around too
long it loses it's luster. That same cup o 'Joe isn't the same if it's cooled down. I'd
rather brew a new pot than be made to gulp it down lukewarm, no matter the
brand or blend. That's the image I get when Jesus says "you are neither hot nor
cold." When your faith is lukewarm, you don't realize how pitiful you've become.

Part of the problem is that when you have acquired a few bucks in the bank
account, then you think you have what you need. You are self-sufficient. You're
becoming indifferent. You don't realize it when it happens, but you drift from
passionate to lackadaisical. The treasure you value is not the eternal treasure
of prayer and holiness that it once was. Jesus says in verse 18: *"Acquire a faith*
that is tried as gold in the fire." That's worth plenty. *"Put on His righteousness as a*
garment." Let folks see what you are made of. And *"let Jesus heal your spirit eyes, "*
so you can see and perceive the spiritual realities again; because right now, you're
not seeing clearly. Stay the status quo and get spewed out.

Jesus lays it down: Be earnest and repent. Don't be half-hearted and complacent.
It's not a place you want to get stuck in. Did you even notice Jesus standing at
the door? Did you hear him knocking? Sweet fellowship awaits the one who will
open the door and overcome.

Jesus, faithful and true witness, You are sculpting my faith to value what is truly
valuable. I will not lean on my own strength. I will earnestly seek You.

December 13

Obadiah 1:1–21; Revelation 4:1–11; Psalm 132:1–18; Proverbs 29:24–25

Too Awesome to Describe

At once I was in the Spirit, and there before me was a throne in heaven with someone sitting on it. And the one who sat there had the appearance of jasper and carnelian. A rainbow, resembling an emerald, encircled the throne. From the throne came flashes of lightning, rumbling and peals of thunder.
—*Revelation 4:2–3,5*

Allow yourself to be consumed with the vision John was permitted to see, while in the Spirit, of the throne room in heaven. On the throne before him was the Lord of heaven and earth, the everlasting God. He is described as One who had the appearance of a semi-transparent jasper and carnelian (or fiery-red sardius stone). He is not described in human features that we would understand, but the pure brightness of brilliant light and color. An entire rainbow encircled the throne, resembling an emerald. Flashes of lightning and peals of thunder exuded from his throne, and before it all was a sea of glass.

Around the throne are twenty–four elders on twenty–four thrones wearing white with crowns of gold that they lay at his feet in worship. Four living creatures, with four faces (resembling those in Ezekiel 1), having six wings and covered with eyes all around, never stop giving glory to the One who sits on the throne. Day and night, they never stopped saying: *"Holy, holy, holy…" (v.8).*

These descriptions are simply off the charts. John makes his best attempt to document the glory he witnessed, but words fall short. How can you adequately describe the majesty and splendor of the Lord God Almighty? Can anyone grasp this glory for a minute?

Words cannot adequately describe Your dwelling place, but this vision has magnified my perspective on worship. I will fill my mind with the glories of heaven and give You praise. I long for the day to witness this unceasing glory.

December 14

Jonah 1:1–4:11; Revelation 5:1–14; Psalm 133:1–3; Proverbs 29:26–27

Only One Worthy

"Who is worthy to break the seals and open the scroll?" He (a Lamb) came and took the scroll from him who sat on the throne. And the four living creatures and the twenty-four elders fell down ... Each one had a harp and they were holding golden bowls full of incense, which are the prayers of the saints.
—Revelation 5:2,7–8

Further drama of the throne room unfolds in the vision John witnesses. The One who sits on the throne held a scroll with writing on both sides and sealed with seven seals, but no one was worthy to open the scroll except one—the Lion of the tribe of Judah. Yet it was a Lamb that stood before the throne and the four living creatures and the elders. This Lamb looked as if it had been slain. Jesus was the Lion, the promised Messiah from David's line, but He was also the perfect sacrificial Lamb who bore the sins of all mankind. He was the only one found worthy to open the scroll and reveal the events of the end. When He took the scroll, the creatures and the elders fell down before the Lamb and sang a new song. They each had a harp and golden bowls of incense, which were described as the prayers of the saints. The offering they brought before the throne were songs of worship and intercession from the saints that arose as incense. As a violinist, I am glad to know that the Lord welcomes my offering as worship.

It was the slain lamb who purchased men for God from every tribe and nation to serve our God and to rule and reign on the earth. Joining the chorus around the throne were the voices of a multitude of thousands (times ten thousand) of angels singing in a loud voice: *"Worthy is the Lamb, who was slain, to receive power and wealth and wisdom and strength and honor and glory and praise!" (v.12).*

Jesus, You alone are worthy. I offer my earnest prayers as incense before the throne, knowing that they are precious and they matter to You. Amen.

December 15

Micah 1:1–4:13; Revelation 6:1–17; Psalm 134:1–3; Proverbs 30:1–4

Seal Judgments Begin

When he opened the fifth seal, I saw under the altar the souls of those who had been slain because of the word of God and the testimony they had maintained. They called out in a loud voice, "How long ... until you judge the inhabitants of the earth and avenge our blood?" Each of them was given a white robe ...
—Revelation 6:9–11

With the Lamb stepping forward as the only one worthy to open the seals, now I want to know what it is that is so exclusive. The time has come ... We find out as the Lamb opens each seal, He sets in motion each judgment event. Future judgments will follow, but the seals begin the righteous judgments of God upon the sin of the earth.

The first seal reveals a white horse with it's rider set out to make war. The second seal releases a fiery red horse with it's rider given power to remove peace with rampant bloodshed. The third seal brings forth a black horse. It's rider holds a pair of scales to illustrate the impact on prices of grain in famine. The fourth seal shows the pale horse of death, with power for it's rider over a quarter of the earth. (The fifth seal in a minute.) The sixth seal unleashes a great earthquake as never before, with stars from the sky falling to the earth and mountains being leveled. Pandemonium ensues for self-preservation.

The fifth seal reveals the souls of the martyrs. These who have honored the Word of God and have stood up for their faith in the face of death call out, *"How long?"* How long until their blood is avenged? The number of martyrs has not yet been completed, so they must tarry a little longer, but they shall receive great honor. The peril we face as believers is real, but as has been said many times, *"You won't have a faith worth living for unless it is also worth dying for."*

Righteous Judge, prepare my heart so that I may be true to the end. Amen.

December 16

Micah 5:1–7:20; Revelation 7:1–17; Psalm 135:1–21; Proverbs 30:5–6

Every Tribe and Nation

After this I looked and there before me was a great multitude that no one could count, from every nation, tribe, people and language, standing before the throne and in front of the Lamb. They were wearing white robes and were holding palm branches in their hands. And they cried out in a loud voice: "Salvation belongs to our God, who sits on the throne, and to the Lamb."
—Revelation 7:9–10

What John saw in his vision of the heavenly sanctuary is breathtaking, to say the least. The splendor, the awe, the visual glory and the participants engaging in worship and exaltation fill the senses.

What I so look forward to is the reality of this gathering of saints from every corner of the earth. What we will witness is the climax of the gospel's mission to make disciples of all nations, tribes and people. Those who believed that Jesus was God's answer for salvation and then confessed His Lordship will be called together for this glorious reunion. Here, they cried out in a loud voice as one. The prior worship from chapter five has them singing. It was both. It was passionate worship all focused around the Lamb that was slain and the blood that was spilled to make their robes white with the righteousness and holiness of Christ. This is a massive celebration for the ages.

The praise will be glorious. Can you imagine the stoic Englishman liberated and lifting his hands? Visualize for a moment the island nations moving to a Jamaican beat. The Polish brothers are dancing a polka to an accordion. A black choir (with white robes) is swaying in rhythm to a chorus and the cowboys are humming praise to a harmonica. My intention is not to trivialize this holy moment, only to highlight the international flavor of our great gathering to come.

To the One who sits on the throne, I join You in celebrating Jesus. Amen.

December 17

Nahum 1:1–3:19; Revelation 8:1–13; Psalm 136:1–26; Proverbs 30:7–9

Silence in Heaven

When he opened the seventh seal, there was silence in heaven for about half an hour. Another angel … was given much incense to offer, with the prayers of all the saints, on the golden alter before the throne. The smoke of the incense, together with the prayers of the saints, went up before God.
—Revelation 8:1,3–4

We finally made it to the seventh and final seal. I mean, we can't list the first six and leave out the last one, right? But the opening of the seventh seal really is the ushering in of the next set of judgments, called the trumpet judgments. They are released upon the anti-Christ.

The unique mark of the seventh seal was that (by John's earthly estimation) there was silence in heaven for about a half an hour. But what do you suppose was meant by this? Just moments prior, there was exuberant praise by every people group of the world. Was it now the glory perceived as a holy hush before the presence of Almighty God? Was it just an overwhelming few moments to ponder all the judgments as they were transpiring? Was it a time of contemplation of all that had culminated? Was the mood one of joy or sadness? Was it a pause leading to the next big thing? What was the purpose in the half hour of silence? I believe it had to do with the next recorded act.

An offering of much incense and the prayers of the saints went up before God from the angel's hand. It is estimated that it took a priest about a half an hour to offer incense in the temple *(Leviticus 16:13)*. The power of God has historically been released through prayer, and so it is that the prayers of the saints assist the release in the next series of judgments. The censor of prayers is mixed with fire and is hurled to the earth, bringing about lightning, thunder and a great earthquake.

Father, bring an end to the deceiver. Inaugurate the reign of Jesus. Amen.

December 18

Habakkuk 1:1–3:19; Revelation 9:1–21; Psalm 137:1–9; Proverbs 30:10

Write Down the Revelation

How long, O Lord, must I call out for help, but you do not listen? Why do you tolerate wrong? Then the Lord replied: "Write down the revelation and make it plain on tablets so that a herald may run with it. For the revelation awaits an appointed time; it speaks of the end and will not prove false ... wait for it.
   —Habakkuk 1:2–3; 2:2–3

The prophet Habakkuk witnessed the decline of his nation just as Jeremiah did. He saw the shift in global power and how it was encroaching upon Judah. While Jeremiah dramatically spoke out the hard message of the sins they were committing, Habakkuk took his case to God and asked the hard and honest questions.

God was not silent. Both prophets were heard, but in different ways. God answered Habakkuk. He was raising up Babylon for His purposes, but their domination would be short-lived. *"Because you have plundered many nations, the people who are left will plunder you" (2:8).* God's answer was that deliverance will come, but there is a time frame God has ordained. In the meantime, the righteous will live by faith, and they will wait for the Lord; but His word is sure.

What Habakkuk did by writing down the revelation is what I have found to be a priceless practice in my discernment of revelation given by the Holy Spirit. In my personal devotions of Scripture, writing goes well beyond just reading, because now I am going beneath the surface in my pursuit of the context and meaning. As I meditate on a passage, the Spirit illuminates what I need for the moment and makes the application personal. Writing down the revelation has taken me to a new level. Could this be a way for you to go deeper too?

Father, You speak to me from Your Word by the Holy Spirit. Make it plain, as I meditate and process Your words. May the herald run with its news. Amen.

December 19

Zephaniah 1:1–3:20; Revelation 10:1–11; Psalm 138:1–8; Proverbs 30:11–14

God Sings

Seek the Lord, all you humble of the land, you who do what he commands … perhaps you will be sheltered on the day of the Lord's anger. The Lord is with you, he is mighty to save. He will take great delight in you, he will quiet you with his love, he will rejoice over you with singing.
—Zephaniah 2:3; 3:17

The climate around Zephaniah's ministry was the abandonment of true worship under the evil kings, Manasseh and Amon. Their leadership caused Judah to plunge to new lows. Zephaniah's mandate was to draw Judah out of complacency, to proclaim the coming judgment upon their sin and to bring hope of a national awakening.

What is striking is the weight Zephaniah puts on the remnant, those who seek the Lord, who by their obedience and perseverance, in the face of this moral breakdown, bring back the hope and promise of restoration for the nation. It is the people of God who attract the blessing of God to regain greatness. Sin is a big deal to God. The consequences are far-reaching. Evil must be purged. The remnant understands that it is a just and righteous God who deals with sin in order to purify a people. While the tumult transpires, the righteous will seek the Lord. It is those who call upon His name that set the tone for revival. And indeed, Zephaniah watched as a young King Josiah grew to be a man of God, bringing reforms and great revival.

The tone of God's endearment crescendos in the final chapter. Not only will the Lord turn back their enemy, but He will personally comfort and save His beloved. Because God delights in His own, He will rejoice over us with singing. You didn't know God could sing?

Dear Father, how you love me! You take the personal measures to calm my heart in the midst of darkness. You also hear me when I cry out to You. Amen.

December 20

Haggai 1:1–2:23; Revelation 11:1–19; Psalm 139:1–24; Proverbs 30:15–16

A Temple of Glory

"Is it a time for you yourselves to be living in your paneled houses, while this house remains a ruin? I will shake all nations, and the desired of all nations will come, and I will fill this house with glory. The glory of this present house will be greater than the glory of the former house," says the Lord Almighty.
—Haggai 1:4; 2:7,9

The destruction of the temple in Jerusalem and the captivity to Babylon are all behind us now. King Cyrus of Persia has defeated the Babylonians, and now has authorized the Jews to return so they might rebuild the temple. This is significant because the house of God is the center of their livelihood and the place of God's presence.

The rebuilding continues upon the urging of the prophets Haggai and Zechariah. As we remember from Ezra, they had run into snags that delayed the work. Opposition from the local leaders and a lost sense of urgency stopped it dead in the water. So Haggai reminds governor Zerubbabel and the high priest, Joshua, of their priorities. The whole remnant of the people obeyed, and the Lord stirred up their spirit.

Haggai prophesied of a day when the Messiah would come. He is called "the desired of all nations," and His glory would fill the house. What we have come to know is that the temple God comes to dwell in is no longer a temple made of hands *(Acts 17:24)*. Paul informs us that the members of God's family are being joined together to become a dwelling that God inhabits by his Spirit *(Ephesians 2:19-22)*. In fact, your body is a temple of the Holy Spirit. He lives within you *(1 Corinthians 3:16; 6:19)*. God has chosen to reveal His glory in and through His people. Giving God His rightful place is my new priority.

Father of glory, I make ready my heart to be a resting place for Your Spirit. Let Your glory fill me and the body of Christ to whom I am joined. Amen.

December 21

Zechariah 1:1–21; Revelation 12:1–13:1a; Psalm 140:1–13; Proverbs 30:17

We Overcome the Devil

I heard a loud voice in heaven say: "Now have come the salvation and the power and the kingdom of our God … For the accuser of our brothers has been hurled down. They overcame him by the blood of the Lamb and by the word of their testimony; they did not love their lives so much as to shrink from death."
—Revelation 12:10–11

The apostle John is still seeing signs and visions in heaven. It was Michael and his angels that threw the dragon—that ancient serpent called the devil or Satan—and his angels unto the earth. After that skirmish in heaven, then came the loud proclamation. The one who accuses us before God night and day has been overcome and is no longer allowed access to the heavens. (Remember how Satan brought accusation against Job?) The war he would make now was against the remaining believers on the earth, but, at this point, his time is short.

What overcomes the devil then is the same that overcomes the devil now—the blood of the Lamb and the word of our testimony. When Jesus died on the cross, He was the spotless Lamb, the perfect sacrifice, whose blood paid the penalty for our sins. It is forever the trump card that wins the victory. The word of our testimony is our witness of the Lord Jesus. It is unashamedly proclaimed and, more importantly, lived out in our lives. Jesus declared, at the time of His ascension, that we would receive power when the Holy Spirit came upon us so that we would be His ambassadors to the ends of the earth *(Acts 1:8)*. He gives us the authority to represent Him rightly. Don't ever underestimate your most effective tool. Your testimony is yours—it can never be taken from you. Satan is still on the prowl with the intent to attack vulnerable believers *(1 Peter 5:9)*, but, until he is bound forever (and he will be), we have what we need to overcome.

Father, let my life validate what Your Son accomplished on the cross. Amen.

December 22

Zechariah 2:1–3:10; Revelation 13:1b–18; Psalm 141:1–10; Proverbs 30:18–20

Perimeters for Purity

Set a guard over my mouth, O Lord; keep watch over the door of my lips. Let not my heart be drawn to what is evil… Let a righteous man strike me—it is a kindness; let him rebuke me—it is oil on my head. My head will not refuse it.
—Psalm 141:3–5

David prays earnestly to the Lord to keep his heart from being drawn into what is evil. In his plea, David relates three very wise principles.

First, David acknowledges his vulnerability to temptations that are around him. He knows firsthand how weak the flesh can be. He is asking for help from the right source. He does not want to be a victim of the entrapments of sin. He calls out for divine assistance.

Second, David realizes that it is our words that are what most often get us into trouble. We need a guard to monitor our mouth. The words we speak reflect what is going on in our heart and through our mind, so we need the self-control to push the "Pause" button. That is why James said: *"Be quick to listen, slow to speak and slow to become angry"* (1:19). Even Jesus, in the face of His accusers, said nothing.

Lastly, David was open to correction, even if it was from another individual; not just anyone, but a truly righteous friend who has your best interest in mind. There should be a mutual high regard for each other. The beauty of godly relationships is that sometimes another mature believer can speak into your life in an area that may be in your blind spot. If he brings to light something that needs your attention, it is a kindness. We are better for it and we welcome that.

O Lord, I welcome Your dealings in my life that enable me to overcome sin and temptation. When I need to speak, may my words be helpful and hopeful. Amen.

December 23

Zechariah 4:1–5:11; Revelation 14:1–20; Psalm 142:1–7; Proverbs 30:21–23

Spirit Empowered

So he said to me, "This is the word of the Lord to Zerubbabel: 'Not by might nor by power, but by my Spirit,'" says the Lord Almighty. "The hands of Zerubbabel have laid the foundation of this temple; his hands will also complete it. Who despises the day of small things?"
—Zechariah 4:6,9–10

Zechariah, like Haggai, ministered to the Jews who were returning to Jerusalem to rebuild the temple and their nation. Now that their captivity was over, the hope of a new day was being ushered in. Zechariah reports the heart of God for His people. He has already called them *"the apple of his eye" (2:8).* He has already declared, *"I will live among you,"* and *"I will be [Jerusalem's] glory within" (2:5,10).*

The word the angel brought to Zechariah was to encourage Zerubbabel, their governor and leader, that it is by the Spirit of God that the temple will be completed. It will not be accomplished by a power struggle or smooth deliberation. The work God started will be the result of supernatural intervention by the Holy Spirit. This is equally true of whatever God has initiated in our lives. Our best efforts cannot produce spiritual results that endure. Only by obedience will God anoint it and bless it and accomplishes His purposes, so that His name is glorified. Slick strategies won't do that.

It matters not that the temple looked small at first. They were comparing it with the splendor of Solomon's temple. Most things that God initiates are small. Smallness or bigness are not measures of success in God's eyes. Your obedience is. Do not judge a ministry by its size, but by the anointing upon it and the fruit that results.

Lord Almighty, You call me to a higher obedience that relies upon Your Spirit to bring about Your plans and purposes. Lead me by Your Spirit today. Amen.

December 24

Zechariah 6:1–7:14; Revelation 15:1–8; Psalm 143:1–12; Proverbs 30:24–28

The Branch

Take the silver and the gold and make a crown, and set it on the head of the high priest, Joshua son of Jehozadak. Tell him; 'Here is the man whose name is the Branch, and he will branch out from his place and build the temple of the Lord, and he will be clothed with majesty and will sit and rule on his throne ... he will be a priest on his throne. And there will be harmony between the two.'
—Zechariah 6:11–13

Here, on the eve of Christmas, we read of the prophetic word of the Lord from Zechariah that a Messiah would come. His vantage point in history is about 500 years before Jesus came to fulfill these words.

Zechariah was to collect silver and gold from some of the named family groups of the returning exiles to fashion a crown. There was some urgency to it, as they went the same day to Josiah's house to create it. It would then be placed on the head of the current high priest, Joshua, as a prophetic sign. They would place the crown on one who they could see and spoke of one who would come that they could not see. His name is the Branch. The unique characteristic of the Branch is that He will be worthy to rule as both king and priest.

Isaiah spoke of the Branch of the Lord as one who will be beautiful and glorious *(4:2; 11:1)*. Jeremiah gives us the clearest depiction, describing the righteous Branch who will come as a King and will reign wisely. He is called the Branch because he is raised up from the stump, or the family line, of David *(23:5-6)*. Zechariah has already proclaimed that Joshua and his associates were men symbolic of things to come, speaking again of the Branch *(3:8)*. Jesus, the Messiah we celebrate, will build His kingdom and bring His righteous rule.

Jesus, I celebrate Your entry into the world. You are the priest who brought redemption. You are the King of my life. Bring Your righteous rule. Amen.

December 25

Zechariah 8:1–23; Revelation 16:1–21; Psalm 144:1–15; Proverbs 30:29–31

A Battle to Fight

Praise be to the Lord my Rock, who trains my hands for war, my fingers for battle. He is my loving God and my fortress, my stronghold and my deliverer, my shield, in whom I take refuge, who subdues people under me. Reach down your hand from on high; deliver me … from the hands of foreigners …
—Psalm 144:1–2; 7

David is a skilled leader and warrior. As king, He has gone forth into battle many times. The warring is necessary to protect a people from encroaching enemies and to seize what God has authorized. But it was never David's battle to fight. In this Psalm we see a commander who has a right perspective. David knows where his help comes from. He has witnessed the mighty hand of God to intervene. He cries out, *"Part your heavens. Reach down your hand from on high; deliver me and rescue me. You are the One who gives victory to kings" (v.7,10)*.

Look at David's descriptions of the God in charge: stronghold, shield, fortress, deliverer, refuge and Rock. He also is the One who trains and equips David to subdue his enemy. It is God who brings victory, but it is still worked out through the willing participation of His servants.

David has seen the lives cut short from such warring. There are casualties. He is reminded that all our days are like a fleeting shadow, a mere breath. In the grand scheme of life, why is it that God cares and takes such interest in man? Because He does, that is why David calls Him *"my loving God" (v.2)*. As we gleaned from 1 John 3:8, the reason the Son of God came was to destroy the devil's work. We don't pick fights with the devil, but we take what's ours and defend what's ours by the power of the Holy Spirit to make His name great on the earth. That is a good reason to celebrate Jesus today!

Jesus, You are my deliverer. Train my hands for righteousness. Amen.

December 26

Zechariah 9:1–17; Revelation 17:1–18; Psalm 145:1–21; Proverbs 30:32

Intentional Praise

Every day I will praise you and extol your name forever. One generation will commend your works to another; they will tell of your mighty acts. They will speak of the glorious splendor of your majesty, and I will meditate on your wonderful works. They will celebrate your abundant goodness …
    —Psalm 145:2,4–5,7

The longer David is alive, the more he sees the faithfulness of God. When he witnesses the greatness of God, it resounds into a heart that overflows with praise. Because God is so good and so worthy, praise is the right response. To acknowledge who God is and what God does is to cultivate an attitude of unending gratitude. David says, *"Every day* I will praise you … *forever and ever."* Noticing God's involvement in our lives, big and small, unlocks our heart to truly worship.

Three dynamics factor in. First, you praise Him because you have a reason to. By praising Him we have arrived at the conclusion of His worthiness. We have pondered and meditated upon His goodness *(v.5)*. Next, when we praise Him, we declare God's majesty to the next generation *(v.4)*. His greatness is worth passing on. Our children, and their children, need to hear firsthand how God is at work in my life. So we speak of it. We proclaim it. And when I testify to His awesome deeds, they see that God is alive and active. Lastly, we need to know what it is to celebrate with intentionality *(v.7)*. When praise overflows, it shows. We celebrate many lesser things. Wouldn't you agree that His splendor and majesty and faithfulness is worth celebrating?

People who praise are people who have an awakened awareness of glory. God's greatness—who can fathom, and who can remain silent?

God of splendor, when I consider what You have done, I must extol Your name. Cultivate in me a heart of gratitude, for You are worthy of all praise.

December 27

Zechariah 10:1–11:17; Revelation 18:1–24; Psalm 146:1–10; Proverbs 30:33

The Shepherd's Care

The idols speak deceit, diviners see visions that are false… Therefore the people wander like sheep oppressed for lack of a shepherd. My anger burns against the shepherds, and I will punish the leaders; for the Lord Almighty will care for His flock, the house of Judah … From Judah will come the cornerstone, from him the tent peg, from him the battle bow, from him every ruler."
—*Zechariah 10:2–4*

Shepherds are those who lead us, just as a shepherd leads and cares for his sheep. They are leaders whom we look to for moral and spiritual guidance. Historically, some shepherds who led Israel were good. Like David, he was an exemplary shepherd over the people of Israel *(Psalm 78:72)*. Others were evil, self-serving and ruled harshly over God's people *(Ezekiel 34, Zechariah 11)*. And then, sometimes, it was the sheep who were the obstinate ones. But it was the worthless, oppressive shepherds who gained God's attention, not in a good way.

Shepherds are held to a higher standard. They are accountable to God for the manner in which they care for His people. When much is given, then much is required *(Luke 12:48)*. Peter exhorted pastors to be willing shepherds of God's flock showing forth by example what it means to serve *(1 Peter 5:2–3)*.

It is the Lord Almighty who ensures the care for His flock. He places and removes shepherds strategically so that His care and compassion are administrated. From Judah, God brought forth the Messiah Jesus. He would be many things: the cornerstone *(Isaiah 28:16)*, the tent peg *(Isaiah 22:23)* and the One to rule over Israel *(Micah 5:2)*, but Jesus would be the Chief Shepherd to lead God's flock in truth *(1 Peter 5:4)*.

Shepherd of my soul, You searched for me and rescued me. You give me confidence to overcome. You are my good, good Shepherd. Amen.

December 28

Zechariah 12:1–13:9; Revelation 19:1–21; Psalm 147:1–20; Proverbs 31:1–7

The Wedding Supper

Then I heard what sounded like a great multitude ... shouting: "Hallelujah! ... For the wedding of the Lamb has come, and his bride has made herself ready. Fine linen, bright and clean, was given her to wear." (Fine linen stands for the righteous acts of the saints.) Then the angel said to me, "Write: 'Blessed are those who are invited to the wedding supper of the Lamb!'"
—Revelation 19:6–9

The vision John is witnessing can only be described as overwhelming. This chapter depicts why the day of the Lord is both great and terrible: great for the persevering saints and dreadful for those who receive the righteous wrath of judgment. But aren't you glad the Lord chose to give us this glimpse of this great triumph to come.

The time for the wedding has come—the crowning moment of history. The wedding supper of the Lamb is the union of Jesus and His bride, the church. You've seen extravagant weddings before, but none more breathtaking than this. The bride has made herself ready. She is adorned with fine linen, reflecting her righteousness, made white by the blood of the Lamb *(7:9,14)* and maintained by her life choices.

Jesus gave us teaching for this preparation, in Matthew 25. The virgins who were ready for the bridegroom had oil in their lamps. They had a life empowered by the Holy Spirit that was their own *(vv.1-13)*. The parable of the talents taught us to be faithful with all that God has entrusted to us *(vv.14-30)*. The sheep and goats parable illustrated the importance of serving people in their need *(vv.31-46)*.

We have been given a great invitation. It is the culmination of all that we live for. How will you prepare yourself for the Bridegroom?

Jesus, the wedding day is approaching. I want to be ready for that day! Amen.

December 29

Zechariah 14:1–21; Revelation 20:1–15; Psalm 148:1–14; Proverbs 31:8–9

Final Judgment

And the devil was thrown into the lake of burning sulfur, where the beast and the false prophet had been thrown. They will be tormented day and night forever and ever ... I saw a great white throne and him who was seated on it. And I saw the dead, great and small, and books were opened. If anyone's name was not found written in the book of life, he was thrown into the lake of fire.
—Revelation 20:10–12,15

It may not seem very pleasant to read about judgments, but it is good news to know that the deceiver Satan finally gets his life sentence in the lake of fire. It is also the promised final accounting that will come for everyone who has rejected the salvation offered by the Lord Jesus.

The armies of heaven had already followed the white horse whose rider is called Faithful and True to make swift work of the armies of earth *(ch.19)*. The beast and false prophet were thrown into the lake of burning sulfur. The flesh of the kings, generals and fighting men became the great supper of God for all the birds. Not a pretty sight. The devil is bound and restrained from any deception until the end of a thousand years. When he is released from his prison, his deceptions lead up to the final demise. Satan is defeated and thrown into the lake where all judgments end, the lake of fire. *Satan's end is coming.*

Each person, great and small, who ever lived will stand before the great white throne and the books will tell on them of their deeds. Each will be judged according to what they have done. If their name is not included in the book of life, the lake will consume them. Death and Hades will join them. The enemies of God will meet their end. John's vision allows us to see what we want to avoid. There is finality in our acceptance or rejection of the Savior. Which will you choose?

Judge of all, I accept Your provision of salvation through Jesus. Amen.

December 30

Malachi 1:1–2:17; Revelation 21:1–27; Psalm 149:1–9; Proverbs 31:10–24

The New Jerusalem

I saw the Holy City, the New Jerusalem, coming down out of heaven from God. And I heard a loud voice saying, "Now the dwelling of God is with men, and he will live with them. They will be his people, and God himself will be with them and be their God." He who overcomes will inherit all this …
—Revelation 21:2–3,7

I have always perceived heaven as that place where God dwells above the clouds. We have read John's vision of its glory around the throne. But at the end of days upon the earth, at its consummation, the dwelling of God is coming to the earth. The kingdom of God and the holy city, new Jerusalem, where God's throne is, will enjoin the new earth. The emphasis on all of this needs to be upon "new." *I am making everything new!" (v.5).* The old order of things is passed away.

The next emphasis will be from verse seven: *"He who overcomes will inherit all this."* It will be exclusively prepared for the redeemed. Jesus taught us that it is the meek who will inherit the earth *(Matthew 5:5),* those who walk humbly and confidently in God's grace. What's more, *"God Himself will be with them."* His presence and rule will permeate life forever forward. We will be His people and He will be our God.

Just ponder it. No hint of impurity or shame. No death or pain. Only glory and light and splendor. Imagine no need for the sun *ever.* The glory of the Lamb will make the sun pale. The brilliance of the city will be as clear precious jewels, the streets as pure transparent gold. This will be my new address. I am pretty sure I could get used to this!

To Him who sits on the throne and unto the Lamb, I give You honor and glory. What You have prepared for me is beyond comprehension, yet I set it as my hope and future reality. While I am here, let Your kingdom be represented through me. I long for Your appearing. Come Lord Jesus. Amen.

December 31

Malachi 3:1–4:6; Revelation 22:1–21; Psalm 150:1–6; Proverbs 31:25–31

A Scroll of Remembrance

"But you ask, 'How are we to return? ... How do we rob you?... What have we said against you?'" Then those who feared the Lord talked with each other, and the Lord listened and heard. A scroll of remembrance was written in his presence concerning those who feared the Lord and honored his name.
—Malachi 3:7–8,13,16

What sounds like a dialogue is really a monologue, and it has been going on throughout the book. The word of the Lord brought forth by the prophet Malachi confronts the Jews who have returned to Jerusalem for their contempt and broken faith. What's interesting is how Malachi sets up the conversation. You see, God knows what they are thinking, what their rationale is and their alibi. God lays out His argument. He calls them on their willful disobedience. He answers their weak rebuttal. He explains to them what really matters.

All throughout, God is just looking for a people who will be responsive to Him and will honor His name. You hear the pleas of a faithful God calling to His beloved for a restored relationship and a higher commitment. Instead of a heartfelt devotion, they have made it into a religion of rules and regulations. But God's hands are not tied.

The Lord heard their complaints and every harsh word, but He also heard the conversation of those who reverenced His name. That's because, even in the disappointment of broken covenant, there are the few who are faithful. To these God delights and recalls every deed that went seemingly unnoticed. A scroll of remembrance is recorded. Justice will come to that one who honored the Almighty. He calls them His "treasured possession." To this remnant will He show His favor. The distinction will be made. *It is so worth serving the Lord.*

Abba, nothing I do goes unnoticed. You are just and worthy of my best. Amen.

Printed in the United States
By Bookmasters